DATE DUE			

RURAL SOCIOLOGY

Lowry Nelson

RURAL SOCIOLOGY

Its Origin and Growth in the United States

GREENWOOD PRESS, PUBLISHERS
WESTPORT CONNECTICUT

Library of Congress Cataloging in Publication Data

Nelson, Lowry, 1893-
  Rural sociology, its origin and growth in the
United States.

  Reprint of the ed. published by University of
Minnesota Press, Minneapolis.
  Includes bibliographical references and index.
  1. Sociology, Rural--United States--History.
I. Title.
[HT415.N4 1980] 307.7'2 80-36884
ISBN 0-313-22675-X (lib. bdg.)

© Copyright 1969 by the University of Minnesota.

Material from Howard Odum *American Sociology*, is reprinted on pages 183-84 by permission of David McKay
Company, Inc.

Reprinted with the permission of University of Minnesota
Press.

Reprinted 1980 by Greenwood Press,
A division of Congressional Information Service, Inc.
88 Post Road West, Westport, Connecticut 06881

Printed in the United States of America

10 9 8 7 6 5 4 3 2 1

For Ann, Lowry, Jr., and Janet

Preface

IN THIS work I attempt to account for the origin of rural sociology in the United States and to chart its growth. It is essentially an indigenous discipline that for nearly half a century did not take root in any other country. My central proposition has been that any field of knowledge, any new discipline, comes into being because of the convergence, at the appropriate time, of conditions in the social environment together with the presence of imaginative and forceful men who are stimulated by those conditions to respond creatively in new intellectual formations. The conditions, incidentally, include social instability and even disorganization.

My emphasis is on the founders and the period of pioneering. Like the pioneer land settlers whom they were to study, the early sociologists were primarily engaged in field reconnaissance: they spied out the land; they chose the locale of their future work; they decided upon the essential objects of their search. These intellectual pioneers and their works, at home and abroad, form the central part of the book.

Practical considerations have made it necessary to base the discussion mainly on published work, chiefly research. This has meant that sociologists in teaching and extension work are not as well represented as the author could desire. Many teachers and, to a lesser extent, extension sociologists produce little "copy," and it is on publications that I have largely relied for evaluation. This consideration applies equally to the many rural sociologists who have done important work in foreign countries, but who will receive little if any attention in Chapter 11. In short, I do not pretend to have exhausted the field; there is plenty for other historians to do. It seemed important for me to record as much of the early period as possible.

My debt to many people will be obvious. Fellow sociologists, particularly the older ones, have devoted much time and effort to providing information. I am particularly grateful to the ones who were good enough to write the memoirs included in the appendix. Specific acknowledgment is also due to certain other individuals. Professor George A. Donohue, head of the department of sociology of the St. Paul Campus of the University of Minnesota, provided office space, clerical help, and, above all, ceaseless encouragement. Another colleague, C. E. Ramsey, read several chapters and gave valuable suggestions and encouragement, as did Bert L. Ellenbogen, head of the sociology department at Colorado State University. Louis W. Kutcher, research assistant, gave valuable aid in bibliographic and library reference work as did also Miss Annette Harrison. Lowry Nelson, Jr., of Yale University read several chapters and provided detailed editorial corrections. Miss Nancy Setzler's competent typing of the manuscript is gratefully recorded. Finally, my wife, Florence, assisted with the index, read many of the chapters, and saved me from many errors. Such sins of commission or omission as remain are, inevitably, my responsibility.

L. N.

April, 1969
Coral Gables, Florida

Contents

RURAL SOCIOLOGY

1

The Social Climate

THE appearance on the human scene of a new social movement, a new theory of relations of phenomena, a new method of investigation, or any new phase of knowledge is possible only if certain antecedent conditions have prepared the way for it. The rise of a social science, more than a comparable development in the physical and biological fields, is governed by the state of society itself. The social science requires a social climate in which it can grow.

As an accepted academic discipline, rural sociology is indigenous to the United States. It began to emerge early in the twentieth century, but we must look back to the social climate of America in the last quarter or so of the nineteenth century if we are to understand its inception and rise.

After the Civil War a great gulf opened between the agricultural and the industrial segments of American society. One can almost speak of two worlds: the distressed, unstable agricultural world and the booming world of industry and finance. The largely rural South was left economically prostrate and socially paralyzed by the war, and Reconstruction policies compounded its difficulties. In the West wave on wave of immigrants surged into the vast stretches of land to homestead farms. Their diverse ethnic backgrounds, as well as their numbers, the speed of their movement, and the scattered pattern of settlement, made development of stable community institutions extremely difficult.

The problems of social and physical isolation faced by farmers in the South and West were magnified by economic troubles. As the new lands brought under cultivation yielded excess supplies of corn, wheat, and cotton, the prices of farm commodities steadily declined. Farmers, lacking economical sources of credit, easily fell victim to land speculators and avaricious middlemen. Rural grievances came to center on the railroads, which indulged in discriminatory rate systems and unfair grading practices. The American farmer's dream of prosperity and the good life faded as agricultural debt and tenancy increased. "There are three great crops raised in Nebraska," wrote an embittered editor. "One is a crop of corn, one a crop of freight rates, and one a crop of interest." By 1890 there was, on the average, one mortgage for every family in the Midwest, and in the South the crop-lien system had reduced three-fourths of cotton farmers to a condition of peonage.[1]

In contrast to the rural depression, the urban and industrial world flourished as never before. The railroads — subsidized in their progress across the continent by prodigal disbursements of public lands — amassed immense fortunes for their owners. Other entrepreneurs ruthlessly exploited precious natural resources like the virgin forests and built industrial empires. Unrestrained by government regulation, monopolies developed, particularly in the rail and steel industries, which concentrated unprecedented economic and political power in the hands of a few. The situation was eloquently described by a member of the Farmers' Alliance:

There is something radically wrong in our industrial system. There is a screw loose. The wheels have dropped out of balance. The railroads have never been so prosperous, and yet agriculture languishes. The banks have never done a better or more profitable business, and yet agriculture languishes. Manufacturing enterprises never made more money or were in a more flourishing condition, and yet agriculture languishes. Towns and cities flourish and "boom" and grow and "boom," and yet agriculture languishes. Salaries and fees were never so temptingly high and desirable, and yet agriculture languishes.[2]

Reactions to the Agrarian Situation

In response to the plight of the farmer, a series of agrarian reform movements appeared on the scene. The first important farmers' organization was the Patrons of Husbandry, better known as the Grange. Organized in Washington, D.C., in 1867 by Oliver Hudson Kelley and some associates, the Grange reached a membership of more than 800,000 in thirty-three states by 1875. This society was remarkable not only for the breadth of its appeal throughout the country, but also for its emphasis on satisfying the social needs of farm families. Membership was open to adults and children alike, and the dual delegate plan, making husband and wife equal in representing their local unit, was an innovation. The most important local officer was the lecturer, who took charge of the educational program at the regular meetings in Grange halls. Through the establishment of cooperatives, the Grange endeavored to improve the prices that farmers received for their products and to reduce their costs through large-scale purchasing.

As an organization, the Grange formally eschewed politics, but it sought the intervention of state and federal governments in order to redress the balance between industrial prosperity and agricultural poverty. It proposed railroad and warehouse regulation, control of monopolies, and the establishment of parcel post and postal savings banks — all radical proposals for their time.[3] (Farmers can be "radical" when their interests arc threatened, as well as "conservative" when threatened by what they consider to be the "radical" measure of others.)

The Farmers' Alliance, which succeeded the Grange as a protest movement in the 1880s, worked more aggressively in trying to get the federal government to solve farmers' economic problems, and it finally entered politics directly when its leaders organized the short-lived People's (Populist) party in 1891. Although this development spelled the end of the Alliance as a farm organization, it served, along with the activities of the Grange, to dramatize the conditions of the farmers.[4]

Not only politicians in the nation's capital but also leaders in the social sciences were slow to give attention to agricultural difficulties. Economists, historians, sociologists, and political scientists largely ignored rural issues except as they discussed bimetallism and the farmers' support for it. It was the severe depression of the early 1890s that finally brought forth earnest discussion of the agricultural situation. During that decade members of the American Economic Association discussed at their annual professional meetings such topics as "The Farmers' Movement" and "Is There a Distinct Agricultural Question?" A number of social scientists, including John R. Commons and Richard T. Ely, contributed perceptive and sympathetic remarks at these meetings. Lester F. Ward, the pioneer sociologist, commenting upon the exodus of people from the farms, observed thoughtfully that the problem was "sociological rather than economic." [5]

On the other hand, sociologist Franklin H. Giddings demonstrated considerably less understanding about the problems of rural inhabitants than did some of his colleagues. Said Giddings:

. . . Why throughout these long years of his affliction has he always come off worse in the contest? There must be something wrong in his own make-up, some failing on his part to see what the conditions of life are. I am not saying that the farmer has no grievances. I think that he does not get the same freight rates that other men get, and that he is taxed more than other men are taxed. But there is a reason somewhere why, if he controls more votes than other men control, which we may suppose to be the fact, he is not able to correct these evils. The failing is in himself. If you want to reach the root of the farmers' difficulties, you will have to begin with the farmers' minds.[6]

Giddings' statement reflected the impact of the doctrine of laissez-faire, which in the late nineteenth century dominated economic thought and teaching in the United States. A kindred doctrine was what has been called social Darwinism: the belief that natural selection should be allowed to operate freely among human beings as well as among other forms of organic life and that the survival of the fittest would guarantee progressive improvement of the race.[7]

The chief exponent of social Darwinism was Herbert Spencer, whose *Study of Sociology* was generally used as a textbook. Most sociologists who began their education between 1870 and 1890 were not only influenced by Spencer, but were probably inspired by him to enter the field. Giddings, as we have seen, reflected his ideas, and so did Charles R. Henderson, who taught the first course in the United States on the rural community at the University of Chicago.[8]

Spencer's influence extended far beyond the classroom to the American public. John Commons, recalling his midwestern boyhood, said of his father: "He and his cronies talked politics and science. Every one of them in that Eastern section of Indiana was a Republican . . . and every one was a follower of Herbert Spencer, who was then the shining light of evolution and individualism. . . .¯ [Later] I was shocked, at a meeting of the American Economic Association, to hear Professor [Richard T.] Ely denounce Herbert Spencer . . ."[9]

The churches, like the social scientists, were sluggish in recognizing their responsibility to rural people. Though there was often frenetic competition among denominations to establish congregations on the frontier, often without serious thought about whether there would be enough members to support them, for many years little attention was given to the social and economic problems confronting farm people. Then in 1892 the *Forum* printed the Reverend William DeWitt Hyde's "Impending Paganism in New England," an article which stimulated clergymen to take note of conditions in the rural areas. Josiah Strong, a midwestern Congregational minister, was another churchman who expressed concern about the social evils of his day. In 1893 he published a book that described the abandonment of farms and churches, the depreciation of agricultural property, and the general rural decline.[10]

While academicians tried to diagnose the economic difficulties of agriculture and clergymen bemoaned the decline of the rural church and the exodus from the countryside, it remained for Hamlin Garland, author of *Main-Travelled Roads* (1891), to portray in vivid detail the dismal life of the farm family on the frontier. However Garland's fiction may rank as literature, his short stories were tracts for the times, based as they were upon a firsthand knowledge of rural conditions. Garland's family had taken up prairie land in Iowa in 1869 and later homesteaded in South Dakota. Some years afterward Garland set down his impression of the rural Midwest in the late 1880s.

On my way westward, that summer day in 1887, rural life presented itself from an entirely new angle. The ugliness, the endless drudgery, and the loneliness of the farmer's lot smote me with stern insistence. I was the militant reformer.

The farther I got from Chicago the more depressing the landscape became . . . my pity grew more intense as I passed from northwest Iowa into southern Dakota. The houses, bare as boxes, dropped on the treeless plains, the barbed wire fences running at right angles, and the towns mere assemblages of flimsy wooden sheds with painted-pine battlement, produced on me the effect of an almost helpless and sterile poverty.

My dark mood was deepened into bitterness by my father's farm, where I found my mother imprisoned in a small cabin on the enormous sunburnt, treeless plain, with no expectation of ever living anywhere else. . . . she endured the discomforts of her life uncomplainingly — but my resentment of "things as they are" deepened during my talks with her neighbors who were all housed in the same unshaded cabins in equal poverty and loneliness.[11]

Garland's stories, with their graphic description of the problems of farm people, helped to convince the nation that something was seriously wrong. Discounting the author's exaggeration for dramatic effect, any reader who knew conditions on American farms, even as late as the outbreak of World War I, realized that fact was truly worse than his fiction.

Garland aroused pity for the people on the land, but he hardly inspired admiration for them. His characters were caught in a network of forces from which they could not extricate themselves. Observers of the rural scene could still argue that the farmers' situation was of their own making — they went West to get rich, they gambled on a better outcome, and they failed. What did it matter?

It remained for Frederick Jackson Turner to describe a rural America that was making a positive contribution to the nation. The frontier, said Turner, was the cradle of democratic institutions. "American democracy was born of no theorist's dream; it was not carried in the Susan Constant to Virginia, nor in the Mayflower to Plymouth. It came stark and strong and full of life out of the American forest and it gained new strength each time it touched a new frontier." [12]

Turner's energetic and self-reliant frontiersman was far removed from the stereotyped backwoodsman of some American literature — the "brother to the ox" of Edwin Markham or the ignorant and depraved rustic of other writers. Whether or not Turner's theory of the role of the frontier in shaping American institutions could bear close scrutiny, his hypothesis drew widespread and favorable attention to the people who were settling the West.

The Commission on Country Life

In 1901 Theodore Roosevelt's succession to the presidency of the United States inaugurated a new era in American history and released the pent-up impulses of change. In his first message to Congress President Roosevelt called for federal regulation of trusts and railroads, projects for conservation, irrigation, and reclamation, and a variety of other reforms. Although Roosevelt gained wide recognition as a trust-buster, it is his achievements in the conservation of natural resources that concern us here.

The widespread and wasteful exploitation of forests, waters, and mineral lands by private entrepreneurs had gone virtually unchecked in the years after the Civil War. The battle for government control of public lands was bitterly fought by those who profited from their exploitation, and only a limited measure of success was achieved by conservationists until the Roosevelt administration took office. Then the president and his chief forester, Gifford Pinchot, succeeded in mòbilizing public support for the philosophy of conservation and gave impetus to much new legislation.[13] The Reclamation Act of 1902 and the creation of the National Forest Service in 1905 came during the Roosevelt administration. But the most important event for rural sociology was the appointment in 1908 of the Commission on Country Life. Roosevelt regarded this commission as "full twin brother" to his National Conservation Commission and as the human side of the conservation movement.[14]

We have noted that rural sociology is indigenous to the United States, but its beginnings were not without European influence. Sir Horace Plunkett, a leader in the Irish cooperative movement and a friend of Roosevelt, played a central role in the establishment of the Country Life Commission. Just how central is not widely understood. In his autobiography Roosevelt says of Plunkett: "In various conversations he described to me and my close associates the reconstruction of farm life which had been accomplished by the Agricultural Organization Society of Ireland, of which he was the founder and controlling force; and he discussed the application of similar methods to the improvements of farm life in the United States."[15]

Plunkett came of a family particularly susceptible to tuberculosis and his physicians recommended that he spend part of each year in a dry climate. Leaving Ireland in 1879, at the age of twenty-five he took up ranching in the Powder River district of Wyoming. In 1901 Plunkett and Roosevelt conferred together at the suggestion of the secretary of agriculture, James Wilson. Meeting again in 1905, the two men discussed for more than an hour the problems of rural life, particularly ways of stopping the exodus from the farm to the city.[16]

At this interview Roosevelt asked the Irishman to write out his ideas about what might be done for America's farmers. When he received Plunkett's report, the president responded with typical enthusiasm: "By George," he wrote on July 3, 1906, "I wish you were . . . either in the Senate or my Cabinet. . . . You take an interest in exactly the problems which I regard as vital." Roosevelt was later to include passages from Plunkett's statement in his annual message to Congress.[17]

At various times in the next two years, Plunkett conferred with Roosevelt, Pinchot, and other Washington officials on ways of improving farm life in the United States. The Irishman confided to his diary that he was elated to find his "life's thought and work" being applied to the vast American continent. Out of these conversations emerged the idea for a Commission on Country Life, with the dual goals of directing national attention to farm problems and of gathering information about rural conditions.[18]

In August 1908 Roosevelt appointed the members of the commission, naming as chairman Liberty Hyde Bailey, then dean of Cornell University's College of Agriculture. Other commissioners were Kenyon L. Butterfield, president of Massachusetts State College (now the University of Massachusetts); Henry Wallace, Sr., founder and editor of *Wallace's Farmer*; Walter Hines Page, editor of *World's Work*, a prominent journal of politics and practical affairs; Pinchot, chief of the United States Forest Service and founder of Yale University's School of Forestry; Charles S. Barrett, president of the National Farmers Union; and William A. Beard, editor of *Great Western Magazine*. Horace Plunkett was also made a member.

The commission set to work assembling data. Between November 9 and December 22, 1908, the members held open hearings at thirty cities across the country. The information thus gathered was supplemented by questionnaires mailed to about 550,000 people and by special inquiries and investigations conducted by individual members.[19]

Since Roosevelt's second term of office was drawing to a close, the president was anxious to present the commission's report to Congress before his administration ended in March 1909. This situation lent urgency to the commission's work. A draft version of the findings was hastily prepared by mid-December. Plunkett, who saw the draft in Washington, expressed disappointment with it. In his diary he wrote:

So I went to R. and told him the report I had seen would never do, and that it was impossible to deal with such a mass of material in a few weeks. I suggested that a brief preliminary report giving a general outline of the main conditions . . . should be sent to him and that he should send it to Congress with a message explaining the object he had in view in the appointment of the Commission and the general scope and purpose of their inquiries.[20]

Little is known about how the final version of the report evolved, but it is obvious that the members of the commission faced great difficulties in achieving agreement. One of Bailey's biographers has said: "The report was written by Bailey and was debated vigorously in committee. Some portions were rewritten at least eight times in an effort to reconcile all divergent opinions." The document was eventually finished and transmitted by the president to Congress on February 9, 1909.[21]

The report opened with a summary of the "most prominent deficiencies" of rural life: insufficient technical knowledge of agricultural conditions and possibilities; lack of training for country life in the schools; the monopolization of rivers and forests and the withholding of great tracts of arable land for speculation; inadequate highways; soil depletion; the lack of good leadership; the inadequacy of credit and the shortage of labor; the restricted and burdensome life of farm women; and the lack of public health services.[22]

Moving on to remedies for these conditions, the authors recommended surveys of agricultural regions to provide a factual basis for the development of a scientific and economically sound country life; the encouragement of rural extension work through the land-grant colleges; an investigation of the middleman system of handling farm products, coupled with a general inquiry into taxation, transportation rates, cooperative organizations and credit, and the entire business system; an inquiry into the control of rivers with the object of protecting public ownership; the establishment of an engineering service to advise the states on effective and economical highway systems; and the inauguration of parcel post and postal savings banks.

Succeeding paragraphs called attention to the need for knowledge, education, organization, and the strengthening of "spiritual forces." The main body of the document, consisting of only ninety-two pages, spelled out in more detail the various points raised in the summary. The report's brevity may have resulted from Plunkett's recommendations to Roosevelt after he had read the draft version.

When the document was released, it made only a modest impact on public opinion. Inevitably the magazines *World's Work* and *Wallace's Farmer*, edited by two members of the commission, carried favorable notices. But the important newspapers apparently gave only perfunctory coverage, and no pronounced interest was apparent. Congressmen, obviously unimpressed, ignored Roosevelt's request for $25,000 to circulate the findings and make possible an analysis of the large amount of data assembled by the commission.

11

It must be admitted that the report contained little, if anything, that the commission members and other informed people did not already know. Bailey, Butterfield, and Pinchot had been saying much the same thing for several years. Indeed it is quite possible that these men could have written the account without stirring from their offices in Ithaca and Washington and without the nationwide hearings. The report's significance lay in the fact that it was an official voice from the highest level of government, describing rural conditions and proposing a series of reforms.

At the time, however, this voice went largely unheard. The conditions which brought the commission into existence — economic depression, rural decadence, and, one might say, despair — were rapidly disappearing. By 1908 rural recovery was evident, and agriculture was about to enter what has often been called its golden age, that happy state later known as parity. With the development of a new prosperity, farmers themselves lost interest in reform until another depression brought new economic difficulties after World War I.

Summary

Rural sociology had yet, of course, to be established as a discipline. But the way had been prepared. Through their protest movements, the farmers themselves had focused national attention on their critical problems: lack of credit, inadequate transportation, chaotic markets, poor educational institutions, and social isolation. Economists attempted to diagnose the agricultural malaise; clergymen became alarmed at the decline of country churches and country life. Suddenly it was discovered that farmers were vitally important to the national welfare.

By the beginning of the twentieth century, social Darwinism and laissez-faire were clearly on the wane, and long-overdue reforms were being instituted.[23] The conservation movement had paid off in far-reaching legislation affecting natural resources. The way was open for something to be done about the rural problem. The report of the Commission on Country Life must be recognized as the first important milestone on the way to the establishment of the rural social sciences.

These rural social sciences would be highly practical in orientation and this is, no doubt, one reason why they did not for many years develop in or spread to Europe, where the related fields of general sociology and economics originated. As E. W. Hofstee has pointed out, European sociology before World War II was "highly theoretical and often even spec-

12

ulative in character" and rural sociology as it was developed in America "did not fit into the dominating concept of sociology in Europe before 1940." [24] It should be noted, also, that in contrast to the situation in the United States in the late nineteenth century, stability was for the most part characteristic of rural life in Europe and hence pressures for developing a practical rural sociology did not build up.[25]

2

The Herald-Evangelists of Rural Life

THE two members of the Commission on Country Life who were most important to its work were Liberty Hyde Bailey and Kenyon Leech Butterfield. These two men had much in common. In the first place, both were heads of agricultural colleges: Bailey was dean of the Cornell University College of Agriculture and Butterfield was president of Massachusetts Agricultural College. For years they had had direct contact with the problems of farm people and had been writing and speaking about them. Both men published books on rural problems in 1908, the year the commission was appointed. Coincidentally, both were born in Michigan and graduated from the Michigan agricultural college (now Michigan State University).

As herald-evangelists of a better rural life, these men did much to prepare the way for the emergence of rural sociology.[1] It is true that neither could be called a sociologist, though Butterfield more nearly qualified for that title than Bailey, but their role was nevertheless an influential one.

Liberty Hyde Bailey

Born in 1858 on a farm that had barely emerged from the wilderness of western Michigan, Bailey gained an early familiarity with frontier life.[2]

His father, an orchardist who raised more varieties of fruit trees than any-one else in the area, provided a stimulating environment for the young man who was to become the most famous horticulturist of his day. Bailey received a B.S. degree from Michigan State College in 1882 at the age of twenty-four and an M.S. four years later. After taking his first degree, he spent a year at Harvard as assistant to the famous botanist, Asa Gray. Bailey taught horticulture and landscape gardening at Michigan State from 1885 until 1888, when he was called to Cornell as professor of hor-ticulture. In 1903 he was made dean and director of the College of Agri-culture. Ten years later, although he was only fifty-five, Bailey resigned and devoted all his time to research and writing. His main interest was the study of the palm tree and he visited many parts of the world collecting specimens. He died in 1954 at the age of ninety-seven.

For at least a generation Bailey was the most widely known and re-spected figure in agricultural circles. His reputation came largely through his writings; he was certainly the most prolific agricultural writer and edi-tor of his time, and one would be hard pressed to find his equal. He ac-quired a nationwide reputation as the editor of the Macmillan series of textbooks on agriculture. There was hardly an agricultural college in America that did not claim at least one author in this series and, since Bailey's name appeared on every book, he was known to almost every student who attended an agricultural college. (It is said that he edited 117 titles by 99 authors between 1890 and 1940.[3]) His editorial works also included the multi-volume *Cyclopedia of American Horticulture* (1900–2) and *Cyclopedia of American Agriculture* (1907–9).

As dean of what was in many respects the leading college of agriculture in the United States, Bailey was a widely known and respected educational administrator. He was in great demand as a lecturer and must have visited almost all the land-grant colleges of the country. He was also a poet whose verse, collected in the volume *Wind and Weather* (1916), was widely quoted and read.

Throughout his life a true Jeffersonian agrarian, Bailey idealized the farmer who owned his land. "It would be a great gain," he wrote, "if many persons could look forward to the ownership of a bit of the earth, to share in the partition, to partake of the brotherhood." [4] He did not apologize for his almost lyric idealism. "I am sometimes told when I make remarks similar to these, that I am idealizing. I hope that I am, for if farm life cannot be idealized, it cannot be recommended; but I hope the ideas are attainable." [5]

Bailey's regard for the beauty and wisdom to be found in nature approached a passion. He believed that every farmer ought to be a naturalist. "To the extent that he is a good naturalist, he is a good farmer. I sometimes think that, as a race, our real outlook to nature is to rest largely on the farming occupation, and therefore that we need to conserve this occupation in order to recruit the native strength of our civilization as well as to provide a source of material supplies." [6]

Holding such strong opinions on the importance of nature and the idealized life of the country, Bailey could hardly view the city with enthusiasm:

The fundamental weakness in our civilization is the fact that the city and the country represent antagonistic forces. . . . The city sits like a parasite, running out its roots into the open country and draining it of its substance. The city takes everything to itself — materials, money, men — and gives back only what it does not want; it does not reconstruct or even maintain its contributory country. Many country places are already sucked dry. [7]

Like Turner, he believed that the moral strength and political virtue of Americans derived from their association with the land. "It is doubtful," he once said, "whether a nation of cities could be a democracy." [8]

Although Bailey was convinced of the superiority of farm life and farm people, he was willing to admit that actual conditions left something to be desired. His definition of the problem of rural life, however, was typically stated in broad generalities. The rural problem, in his opinion, was that of "developing and maintaining on our farms a civilization in full harmony with the best of American ideals." But if Bailey was seldom concrete or specific in his analysis of rural difficulties or in his proposals for remedying them, he did recognize two general areas — education and community life — where improvement was necessary.

The most fundamental need, he wrote in *The Country-Life Movement*, was to "place effectively educated men and women into the open country." [9] Everything else depended upon this first step. With an educated population on the land, all other problems could be solved; in its absence rural institutions and community life would never reach a high point of development.

He urged the teaching of agriculture in the public schools, not merely as a concession to farmers but as a school subject in its own right. He wanted to see the school adapt its curriculum to the life experience of students:

The schools, if they are to be really effective, must represent the civilization of their time and place. This does not mean that every school is to introduce all the subjects that engage men's attention, or are capable of being put into educational form; it means that it must express the main activities, progress, and outlook of its people. Agriculture is not a technical profession or merely an industry, but a civilization.[10]

All of Bailey's thinking about rural education apparently had reference to the simple country school. In *The State and the Farmer*, published in 1908, he discussed the consolidation of schools. "I fear," he wrote, "that much of the impulse for the consolidation of schools is a reflection of the centralized formal city graded school; but it is by no means certain that these institutions are to be the most important or dominating public schools of the future. The small rural school, with all its weaknesses, has the tremendous advantage of directness and simplicity." [11] In a larger sense, he was expressing not only his concern for the rural school, but also his misgivings about removing any existing institution from the rural neighborhood.

Bailey's emphasis on retaining local institutions was part of his deep interest in strengthening rural community life. "It is generally agreed," he said, "that one of the greatest insufficiencies in country life is its lack of organization or cohesion, both in a social and economic way. . . . There is a general absence of such common feeling as would cause them to act together unitedly and quickly on questions that concern the whole community, or on matters of public moment." [12]

Bailey rejected the idea, suggested by others, that American farmers should live in hamlets, like European peasants. Modern means of communication and a growing population would, he felt, eventually produce social solidarity. He also believed that the dividing up of large farms would help to achieve this result, an idea which seems somewhat naïve in the light of historical experience. In the interests of improving neighborhood life, Bailey listed a great many things that farm people ought to do (with emphasis on the *ought*). They should participate in local politics, establish community health programs, extend economic and business cooperation. The country store and the rural press, Bailey said, should be used to promote "rural betterment" and "community action." In short, the strengthening of all kinds of local institutions would result "in evolving a

17

good community sense." All these "oughts" and "musts" required articulation, but, as Bailey himself surely realized, there was a wide gap between setting up goals and providing the means to attain them.

In evaluating Bailey's contribution to the development of the rural social sciences, it must be remembered that he seldom dwelled upon the sordid aspects of rural life, its drudgery, crudities, and monotony, preferring to speak of the ideal farmer and the ideal farm.

Most of his criticism — if it can be called that — of the conditions of rural life was made only by implication. Although he enumerated scores of activities that farm people ought to undertake, he seldom specifically stated how a problem could be studied in order to find a solution, nor did he suggest a need for research. Bailey's strong emphasis on the improvement of schools, from the elementary to the highest level, must be considered a contribution, but it is not apparent that he used his administrative authority at Cornell to encourage the development of the social sciences. The first professor of "rural social organization" was appointed in 1915, two years after Bailey retired.[13]

Yet his books about country life helped to upgrade and dignify the occupation of farming and to set ideals for the development of rural social life. Although his books contain few references to sociology or economics as scholarly disciplines, what he wrote about was essentially the subject matter of both, particularly of sociology. He popularized the themes of the field and his great prestige lent dignity to the subject matter. And it is important to record that volume four of his *Cyclopedia of American Agriculture* was devoted to social and economic questions.

Kenyon Leech Butterfield

There can be no question that Bailey was no more than a herald of sociology. His contemporary, Kenyon Butterfield, however, came somewhat closer to achieving a professional approach to the field. Born in Michigan in 1868, Butterfield also attended Michigan Agricultural College and received a bachelor of science degree in 1891. Although he was born and reared on a farm, he apparently did not take much interest in technical agricultural courses. During the 1890s he edited the *Michigan Grange Visitor* and the Grange department of the *Michigan Farmer*. He served also as superintendent of the Michigan Farmers' Institute and field agent for the Agricultural College. In 1902 he received a master's degree at the University of Michigan, and the next year that institution hired him as an instructor in rural sociology. He must have been the first man to hold such a position.[14]

In the following decades he served as president of Rhode Island State College (1903–6), of Massachusetts Agricultural College (1906–24), and of Michigan State College (1924–28), where he remained until his retirement. During his later years he devoted much attention to the American Country Life Association and took an interest in a number of other activities, including the International Missionary Council. He was the author of four books, of which the earliest — *Chapters in Rural Progress*, published in 1908 — is the most important for our purposes.[15] Most of the material in this volume had already reached a wide audience through publication in such journals as the *Chautauquan*, the *Forum*, *Popular Science Monthly*, the *New England Farmer*, and the *Cornell Countryman*.

Along with other writers of the period, Butterfield attempted to define what was variously called the farm problem, the rural problem, or the country problem. In *Chapters in Rural Progress*, he wrote:

Perhaps the most common error in studying rural conditions is the failure to distinguish the vital difference between the urban problem and the rural problem. *Sociologically the city problem is that of congestion: the rural problem is that of isolation.* . . . We conclude, then, that the farm problem consists in maintaining upon our farms a class of people who have succeeded in procuring for themselves the highest possible class status, not only in the industrial, but in the political and social order — a relative status, moreover, that is measured by demands of American ideals.[16]

, Like Bailey, Butterfield felt it necessary to emphasize the advantages of rural life:

City life goes to extremes; country life, while varied, is more even. In the country there is little of large wealth, luxury, and ease; little also of extreme poverty, reeking crime, unutterable filth, moral sewage. Farmers are essentially a middle class and no comparison is fair that does not keep this fact ever in mind. . . .

Much country life is truly barren; but much more of it is so only relatively and not essentially. . . .

I do not justify neglect of the finer material things of life, nor plead for drab and homespun as passports to the courts of excellence; but I insist that the plainness, simple living, absence of luxury, lack of polish that may be met with in the country, do not necessarily accompany a condition barren of the essentials of the higher life.[17]

19

Butterfield apparently viewed the rural-urban dichotomy in terms of class. He insisted that farmers were "middle class" and that part of the rural problem was their isolation from other "classes." "The well-known conservatism of the farming class," he wrote, "is largely due to class isolation," the effects of which were difficult to eliminate.[18]

Extreme isolation was, indeed, the "bane of country living. Undue conservatism, lack of conformity to progressive views, undue prominence of class feeling, and a tendency to be less alert are things that grow out of this isolation."[19]

Since Butterfield emphasized the social and physical isolation of farm people, he naturally stressed too the need for remedial measures, including "better organization, fuller and richer education, quicker communication." There is no such thing as a lone farmer, he said; "we must have co-operating individuals." Above all, he emphasized the importance of improving human resources through education. Quoting the Grange proverb, "the farmer is of more consequence than the farm and should be first improved," he insisted that the mind must be cultivated before the soil.[20]

The farm question then, in Butterfield's view, was a social question:

. . . the real end is not merely to utilize each acre to its utmost, nor to provide cheap food for the people who do not farm, nor yet to render agriculture industrially strong. The gravest and most far-reaching consideration is the social and patriotic one of endeavoring to develop and maintain an agricultural class which represents the very best type of American manhood and womanhood, to make the farm home the ideal home, to bring agriculture to such a state that the business will always attract the keen and the strong, who at the same time care more for home and children and state and freedom than for millions.[21]

Butterfield's evangelism for rural sociology was specific and direct, and he frequently used the term in his writings. He urged the agricultural colleges to introduce courses in rural sociology and agricultural economics and repeatedly criticized the schools for their failure to provide instruction in these fields. The colleges' responsibility, he pointed out, did not end with training their students in the technical aspects of farming. Educators, he said, "must help the farmer solve all his problems, whether these problems are scientific, or economic, or social, or political."[22]

On many occasions Butterfield seized the opportunity to promote the social sciences. He advocated training in sociology for clergymen and suggested that rural sociology should be a required subject in the teachers' colleges. In 1912 he wrote an article on the subject of rural sociology as a college discipline which represented probably the most sophisticated description of the field to be published up to that time.[23]

In his article Butterfield suggested twelve courses for the new discipline. His list represents a serious effort to describe aspects of rural sociology which students still regard as its proper subject matter. The content of some of the courses he proposed deserves comment. Two of them, "The Rural Problem" and the "Social Status of Rural People," now play an inconspicuous part as separate courses. Except as "Rural Government" is studied in courses on rural institutions, it lies today in the field of political science, and "Rural Law" is no longer considered to be an aspect of rural sociology. But the "Social Aspects of Current Agricultural Questions" have received more and more attention over the years, and the "Social Psychology of Rural Life" has yet to find its proper place in the curriculum. As a whole, Butterfield's list is impressive, showing that he was closer to present-day trends than his co-worker Bailey, who never attempted a definition of rural sociology.

Butterfield was trying to deal with the field as a college discipline, to define its scope and indicate its content. Because of his prestige as a college president, as a member of the Commission on Country Life, and as a well-known lecturer and writer, it meant a good deal to have him preach the necessity for the establishment of rural sociology as part of the academic curriculum.

Equally important, perhaps, is the fact that he used his administrative position, especially at Massachusetts Agricultural College, to see that courses in the field were offered. In 1920 he hired Newell L. Sims to teach rural sociology exclusively. The faculty at Massachusetts also included John Phelan and E. L. Morgan, two men who were later to make important contributions to the science.

Summary

The influence of Bailey and Butterfield was indeed very great. They were well aware of the shortcomings of farm life: the narrowness of outlook, the provincialism, the drudgery, and the crudities. But they also had a vision of what it could be at its best. If they often painted farm life in idyllic terms, as true sons of their time they also believed in progress and had faith that the ideal could be realized. Butterfield's work, particularly, must be regarded as important to the emerging rural social sciences, especially rural sociology.

It is, however, ironic that two such influential persons in the land-grant college organization had so little impact on their colleagues. Few agricultural college administrators were ready to introduce the social sciences into their curricula. It was the teachers' colleges, the theological seminaries, and the organized church groups which were the first to hear the message. The colleges of agriculture limped along uncertainly for decades after Bailey retired in 1913.

3

The Academic Milieu

RURAL sociology would not have developed as a college discipline had it not been for the growth of the other social sciences during the latter part of the nineteenth century. No doubt there would have been continued agitation for rural betterment, both on the campuses and off, and the work of L. H. Bailey and Kenyon Butterfield made an important contribution, as did the reform movement among farmers and the report of the Commission on Country Life. But the development of a scientific discipline requires something more. It is important, therefore, that we give some attention to the development of the social sciences in general and in particular note the beginnings of rural life studies in the fields of sociology and agricultural economics.

Emergence of the Social Sciences

During the last quarter of the nineteenth century such subjects as economics, political science, sociology, and anthropology were only beginning to emerge as recognizable disciplines in the United States. In 1876 John W. Burgess created the department of political science and constitutional law at Columbia University; when he retired thirty-six years later, that single department had become the four departments of history, public law, economics, and sociology.[1] In the year 1892 Richard T. Ely organized a department of economics at the University of Wisconsin and Albion W. Small started at Chicago the first department of sociology to be established anywhere in the world.

In another respect, too, American scholarship was still in its infancy. "It is difficult to realize," one historian commented, "that prior to 1880 there had been no systematic organization of research in the United States either in the field of history or of government,"[2] and the statement was true of other disciplines as well. The training of scholars was then greatly dependent upon European universities, and most men who planned a career in history, political science, or economics considered it necessary to take advanced study in the great German schools.

From their German mentors Americans learned to take a new outlook on society and the economy, as old dogmas were abandoned in favor of a vital study of the actual behavior of economic life. Students returning from abroad brought with them not only a fresh point of view, but also new methods of study, most notably a concern for the accurate gathering of "scientific" facts.

A great impetus to graduate study in the United States came with the establishment of Johns Hopkins University, which opened its doors in 1876 with a primary commitment to graduate education and research. Generally organized on the European model, the new school was regarded by some observers as the first genuine university in the United States.

H. B. ADAMS AND STUDIES OF RURAL COMMUNITIES

A whole generation of scholars was trained at Johns Hopkins by the historian and political scientist Herbert Baxter Adams, who had received a doctoral degree at the University of Heidelberg. In Germany Adams had become interested in the origin and diffusion of political institutions and had written his thesis on the origin of the New England town, which he traced back to England and thence to its "germ" among the early Teutonic tribes. At Johns Hopkins Adams continued his study of American local institutions and drew to his seminars a remarkable group of students who carried on his work by investigating colonial settlements in Connecticut, New York, Pennsylvania, and other areas. The results of their research were published in a famous series called the Johns Hopkins Studies in Historical and Political Science, which was edited by Adams until his death. Richard T. Ely called these studies the "mother of similar series in every part of the United States." [3]

Although Adams himself was especially interested in the political features of early communities, landholding and settlement patterns were inextricably associated, and these aspects were always described in the Johns Hopkins Studies. Thus Adams and his students provided the first descriptions of the earliest rural communities in America. The studies not only constituted a bench mark for the investigation of social change, but also revealed rich sources for research in the archives of early settlements.

RICHARD T. ELY AND LAND ECONOMICS

Another noteworthy scholar associated with Johns Hopkins was Richard T. Ely, who, it will be recalled, established the department of economics at the University of Wisconsin. Ely's great interest was land and the human relationships involved in its use.

Ely also attended the University of Heidelberg, where he studied both economics and political history, receiving a Ph.D. in 1879. He held a position on the faculty at Johns Hopkins from 1881 until 1892, when he received his appointment at Wisconsin. In his autobiography Ely recalled, "It was an historian, Frederick J. Turner, who was responsible for influencing [President Thomas C.] Chamberlin to call me to Wisconsin. Turner had been in my graduate classes at the Johns Hopkins, and though he was, primarily, an historian, he was also a good economist." [4]

Ely's wide-ranging intellectual and social concerns included a basic interest in the institutions of property, particularly the economics of property in land. Soon after his arrival at Wisconsin, he wrote in his autobiography, "we began a systematic treatment of what is now called Land Economics. I treated the whole subject under the awkward title, 'Land Property and the Rent of Land.' " [5]

His preoccupation with the place of land in economic and social life led him to establish the Institute for Research in Land and Public Utility Economics, which took as its motto, "Under all, the Land." In Ely's thinking, land was basic to society and the nature of its tenure and distribution a matter of major social concern. Land was held by people and therefore the human being and his behavior became the center of studies of economic activity.

Like Adams, Ely attracted many able students, a number of whom were to distinguish themselves in later life through their investigations of land economics. One was Henry C. Taylor, who became an avid student of land tenure and later broadened his interests to include other aspects of what eventually came to be called agricultural economics.

PROFESSIONAL RELATIONSHIPS

This brief survey of the early and, it must be admitted indirect, influences of the infant social sciences upon the development of rural sociology would not be complete without some mention of the cross-connections between disciplines and the intellectual contacts among their practitioners. None of the social sciences was highly specialized at the time when these men were finishing their graduate work and launching their careers, and students had easy access to stimulating thinkers in various fields. We have seen that Turner was both a historian and an economist. Ely gave lectures at Wisconsin on "charities and corrections" and taught at least one course in sociology. Taylor studied sociology, reading the works of Spencer and Ward, before he found the field unsatisfactory and turned to economics; these earlier studies may well have been responsible for his continuing interest in the problems of rural people. Scholars from many different fields exchanged ideas at Johns Hopkins, among them Adams, Turner, and Ely.

Another gathering place for social scientists was Chautauqua, that uniquely American institution of popular education. Founded in 1873 by Methodist bishop John H. Vincent as a summer camp for training Sunday-school teachers, it soon broadened its program to include the arts, sciences, and humanities. Distinguished teachers offered lectures and courses in economics, politics, literature, music, and science. "No one," commented Ely in 1938, "can understand the history of this country and the forces which have been shaping it for the last half century without some comprehension of the important work of that splendid institution that was, and is, Chautauqua." [6]

Many outstanding men who contributed in some way to the development of rural sociology came to know each other through Chautauqua. Ely first taught there in 1884 and Adams was a lecturer for many years. Other colleagues were George E. Vincent, the son of Chautauqua's founder and a future sociologist, and William Rainey Harper, who, when he became the first president of the University of Chicago, recruited Vincent for his sociology faculty. Here were contacts of importance for the leaders of social science.

The general development of the social sciences under the leadership of such men as Adams and Ely was important in preparing the way for the special science of rural sociology. More specific influences, however, can be traced to two of the emerging disciplines, general sociology and agricultural economics. These fields are worth examining in somewhat greater detail.

Early Departments of Sociology

The field of sociology first gained a foothold at the private institutions, notably the universities of Columbia and Chicago. When the latter school opened in 1892 under the presidency of William Harper, it initiated a department of sociology, the first in any university in the world. At that time, indeed, there were few places where students could receive any instruction at all in the subject.

The head of the new department at Chicago was Albion Small, who in the early 1880s had studied at the universities of Berlin and Leipzig and later spent a year as a member of Adams' seminar at Johns Hopkins.[7] In 1890 Small had become president of Colby College in Maine, where he taught a course in sociology, apparently the second such course to be given anywhere (the first had been offered by William Graham Summer at Yale in 1876). Small's most noteworthy contribution to the field of sociology lay in his efforts to establish its academic respectability, but for our purposes it is more important to note that he recruited for his staff at Chicago two men who had an interest in rural problems, George Vincent and Charles R. Henderson.

Vincent, after his graduation from Yale, started postgraduate study in sociology at Chicago in 1892. Very soon thereafter he was invited by Small to collaborate in the writing of *An Introduction to the Study of Society* (1894), the first textbook on the subject published in the United States. In a section entitled "The Natural History of a Society," the work contained what was undoubtedly the earliest textbook treatment of the characteristics and problems of rural life. These chapters were almost certainly the work of Vincent. Small seems to have had no special interest in rural problems; Vincent, on the other hand, was a native of Illinois and had lived there at a time when it was still possible to observe something of the pioneering process.[8]

As the section title suggests, the approach was a historical reconstruction of the beginning and development of society from the initial settle-

27

ment of a family on the land to the growth of a city. The setting was the Middle West. Accompanying the text was a series of hypothetical maps showing the isolated farm, a number of farms connected by paths and roads (called by the author a "rural group" but known to sociologists today as a neighborhood), and a village with outlying farmsteads. A schematic plan of a hypothetical city completed the map series.

At the conclusion of each chapter, the author presented a list of subjects for investigation. Among the topics suggested for the chapter "The Rural Group" are the following:

(1) natural conditions; (2) relation to the soil; (3) artificial arrangements (buildings, barns, roads and footpaths); (4) personal elements (general character of each family as a unit, nationalities, economic condition of each family, educational experience, religious and ecclesiastical characteristics, political affiliation); (5) groupings of population (economic, racial, religious, political, according to education, according to age, according to sex, intermarriage between children of different families).

Although some of the suggestions seem naïve in the light of present knowledge, they nevertheless contained the germinal ideas of most of what has become the sociology of rural groups and institutions.

In 1894, the year that saw the publication of Small and Vincent's textbook, Charles R. Henderson, an associate professor of sociology at Chicago, offered the first course on rural social life to be taught in any American university. Sixteen students enrolled for the course, which was called "Social Conditions in American Rural Life" and was concerned with "some problems of amelioration, presented by life on American farms and in villages . . ."[9]

Henderson does not seem to have encouraged his graduate students to undertake field work, but he was apparently the first person to direct the attention of other sociologists to the importance of the rural studies. In 1901 he wrote: "We actually have more and better books on breeding cattle and marketing corn than on forming citizens or organizing culture. Is it not worthwhile to attempt social technology of the rural community?"[10] Despite Henderson's pioneering work, it is obvious that rural life was only a minor interest for him. An ordained minister and chaplain at the University of Chicago, he was also head of the department of practical sociology (what would now be called social work), and his writing was almost entirely in this field.[11]

While Chicago pioneered in the teaching of sociology, Columbia University sponsored the first published research on American rural communities, aside from the historical reconstructions initiated by Adams at Johns Hopkins. Oddly enough, these books came from students of Franklin H. Giddings, an eminent pioneer sociologist but a man who had no interest in rural sociology or its study. Giddings' laissez-faire notions of society and his accompanying lack of sympathy for the farmer's problems have been mentioned earlier. "I think we shall all agree," he once said, "that the farmer has mixed his difficulties with his misunderstandings and made a pretty bad compound . . . The failing is in himself." [12]

In view of such statements, Giddings' role in the development of rural sociology requires some clarification. His position was ably summarized by one of his students, Newell Sims, who wrote in 1957:

He had no particular interest in or special knowledge of country life. Nor did he make any contribution theoretically or otherwise to the subject. . . . Still it must be said in all fairness that he had developed a true scientific approach . . . [which] he communicated to his students. He was definitely trying to develop a quantitative instead of a purely qualitative sociology. . . . To find ways of measuring and weighing sociological data was his chief interest. [13]

Sims also commented specifically on the contradictory relationship between Giddings' Spencer-derived philosophy and his emphasis on a quantitative methodology:

. . . Giddings had little use for social reform efforts. . . . He believed that one served best who could stand and wait the fulfillment of the evolutionary process. The assumption that such a process was operative in the social sphere was of course fallacious and lacked any basis in empirical observation. Thus Giddings' position was strangely paradoxical, his system proceeding from one set of assumptions while his current teachings stressed a diametrically opposed method.

It was therefore Giddings' emphasis on the value of community field studies — for the training they provided in the collection and interpretation of data, as well as for their substantive contribution to the sum of knowledge — that constitutes his importance to the development of rural sociology. Not only Sims, but two other students of Giddings, James M. Williams and Warren H. Wilson, were encouraged to base their doctoral dissertations on field studies of particular communities. That these communities happened to be rural ones was, in a sense, entirely accidental. "We chose rural communities," wrote Sims, "because they were the ones with which we were best acquainted and understood better than any others." The work of these men produced three milestones in the study of rural communities: Williams' *An American Town* (1906), Wilson's *Quaker Hill* (1908), and Sims's *A Hoosier Village* (1912).

Thus at the private universities of Chicago and Columbia an interest in rural life studies began to develop in departments of sociology. A decade or two later a similar regard became apparent among agricultural economists at the land-grant schools.

Agricultural Economists and Rural Social Life

The earliest indication of concern on the part of economists came toward the close of the first decade of the twentieth century, as rural social scientists struggled to define the content and scope of their field. It is significant that the Farm Management Association (the original professional association of agricultural economists), meeting at Iowa State College in 1910, included rural sociology as one aspect of the proper subject matter of the agricultural social sciences. The "Community Aspect," as it was described in a statement prepared by Butterfield and adopted by the association, involved the following questions: "How can the people who farm, best utilize their industrial and social environment in the development of personal character, best co-operate for their common welfare, and so best maintain permanent institutions which are to minister to the continued improvement of the common or community life?" [14]

A year later another professional group, the committee on agricultural instruction of the American Association of Land-Grant Colleges and Universities, attempted to analyze the subject matter of rural economics. This group too concluded that the study of social life should receive attention. The committee's report noted the existence of a "group of rural problems which is quite clearly differentiated from rural economics and forms a branch of social science or sociology, to which the name of rural sociology may be appropriately applied." The development of "strong courses" in this subject was vigorously recommended in order to "raise the college courses in agriculture above the materialistic plane" and emphasize the "vital connection between agricultural science and the welfare of rural people." [15]

Henry C. Taylor, the pioneer of agricultural economics, also recognized from an early date the importance of rural sociology, though he never became reconciled to the use of the term and conceived of what he called

30

"rural life" as the outcome or culminating interest of other phases of agricultural economics.[16] Nevertheless he encouraged the work of men who were interested in the social aspects of farm life, both at the University of Wisconsin, while he was chairman of the department of agricultural economics, and later in Washington, when he became head of the Bureau of Agricultural Economics. Taylor achieved his most notable service to the field when he appointed his former student, Charles J. Galpin, as head of the bureau's Division of Rural Life Studies.

Meanwhile men trained in economics conducted at the University of Minnesota three pioneer social and economic surveys of rural communities in that state.[17] The studies were sponsored by the Bureau of Research in Agricultural Economics of the university's Department of Agriculture. This Bureau of Research, it should be noted, was established in 1911 upon the recommendation of George Vincent, who had just left the University of Chicago to become president at Minnesota.

The Minnesota studies were in the survey tradition and covered a wide range. The first one, produced in 1913 by Carl W. Thompson and Gustav P. Warber, included occupations, business relationships, farmers' organizations, civic relations, roads, education, and religious and social activities. Like the other two monographs, it was illustrated with photographs, charts, and maps.

The 1913 study used the township as the basic area for analysis. The second and third investigations, published in 1915, departed somewhat from this pattern and focused on the community — an important advance. The author of the second study, Louis D. H. Weld, explained the method in his preface: "A village has been selected as the center of economic activities, and the territory covered is that which is tributary to the village . . . In this way it has been intended not only to bring out a comparison between life on the farm and life in a small Minnesota village, but also to bring out the economic dependence of one on the other." The extent of the trade area was presumably a rough approximation; it is not clear that any attempt was made to define its boundaries precisely.

In sponsoring these community surveys agricultural economics pioneered in a type of research which rural sociology later claimed as its own, though it was ten years before further research by a sociologist was done at Minnesota.

At about the same time the first course in rural sociology was offered at Minnesota. Though it was given in 1915–16 on the agricultural campus, it was listed in the department of sociology and anthropology in the College of Science, Literature, and the Arts. The instructor was Paul I. Neergaard. Two years later the course was also offered on the main campus. Thus while research at Minnesota was sponsored by agricultural economics, instruction was provided by the department of sociology and anthropology, although the first course was only for agricultural students.

In summary, we can say that the social sciences in the modern sense began to take definitive shape late in the nineteenth century. Stimulated by an infusion of German scholarship, which provided both a new spirit and a new method, economics and sociology started to gain academic acceptance and respectability. German-trained scholars produced a distinguished group of teachers and innovators. Herbert B. Adams' seminal instruction at Johns Hopkins University resulted in a series of studies of rural colonial communities. Richard Ely learned from his German tutors a preoccupation with land tenure and land economics. In what might be called a second generation of thought, Ely's student Henry Taylor enlarged his teacher's ideas into the field that became agricultural economics and that acted as an elder brother to rural sociology in some institutions. In addition, the new field received significant sponsorship, in both instruction and research, from departments of general sociology, which had gained a foothold at Chicago under Albion Small and at the University of Columbia under Franklin Giddings.

Why Call It Rural Sociology?

As already noted, the first course in rural sociology was taught at Chicago in 1894–95 by Henderson, and the University of Michigan followed suit in 1902 when it hired Kenyon Butterfield. The agricultural colleges, on the other hand, were less ready to adopt the new subject. Rural sociology entered their curricula very slowly and often under other names. A survey made in 1916 showed that of fifty-seven institutions which responded to a questionnaire, forty-four were teaching some form of rural sociology. Significantly, however, some of the schools with the biggest and oldest departments of sociology did not use the term rural sociology.[18]

This reluctance to give the field its name is illustrated by early departmental appointments at Wisconsin and Cornell. The door of Galpin's office at Wisconsin bore the words "Rural Life." Taylor, as we have seen, was opposed to the phrase rural sociology, and when he set up the social research division in the Bureau of Agricultural Economics he called it "Farm Life Studies." A similar reluctance prevailed at Cornell. Albert R. Mann was named professor of "Rural Social Organization" at that school in 1915, and the title was not changed to "Rural Sociology" until 1939.

The opposition to using the term rural sociology in the early years probably arose from two factors. In the first place, sociology was not well developed as a science and the word itself meant practically nothing to the layman, unless he mistakenly identified it with "socialism," as some persons did. A second reason is that the term implied the *study* of rural society, rather than the solution of its problems. To many people the name sociology was both meaningless and cold. Such terms as farm life, country life, and rural life were warm and concrete. Undoubtedly many an administrator, when approving appointments, responded more readily to a title containing "rural life" or "rural social organization," words which he could easily explain to his board of regents.

At the historic annual meeting of the American Sociological Society in 1916, devoted to the theme of the sociology of rural life, John M. Gillette took note of the controversy over the name. He raised another and persistent problem when he questioned the use of the descriptive adjective. "In the vernacular," remarked Gillette, "it has been said of rural sociology, 'There ain't no such animal.' It is asserted that there is but one sociology, and that is the general science of sociology . . . [I] suggest that rural social study is only in its primitive stage, and that in its maturity it may adopt a title which is more formal and less descriptive than that of rural sociology." [19]

It is worth noting that, fifty years later, there are still those who dislike the use of the adjective "rural." It has invariably tagged workers in the field as something other than true sociologists. A man whose specialty is social psychology may be overlooked by a faculty trying to fill a vacancy in that field because he currently holds the title of professor of rural sociology. More annoying perhaps is the fact that some people persist in classifying rural sociology as a specialized field, along with such true specialties as social stratification, the family, and social change.

However, the title with its descriptive adjective has become a matter of firmly established usage. The fact that rural sociology is associated with the colleges of agriculture makes the use of the word "rural" desirable, perhaps, as a tactical matter. But it is not unreasonable to expect that it may sometime be discontinued.

4

Charles Josiah Galpin

As the agricultural sciences developed in the early twentieth century, rural economists seem to have been more alert to the social problems of farm life than were other rural specialists. A line of development can be traced from Richard Ely through Henry Taylor to Charles J. Galpin, a man who deserves a central place in the history of rural sociology. As head of agricultural economics at the University of Wisconsin, Taylor recruited Galpin to teach and to conduct research in rural life. When, by great good fortune, Taylor became the first chief of the Department of Agriculture's Bureau of Agricultural Economics, his admiration for Galpin's work and his appreciation of its importance led him to invite Galpin to join his staff in Washington, D.C. Moving to the nation's capital, Galpin became in 1919 the head of the newly created Division of Farm Life Studies.

Galpin was to make two major contributions to the field of rural sociology. The first lay in his development of a method for delineating the boundaries of what he called the "rurban" community. The second resulted from his stimulation of research projects both at the state level and in the Department of Agriculture.

Early Career and Publications

Galpin was born in Hamilton, New York, on March 16, 1865. His father, a minister, spent virtually his entire life in rural parishes, and the family lived in close association with farm people. The younger Galpin received a bachelor's degree from Colgate University in 1885 and in later years took postgraduate work at Colgate, Harvard, and Clark University. At Harvard he studied psychology with William James and Hugo Münsterberg, and at Clark with G. Stanley Hall.[1]

For many years Galpin was associated with Union Academy in Belleville, New York, first as a teacher of mathematics and science and then as headmaster. During the time he lived in Belleville, Galpin absorbed the country life of his surroundings. "The agricultural background of a scientific character for rural sociology was sketched into my own life pattern while I lived in this unique community," he wrote in his memoirs. "The farming I had seen in childhood was traditional. Here I saw understanding at work in soils and with plants and animals, just as I had seen chemical reactions in the University laboratory, and I became an enthusiast for agriculture as a scientific occupation." [2]

Illness forced Galpin to leave Union Academy in 1901 and seek recovery on a forty-acre farm of cutover land in Michigan. Three years later he was rescued from the "Skims," as he called the cutover area, by a brother who had a part interest in a milk-processing plant at Delavan, a small town in Walworth County, Wisconsin. As manager of the plant, Galpin traveled the countryside, talking to farmers and soliciting new business. He left his job after a year and in 1905 became the student pastor of a church in Madison, Wisconsin. Here he made the acquaintance of Henry C. Taylor, then chairman of the university's agricultural economics department and later the organizer of the Bureau of Agricultural Economics in the Department of Agriculture.

The friendship with Taylor stimulated the student pastor's thinking about rural life, especially its social aspects. In the summer of 1910, at the age of 46, Galpin conceived the idea for a research project that was to be the prototype of his classic 1915 study. He asked the librarian at Belleville, New York, where he had taught for so many years, to obtain for him the membership lists of farm organizations in the village, as well as data giving the location of farm and village homes. "I wanted to see," he later recalled, "which homes, when plotted on a road map, contained the largest number of memberships in the organizations; which the least; which, none. Then I hoped some new kind of social meaning would be disclosed." [3]

With Taylor's encouragement Galpin presented the results of his investigation at the first Wisconsin Country Life Conference in January 1911. It was on the strength of this report that Taylor invited him to join the staff at Wisconsin in the fall of 1911. Giving up his career in the ministry, Galpin worked at the university until 1919, when Taylor invited his protégé to join him in Washington as head of the Division of Farm Life Studies, a position he held until his retirement in 1934.

During the summer of 1911, before assuming his position at the University of Wisconsin, Galpin decided to revisit Walworth County, the scene of his earlier career as milk-plant manager. He wanted to try out, as he put it, "a New York fly in Wisconsin waters." He traveled to Delavan without an idea in his head, he later observed, and spent two days in a hotel room working out the details of a new project in mapping social relationships. The idea brewing in his head was that the rural community was a combination of the trade center and the farm families in the open country who patronized it. It occurred to Galpin that Delavan was a "fine trading town for farmers. The social significance of goods, services, and trade began to trickle in on me for the first time. I decided to make trade and services central." [4]

Little by little he began to build up a questionnaire, modifying and adapting the one used for the Belleville project. By the end of the second day in Delavan he had devised his schedule, a simple 4 by 6 card containing ten items. A local printer made up 3,000 copies — enough, Galpin said, to give him a total of 30,000 facts.

With a county map in hand, Galpin distributed his schedules in the Delavan region before returning to the university. He relied on a volunteer group, mustered from among his acquaintances in the area, to cover the rest of the county. The data collected in this way were assembled at the university and plotted on a county map under Galpin's direction. Thus came into being *The Social Anatomy of an Agricultural Community*. [5]

In evaluating his results, Galpin posed several questions:

Is there such a thing as a rural community? If so, what are its characteristics? Can the farm population as a class be considered a community? Or can you cut out of the open country any piece, large or small, square, triangular, or irregular in shape, and treat the farm families in this section as a community, and plan institutions for them? Would the Norwegian

36

settlement, bound together by one church organization, form a community? Has each farm a community of its own, differing from that of every other? What is the social nature of the ordinary country school district? What sort of social unit is the agricultural township?

. . . Are the villages communities by themselves? Can you safely treat them socially as complete units? How are they related to one another? What is the real meaning of these picturesque human clusters? [6]

Galpin found at least some answers to these important questions through his demonstration of the interdependence of town and country and his delineation of the boundaries of that interdependence.

It is difficult, if not impossible, to avoid the conclusion that the trade zone about one of these rather complete agricultural centers forms the boundary of an actual, if not legal community, within which the apparent entanglement of human life is resolved into a fairly unitary system of interrelatedness. The fundamental community is a composite of many expanding and contracting feature communities, possessing the characteristic, pulsating instability of all real life. [7]

This study had a great impact on rural social research in the United States. For the first time it became possible to view the areas of rural association as discrete units. What had appeared to less perceptive observers as hundreds of indiscriminately scattered farm homes in Walworth County were now revealed as patterned forms of associative life around the village centers. Galpin's method, if not his concept of the community, was a true social invention. Like many developments in science, its simplicity was its strongest and most important feature. Other observers of the rural scene had conceived of the rural community in similar terms but had not developed a precise method of description. Warren H. Wilson, for example, defined the country community as "that territory, with its people, which lies within the team haul of a given center." [8] The "team haul" was at best a picturesque but imprecise definition of boundaries; in the automobile age it would become meaningless. To thoughtful observers of the time, the concept of the village–open country community was fairly obvious, but surprisingly few persons attempted a definition of the relationships in exact terms. Galpin defined the rural community as a rurban complex and developed a method of delineating its boundaries.

Although the *Social Anatomy of an Agricultural Community* was Galpin's major achievement at Wisconsin, it was not the only one. His first publication, *Rural Social Centers in Wisconsin*, was largely the outgrowth of a semester of travel throughout the state and of his conversations with farmers. On the basis of his observations, he described a number of rural institutions, or social centers, that he believed could provide wider social contacts for farm families. His list included the schools, the Grange hall, the community hall, the township municipal hall, the theater, and others.[9]

The Walworth County study was followed in 1917 by a study of churches. This work originated in a quite different sort of project — a biography of John Frederick Oberlin, the Alsatian Lutheran minister for whom Oberlin College was named. In order to obtain funds for publishing Oberlin's life, Galpin, on Taylor's advice, selected a dozen outstanding rural churches, described them, and wrote a preface on the church as an agent of social control. Oberlin's biography appeared only at the end of *The Country Church, and Social and Economic Forces*. Other minor publications included a mimeographed report on retirement among farmers, for years virtually the only study of the subject; a bulletin on the *Rural Relations of High Schools*; and *Farm Tenancy*, one of the earliest studies of tenancy to be written by a sociologist.[10]

In preparing for his teaching assignment at Wisconsin, Galpin had sifted through the few books then available on country life and found them characterized by opinion and bias.[11] His impatience with hollow generalization and his determination to think independently are apparent in his major books, *Rural Life* and *Rural Social Problems*. Neither of them contained a single footnote. His omission of bibliographical apparatus was deliberate, though admittedly experimental. His purpose, he wrote in the preface to *Rural Life*, was to avoid erecting a "false educational ideal" and to "instigate observation of local conditions, study of one's community, and action, — confident, self-reliant action."

Rural Life, published in 1918, contained fourteen chapters, at least seven of which grew directly out of his earlier studies at Wisconsin. In spite of the many changes in rural life since the book was written, it contains many observations that are still relevant. Although it was more concerned with promoting social action than are modern textbooks, it laid a philosophical and factual basis for the reforms advocated by the author.

Rural Social Problems, published in 1924 after Galpin had gone to Washington, was viewed by its author as a "forebook." Each chapter represented the preliminary discussion of a topic which was to be treated at greater depth in a series of books on rural life projected with the Century Company. Galpin arranged for eight books in the series besides his own, though only five ever saw the light of day. They were *The Woman on the*

Farm by Mary Meek Atkinson, *The Farmer's Standard of Living* by E. L. Kirkpatrick, *Rural Municipalities* by Theodore B. Manny, *The Suburban Trend* by H. Paul Douglass, and *The Farmer's Church* by Warren Wilson.

The Washington Years

Galpin's years of teaching and research at Wisconsin had prepared him well for his unexpected role on a vastly broader stage as the head of the Division of Farm Life Studies.[12] In the study of Walworth County he had not only developed a new method but also suggested ideas and relationships that required further study. Equally useful in his new position were his great enthusiasm and the reach of his warm personality. He aggressively searched for potential collaborators who, with encouragement and a small grant of funds, might undertake studies in their own localities.

The interest in rural social institutions which developed in his Wisconsin days led Galpin to encourage Wayne C. Nason, a member of his Washington staff, to make studies of rural community centers, including libraries, hospitals, fire fighting facilities, and industries. These studies, published as Farmers' Bulletins by the Department of Agriculture, were designed to publicize the "prideful features in rural life, to neutralize the prevailing pessimism about farm people, to hearten discouraged farm women, to stir up emulation among farm youth." More than a million copies were distributed.[13]

In 1922 Galpin added Ellis L. Kirkpatrick to his staff and assigned him the task of investigating the farmer's standard of living. Kirkpatrick had already made a pioneer study of this problem in his doctoral thesis at Cornell.[14] With characteristic energy he now arranged for further studies of farm-family living in eleven states in New England, the Middle Atlantic area, the South, and the Middle West, obtaining in all data on 2,886 families. The results were brought together in a book that was included in the previously mentioned series edited by Galpin.[15] Earlier investigations of family budgets in the United States had been concerned chiefly with non-farm groups — urban slum-dwellers and members of the working class. To Kirkpatrick belongs the distinction of adapting and applying the methodology of earlier studies to farm families.

Another recruit to the Washington staff during the 1920s was Theodore B. Manny, a teacher of rural life at Hendrix College in Conway, Arkansas. Galpin arranged a cooperative project for Manny in Arkansas and in 1928 brought him to Washington to study the "social psychology of farmers' economic organizations, particularly the marketing cooperatives." [16] Later Manny studied the social psychology of rural local government and became the author of *Rural Municipalities*, one of the volumes in the series which Galpin edited.

After putting his staff to work on various projects, Galpin visited state colleges in the Midwest and on the Pacific Coast. His trip convinced him of the importance of having sociologists on every college staff, men who would come to understand the sociology of the state and of the communities just as other kinds of agricultural specialists came to understand problems in their respective fields. But for all his enthusiasm, he found deans and directors unreceptive to his idea. "I failed to interpret correctly the glassy look of boredom that stole into their eyes, gently masked by a fine courtesy," he recounted. "When their interest failed to kindle, I thought it a perverse hardness of heart. Little then did I suspect that it might take 50 years to get the seed of rural sociology planted and growing in all the state colleges of agriculture." [17]

Galpin achieved greater success in another of his projects, that of persuading the Bureau of the Census to provide more complete statistics on farm populations. In his book *Rural Life* he had argued eloquently for a separate census classification of farm and rural nonfarm categories. Calling attention to the 1910 census, he noted the elaborate tabulation of farm animals and its usefulness for the rural economist: "Horses, mules, goats, and bees are listed separately and later tabulated geographically in separate totals. . . . Does the rural sociologist, however, get this clean-cut analysis in the population schedule and tabulation? No. Speaking figuratively, his horses and mules are added together in one total, and this total is diluted with bees and goats." [18]

As head of the rural life division, Galpin persuaded the census bureau to tabulate farm and rural nonfarm statistics in the 1920 census. To his dismay, however, the tabulation was made by states only, and not by counties, and included only a few simple characteristics. In order to demonstrate the usefulness of county data, he prevailed upon the census bureau to permit five members of his staff to make a further analysis of the schedules. Two years of work produced a detailed tabulation of data concerning composition, characteristics, and occupations for eight selected counties. [19] After that experience, the Bureau of the Census adopted the two rural categories, farm and nonfarm, together with a complete reporting by counties and by characteristics. For many years, however, the division at its own expense collected the data on which it based its annual estimates of the movement of population to and from farms during the intercensal years.

The Cooperative Studies

The achievements wrought in Washington by Galpin and his staff, important as they were, are secondary in significance to the cooperative research which the Division of Farm Life Studies promoted with individuals in several states. The first and historically most important were four neighborhood studies undertaken in Wisconsin, New York, North Carolina, and Missouri. The method employed in the Walworth County study to locate the rural community left untouched the numerous smaller social groups which observers knew to exist. Could they be located and their boundaries mapped? To find the answer became the objective of the neighborhood studies.

PRIMARY GROUPS IN WISCONSIN

John H. Kolb's investigation of agricultural neighborhoods in Wisconsin, published in 1921, was the first of the cooperative studies to appear. The method employed by Kolb was simple: each farm family in the study was asked to give the "name" of the country neighborhood in which it lived. On the basis of the replies, Kolb was able to map out boundaries which included all the farms presumed to lie within the same "name" group. The boundaries were further checked by personal interviews with knowledgeable farmers in each neighborhood.[20]

The 121 neighborhoods thus located were classified according to the factors which originally caused their formation and which were still important. These factors included "common former residence," "economic purpose," "educational purpose," "leading family," "mail distribution," "nationality bonds," "religious purpose," "social purpose," and "topography." Nationality, religion, and social purpose were found to be the principal bonds of neighborhoods.

Following Galpin's method, Kolb also asked the families where they went for trade and services. This information made it possible to relate the neighborhood to its village or trade center. Kolb concluded that the village was the farmers' "service station" and that the formation of a community required the federation of village and open country groups.

41

Kolb defined a primary group as "that first group beyond the family which has social significance and which is conscious of some local unity." [21] He did not consider the neighborhood to be a community, but rather a much simpler unit, many of which might be involved in a single community. He was convinced, however, that the smaller units were identifiable as geographic entities because the members of the neighborhood themselves were able to designate the spatial limits of their unit. Such geographic limits were not hard and fast, he advised, because groups were "psychological" in character and constantly changing.

NAME COMMUNITIES IN NORTH CAROLINA

Eight months after the Kolb bulletin appeared, Carle C. Zimmerman and Carl C. Taylor published their study of Wake County, North Carolina. Using a method similar to that employed by Kolb in Wisconsin, they were able to locate 133 so-called "communities," of which 83 were white and 50 were Negro. Ninety-five percent of the names given by the families to these units were those of churches, schools, stores, or old, well-known families. After looking more closely at the mapped units, however, the investigators concluded that the "name" communities were not really sociological communities. Instead they were localities which contained "numerous communities inhabiting the same area" but "separated from each other by race, class status, social practices, and standards of conduct." [22]

To some extent the authors of the North Carolina study appeared to take issue with both Kolb and Galpin on the nature of the geographic community. Part of the difference was semantic, arising from Zimmerman and Taylor's extremely restrictive definition of a community ("only one class of people with one standard of living inhabiting the same area" [23]). Neither Kolb's definition of primary groups nor Galpin's concept of the trading area as a community required complete homogeneity. Zimmerman and Taylor nevertheless brought to the attention of sociologists the fact that conditions in Wisconsin were not typical of the entire country, and that race and class differences were crucial factors affecting the social relationships of rural people in the South.

NEIGHBORHOOD AND COMMUNITY IN NEW YORK

The New York study, conducted by Dwight Sanderson and Warren S. Thompson and published in 1923, was somewhat broader in design than the Wisconsin and North Carolina investigations; it sought to map not

42

only the neighborhoods but the rurban community areas as well. Following the methods used by Kolb and Zimmerman and Taylor, the investigators located 222 locality names employed by 3,177 households. They also raised crucial questions as to what a neighborhood really is.

"It is obvious," they wrote, "that the mere using of the same locality name by six or a dozen farms does not necessarily make them constitute a neighborhood; it may be a mere geographic name of location, and no social ties may exist among the families. Some criterion of what constitutes a neighborhood must therefore be established before we can proceed to any evaluation of its social significance." [24] Sanderson and Thompson set up two attributes for classifying a group as a neighborhood: "the amount of neighborliness and the degree to which it was common to the whole group" and "whether it functioned as a group." They tried to apply these criteria to the 222 name localities, by means of questionnaires and selective interviewing, but the attempt lacked precision and was not entirely convincing. [25]

One result of the study was a classification of neighborhoods into seven categories: hamlet, institutional, business, ethnic, kinship, topographic, and village. The authors found that the hamlet neighborhood was the most persistent, that the business type had virtually disappeared, and that the kinship type was still evident but "passing." "In general," they concluded, "the rural neighborhood in Otsego County is ceasing to function as a social unit except where its life is centered in some local institution." In a second phase of the New York study, community areas of the county were delineated (following Galpin) in terms of trade and services. The authors found 43 such communities and noted that their limits never coincided with the 24 official township boundaries.

The New York and Wisconsin studies reached similar conclusions with respect to mappable social units. The factors determining locality groups varied in the two states, however, with topography playing a major role in New York, and ethnic and religious factors predominating in Wisconsin. The New York investigators agreed with Kolb that there was a difference between a neighborhood and a community. (Zimmerman and Taylor in the North Carolina study seemed less clear on the difference between the two entities, apparently regarding both as communities in the sociological sense.) Sanderson and Thompson also agreed with Kolb that the distinguishing factor was the range of services offered, though they differed on the exact number of services required to make the distinction.

43

GROUP CONSCIOUSNESS IN MISSOURI

Ezra L. Morgan and Owen Howells found "name consciousness" less pronounced in Missouri than had been the case in Wisconsin, New York, or North Carolina.[26] Most frequently rural people responded to the question, "What is the name of this neighborhood?" by asking, "You mean, what school district is this?" Further probing brought the response, "Well I guess you would call it Hinton neighborhood. This is the Brown (school) district, but we get our mail from Columbia and we trade mostly at Hinton." Invariably the interviewers had to explain their aims in detail before they could get the reply they sought. They were able to locate 59 groups, but their map shows large blank spaces where no groups apparently existed. The school, they discovered, was the most important factor in developing primary group consciousness.

The authors attempted a rating of groups in terms of the "intensity of primary group consciousness," using such criteria as the "frequency with which the group came together for any purpose, the readiness with which the group name was accepted and recognized by those within and without the area, and the frequency with which activities occurred that demanded a conscious recognition of group organization." [27] The ratings, as the authors recognized, were on the whole too subjective and arbitrary; nevertheless, their attempt was an interesting innovation.

Summary

Galpin inaugurated what must be called the beginnings of social ecology in the United States. His Walworth County findings, together with the four subsequent studies, revealed an undeniable ecological structure of rural society. There could be no further doubt that the propinquity of rural families was the basis for social interaction among them, though this was true to a greater degree in some areas than in others. The studies also showed that there were many overlapping areas of social groupings — the school district, the Grange membership area, the churches, and other special interest groups — and that neighborhoods were in a state of flux as families moved from place to place.[28] In the South, as the investigations demonstrated, Negro and white neighborhoods occupied the same locality but remained distinct from each other. All the studies pointed to the importance of organizing public services, such as the agricultural extension service, on the basis of the primary group.

5

Support from Church and Lay Groups

THE year 1919, which witnessed the beginning of the Division of Farm Life Studies, also saw the founding of two nationwide, privately supported agencies concerned with the social aspects of agriculture — the Interchurch World Movement and the American Country Life Association. The termination of World War I had released the nation's energies for domestic problems, and professionals and laymen again turned their attention to the countryside. The Interchurch Movement, and its more important successor, the Institute for Social and Religious Research, attempted to bring scientific methods to the study of socioreligious problems. The Country Life Association, organized by representatives of a number of secular groups, helped to focus the nation's attention on the need to reform country life. The history of rural sociology would not be complete without some consideration of the contributions made by these groups.

The Interchurch World Movement

As we have seen, the disquiet of Protestant leaders about rural conditions and their impact on the institutional church was manifested at least

as early as the 1880s. By the second decade of the twentieth century —
years before the land-grant colleges saw fit to sponsor rural social studies
— various religious bodies were engaged in making surveys in a number
of states. Under the leadership of the clergyman and educator Warren H.
Wilson, the Board of Home Missions of the Presbyterian Church in the
United States of America conducted church and community surveys in
counties in Pennsylvania (1910), Indiana and Tennessee (1911), Missouri and Maryland (1912), Arkansas (1914), California (1915), and
Oregon (1916).

In Ohio Paul L. Vogt undertook a series of rural life surveys that were
sponsored jointly by the Ohio Rural Life Association and the Church and
Country Life Department of the Federal Council of Churches. Vogt was
then professor of rural economics and sociology at Ohio State University;
he later became superintendent of rural work for the Board of Home Missions of the Methodist Episcopal Church. Vogt's Ohio surveys, completed
in 1913 and 1914, included *Church Growth and Decline in Ohio* and
Country Churches of Distinction, as well as various regional studies.[1]

These activities of separate denominations contributed to the development of the Interchurch Movement, which arose from a growing conviction among Protestant bodies that greater cooperation was a critical need.[2]
The experience of many religious bodies in united relief work during
World War I had proved the good sense and utility of interchurch cooperation in both domestic and foreign activities. Furthermore, the investigations of men like Wilson and Vogt had demonstrated the value of
surveys in revealing the social context in which churches had to function.
After some preliminary steps toward organization, one hundred representatives of various Protestant groups met in February 1919 to launch
the short-lived Interchurch World Movement.[3]

Its purpose was nothing less than a survey of the entire world to "ascertain the world-task of the Christian churches, and to secure and register as well as train the religious forces to meet the need." As far as the
domestic program was concerned, the sponsors planned to survey every
county and major center in the United States, as well as to study the home,
general and religious education, and industrial relations. To this end, the
most experienced persons available were enlisted to plan schedules. State
and regional conferences were held to acquaint clergy and laymen with
the program. County councils were set up to facilitate the work at the
local level, and a department of education and publicity was organized.

46

The movement was scarcely under way when criticism began. Some church groups feared it as the beginning of an ecumenical movement which would swallow them. Others questioned the methods of raising funds and disliked the high-pressure advertising. One activity which aroused especially bitter controversy was a report on a steel strike in Pennsylvania. At a time when the American labor movement was still young and striking workers received little public sympathy, a few influential industrialists felt that this report went beyond the purpose of the movement. Edwin L. Earp, who later evaluated the program, believed that it was handicapped because of a "lack of practical social engineering, and the lack of ability to cope with the social psychology of the people following the cessation of war." [4]

This extraordinary movement, which completed its organization in February 1919 and did not officially define its purposes until May of that year, had collapsed by August 1920.[5] During its brief existence, however, it created state and county organizations throughout the United States, raised nearly $200,000,000, completed a reported 1,000 county surveys, and published the well-known *Survey of Industrial Relations* (the study of the Pennsylvania steel strike). It involved in its program an estimated one-third of the Protestant ministers and church leaders of the country.

The significance of the Interchurch World Movement lies in the mere fact of its existence. It mobilized interested personnel in the states, counties, and cities and placed in their hands the survey schedules and instructions for using them. Moreover, the population of large sections of the country participated as "interviewees," an educational experience of great, if immeasurable, value. It, as Earp stated, every county in the nation was surveyed, the movement's significance for the emerging field of rural sociology can readily be appreciated.

The Institute for Social and Religious Research

Although the Interchurch Movement disintegrated in mid-career, it possessed a successor and legatee in the Institute for Social and Religious Research, at least so far as domestic studies were concerned. The institute's origins in January 1921 have been described in a brief history published in 1929:

The idea of a permanent religious research and survey organization was

47

conceived by some of the members of the survey staff of the Interchurch World Movement. They held the view that an ecclesiastically controlled agency was not the most competent to conduct unbiased studies in the realm of religion and church organization, and they, therefore, suggested an altogether independent agency. . . . The purpose . . . was to bring the methods of social science to bear upon the solution of religious and socio-religious problems, and also to promote cooperation among the Christian forces of the world.[6]

Searching for funds, the founding committee approached John D. Rockefeller, Jr., who agreed to provide financial backing.

As a research agency, the institute complemented the work of the Division of Farm Life Studies, though its method of operation was somewhat different. Galpin made direct subventions to individuals and left to them the design and execution of projects which they chose — subject, of course, to his approval. The institute planned its studies in the central office and then sought the cooperation of state personnel and institutions in carrying them out.

Much of the institute's success can be attributed to its director of rural research, Edmund deS. Brunner. Since Brunner had been responsibly associated with the rural surveys of the defunct Interchurch World Movement, one of his first endeavors was to salvage as much as possible of the work done by the earlier organization. A number of important studies of church-community relations were published as a result of his efforts.[7] Brunner next launched an extremely important series of studies of American villages. In cooperation with local agencies, including colleges of agriculture and state boards or departments of education and agriculture, 177 villages ranging in population from 250 to 2,500 were selected for intensive study. A special population analysis of the villages was made from the 1920 census schedules. (This tabulation was achieved through the intercession of Galpin, who, it will be remembered, had earlier obtained census bureau permission for a special tabulation of the farm population in eight counties.) Of the 177 villages, 140 were chosen for special study by trained field investigators. The results were brought together and published in the so-called village series.[8]

Although the study centered on villages, these population centers were considered in relation to the countryside they served. As Brunner commented:

. . . It was necessary to ascertain the extent of the community so that its area could be measured and its people counted . . . the community of the agricultural village was defined as the population of that area in which the majority of the people avail themselves of the use of a majority of the social, economic and religious services of the village. The community line enclosing the area in which these people live is not necessarily identical with the line enclosing any given service area, though it may coincide with one or more of such lines. It is rather an average of all the service lines. The various service lines were obtained in the main by questioning villagers and checking their replies by field investigation along every road leading from the village.[9]

In significant follow-up surveys, the 140 villages were restudied in the years 1930 and 1936.[10] The restudies revealed the changes that were taking place not only in the villages but in the adjacent areas as well. Among other important results, they demonstrated that specialization was largely a function of the size of the village and the number of farm families in the trade area; that over a period of time the size of the trade area increased as a result of improved transportation; and that farm families, no longer bound to one locality, used several centers depending on the wants they sought to satisfy. The institute's original studies of villages thus opened up a new field for research and provided an important bench mark for studies of change. Each succeeding census was carefully analyzed for changes, and the trends noted often became the basis of projections for the future.

Another distinctive contribution of Brunner and the workers in the institute concerned the immigrant population. Noting that immigration had been considered an urban problem and that little attention had been paid to foreign-born persons living in rural America, Brunner took advantage of the first analysis of the rural farm population provided by the census of 1920.[11] His study not only showed the distribution by states of immigrants on farms, but also drew together the available information on the process of assimilation. Among other things, Brunner established the facts that immigrant children were as intelligent as children of native-born parents and that intermarriage with other nationalities was not common among immigrant groups. Community participation, Brunner also discovered, was often retarded by language, nationality differences, and preoccupation with individual survival. Such participation as occurred was motivated by economic considerations.

During its lifetime the Institute for Social and Religious Research produced seventy-eight volumes incorporating the results of its rural and urban studies. Brunner and H. Paul Douglass were responsible for half of the forty-eight projects carried out by the institute.[12]

The Country Life Association

While private agencies investigated the rural milieu of religious institutions, a nationwide forum for persons concerned with rural problems was provided by the American Country Life Association. This group grew out of a meeting held in Washington, D.C., in November 1918, which was probably initiated by Kenyon Butterfield. In attendance were representatives of various agencies and governmental bureaus involved with aspects of rural life. The initial meeting in Washington resulted two months later in the first National Conference on Country Life, held in January 1919 at Baltimore. Here the association was formally organized; Butterfield was elected president and C. J. Galpin secretary. A second conference gathered in Chicago in the fall of that year. The two conferences of 1919 inaugurated a series of national meetings that were to be held annually for more than two decades.

Carl C. Taylor has viewed the Country Life Association as part of the so-called country life movement, which emerged in America late in the nineteenth century from a growing awareness of the "social, intellectual, and economic inadequacies of country life." This somewhat amorphous movement was defined by Taylor as a "widely varied group of organized activities" concerned with the "cultural and social welfare of the rural population." [13] Among these early activities, few if any of which were national in scope, it is appropriate to mention the Farmers' Institutes. The institutes — an early expression of the desire of the colleges of agriculture to reach their adult constituencies — predated by some years the creation of the Agricultural Extension Service in 1914. While the institutes emphasized the technology of agriculture and homemaking, there were also discussions of economic problems, of cooperative marketing, and of community problems. Other local programs, which came to be called country life conferences or some equivalent phrase and were more specifically part of the country life movement, were often promoted by the teachers' colleges.

Butterfield and Bailey were, as we have seen, preeminent spokesmen for the country life movement. Butterfield himself had been instrumental in organizing the New England Conference on Rural Progress as early as 1907. Some idea of the proliferation of activity at the local level can be gained from an article in the *Prairie Farmer,* which noted in its issue of June 15, 1915: "There are well up toward a dozen organizations in Chicago that are trying to uplift the farmer."

By 1919 country life associations under various names had been organized in nine states and one Canadian province. The national association, though in no sense a federation of the local, state, and regional groups, became a rallying point for them, providing further stimulus and perhaps guidance.

Throughout its life, the national association's most important function was its sponsorship of the annual conferences. The first meeting, at Baltimore, was attended by 175 persons from a score of states, representing twenty-five national groups and five federal bureaus. By the time of the second conference in the fall of 1919, the association boasted nearly five hundred members.

At that time, the group formulated its purposes as follows: "to facilitate discussion of the problems and objectives of country life and the means of their solution and attainment; to further the efforts and increase the efficiency of agencies and institutions engaged in this field; to disseminate information calculated to promote a better understanding of country life, and to aid in rural improvement." In pursuing these objectives, the association printed the conference proceedings and, after its initial years, employed an executive secretary. It also published *Rural America,* a monthly magazine aimed at a wide readership among farmers, housewives, clergymen, schoolteachers, and academic professionals in all fields of specialization.[14]

Kenyon Butterfield, who served as president during the association's first and most important decade, was probably responsible for its strong orientation toward sociological issues. Between 1919 and 1930 discussions at the annual meetings focused on such topics as rural health, rural organization, town and country relationships, the country community, the rural home, religion in country life, rural youth, and the country life movement.

The importance of the social science disciplines was emphasized at the second national conference, when E. R. Groves, dean of New Hampshire College, reported that the "teaching of rural sociology" could be improved by:

1. Greater emphasis upon the fact that the student needs to be trained through his courses to think socially and to make firsthand use of source-material of social significance.

2. Greater cooperation between members of the teaching staff and extension and research specialists in the rural field at the institutions where teaching, extension and research work are separately maintained.[15]

The late 1920s were the golden years of the Country Life Association. The 1928 conference, held jointly with the American Farm Economics Association, climaxed Butterfield's career as president and celebrated a "Decade of Rural Progress." Prominent agricultural economists read papers stressing the importance of raising the rural standard of living. (Henry Taylor urged the necessity for increased consumption on the part of farm families. Any "class of producers gets only what it consumes," he pointed out, "and farmers must learn this lesson.") More than any other, perhaps, the 1928 conference was notable for the wide representation of farm and nonfarm groups, professional people, and farm men and women among those who attended.

During the subsequent years of depression and war, however, the association suffered increasingly from declining membership and serious budgetary limitations. Lacking from its inception a firm financial basis in membership fees, the organization depended heavily upon support from private contributors and foundations. In 1926, a peak year for income, individual gifts totaled $22,196 and the Russell Sage Foundation, for many years a reliable supporter, contributed $10,000. Membership fees, on the other hand, furnished less than 10 percent of the budget for 1926 and much less in some other years.[16]

Serious troubles began during the 1930s. By 1934 the number of dues-paying members had dropped below 250, and contributions from private individuals virtually disappeared. Foundation awards, in diminishing amounts, kept the organization afloat during the decade of the thirties. In that period, however, the association managed to sponsor annual forums on agricultural issues and policies. Especially in the early days of the New Deal, when agricultural and rural life problems were unusually acute, these forums became important platforms for the explanation and discussion of controversial policies and programs.

Generous grants from the Farm Foundation injected new life into the association during 1939 and 1940. The 1939 grant made possible the assembling of an exhibition of paintings of rural life; an exhibit of several hundred books concerned with rural poetry, fiction, recreation, and rural life generally; the employment of specialists in folk games and folk music; and the procurement of a Danish authority on folk schools.

Through the efforts of the Farm Foundation's director, Henry C. Taylor, the association was able in 1939 to form a committee on rural education and hire an executive director for it. The committee set to work with a budget of about $6,000 and high hopes of influencing rural education in the United States, but it had scarcely begun its program when the deepening crisis of war and other factors brought about its end.[17]

Although the association opened the year of 1941 on an optimistic note, the roof was about to fall in. Early in July the Farm Foundation withdrew its support. Benson Y. Landis, the association's executive secretary, found it necessary to inform his board of directors that he did not "have in sight the resources to carry through the program for the calendar year." The annual conference was cancelled, the national office closed, and the paid personnel dismissed. In November 1942 the executive committee met and reluctantly recommended the dissolution of the American Country Life Association.[18]

Various reasons have been given for the collapse of the association. One critic, the editor of a national farm magazine, claimed that its failure resulted from the fact that rural sociologists had taken control. It is true that rural sociologists were moving spirits in the organization from its inception; however, they provided leadership not because of any interest in manipulating the group for their own benefit, but because of the failure of others to interest themselves in its welfare.

In retrospect, it seems clear that the association had outlived its usefulness. With the passage of time, its purposes were increasingly met by other organizations. By the 1940s farm people themselves were widely served by three major farm organizations and were participating in unprecedented numbers in cooperatives of various types.[19] Then too there had been a vast expansion of federal agencies devoted to improving various aspects of rural life. The agricultural extension service, for example, was giving increased attention to the social problems of home and community. The federal office of education emphasized the provision of rural services to local units through state instrumentalities. Other federal agencies had been created to provide much-needed specialized services — soil conservation, forest conservation, flood control, and rural electrification.

Meanwhile the rural sociologists, who had enthusiastically supported the association, found that their interests and energies were increasingly diverted to other organizations — to the rural section of the American Sociological Association, founded in 1922, and to their own professional association, established in 1937.

During the years of its existence, however, the American Country Life Association served as a rallying point for a variety of individuals and groups who were concerned about rural social problems. It called to the nation's attention the needs of rural people and succeeded in promoting programs of reform.

Directed toward improving those aspects of country life which fell within the field of sociology, the association provided a strong impulse toward the development of the discipline, particularly in its early years. Its annual programs were almost entirely elaborations of the subject matter of the emerging discipline. It served too as a semiprofessional organization for the early rural sociologists. At the annual conferences these men made worthwhile contacts with each other and with rural specialists in such fields as economics, education, and sociology.

Summary

Although the Interchurch World Movement made no real contribution to rural sociology in the form of published research, it served to create a favorable climate for more permanent structures. During its short lifetime it enlisted the participation of millions of people. It convinced philanthropists like John D. Rockefeller, Jr., as well as the leaders of various denominations that studies of the social and economic milieu in which the churches functioned were indispensable.

From the movement's ashes rose the Institute for Social and Religious Research. Brunner's work on the agricultural villages of America greatly enhanced the understanding of rural society on a national scale and supplemented the work on smaller units done by Galpin and his cooperators. Brunner, through his work on immigrants, first called attention to the importance of diverse ethnic groups in the structure of rural society.

At the same time, the American Country Life Association served to keep alive the flame lighted by Roosevelt's Commission on Country Life. Its influence went far beyond the ranks of the professionals who actively participated; thousands of laymen attended the annual meetings, heard the message, and carried it back to their communities.

6

Sending Down the Roots

BY THE year 1920 the teaching of rural sociology was well established in many colleges and institutions, although in some schools the discipline still passed under a variety of other names, such as rural life, rural social organization, and rural social problems. Until the second half of the decade, however, funds for research were extremely limited. Except for sporadic state support, most research, as we have seen, was promoted by church organizations and private institutions.

When Galpin began his administration of the Division of Farm Life Studies, therefore, he provided a much-needed impetus to research activity through financial support to his cooperators at various colleges and universities. Four of these studies have been reviewed in Chapter 4. We need to discuss some additional studies and say something about the lives and subsequent work of the men involved and about others who became associated with them in the early years.

Rural Sociology at Cornell University

Due to the early establishment of a favorable climate for rural sociology at Cornell University, that institution became, and has remained, one of the outstanding centers for research and the training of personnel. In large measure its stature was the result of the work of Ezra Dwight Sanderson. Born in 1878 in a small Michigan village, Sanderson spent his early youth in Detroit. After graduating from Michigan Agricultural College, he went to Cornell to study entomology, taking a second B.S. degree in 1898. During the following twenty years, his career in entomology called him successively to colleges in Maryland, Delaware, New Hampshire, Texas, and West Virginia. He served as director of the New Hampshire Agricultural Experiment Station from 1907 to 1910 and held a similar position at West Virginia from 1912 to 1915. He was author of a number of works in the field of entomology, including some widely used textbooks.

Although Sanderson had no formal contact with rural sociology, he gradually became convinced of the need for studying rural society. This attitude resulted in part from his observation of the difficulty of establishing extension work in West Virginia in 1914–15. Then too he was impressed by the report of the Commission on Country Life and by the progress made by his colleagues in agricultural economics. As a result, he resigned his position in West Virginia in 1917 in order to enroll as a graduate student in sociology at the University of Chicago, where he received his Ph.D. degree in 1921. In the meantime he was appointed head of the recently created department of rural social organization at Cornell, a position he held from 1918 until his retirement in 1943.

For many years Sanderson and his staff at Cornell had little support from the field of general sociology. Indeed, a department of sociology and anthropology was not established in the arts college at Cornell until 1939. (In the same year the name of the earlier department was changed from "Rural Social Organization" to "Rural Sociology.") Sanderson's important study of social areas in New York State appeared as an agricultural experiment station bulletin in 1923. It was followed over the years by several others dealing with social ecology.[1] The analysis of population composition and trends in New York also claimed his attention in his early period at Cornell, and in addition he made a pioneer study of rural health during the late 1920s.[2]

Sanderson's first book-length publication in the field of sociology was *The Farmer and the Community*.[3] The title might well be considered the theme of his work in rural sociology. He spent a good deal of time and effort in defining and locating the community, but he was concerned above all with its organization and with ways of improving its functioning for the benefit of the farm people. Like his contemporaries in rural sociology, Sanderson was basically a reformer, concerned with ameliorating rural life by the provision of better schools, better health facilities, better means of communication, and so on. Sanderson believed that rural sociology must justify itself by the application of sociological principles to the solution of practical problems. This point of view was embodied in the title of his textbook, *Rural Sociology and Rural Social Organization*.[4] "Rural sociology" was the science and "rural social organization" the application.

This is not to suggest that Sanderson did not stress the development of the science. His training in the biological field led to an attempt to utilize some of the methods of that branch of learning in his adopted field. His most pronounced achievement in this respect was the development of a key for classifying and describing human groups, analogous to the keys used for the identification of animal and plant species.[5] While his attempt at arrangement did not come into general use by others, it represented an ingenious attempt to understand the complex range of human group life. As he summed up his point of view:

If we are to have a scientific knowledge of these [various sorts of human] groups, we must first be able to identify them, which will involve a knowledge of those characteristics of structure which make possible their identification. Then if we seek to know how these groups may be controlled, we must know how they act, how they behave. The first is the anatomy and taxonomy, or classification of society; the latter involves its physiology. As in biology, the meaning of anatomy is revealed only with an exact knowledge of physiology, so in the study of human society we must know its physiology as well as its structure. The one is psychology, the other sociology. They are interdependent; both deal with the same phenomena, but each abstracts a different aspect of the phenomena, and, as in biology, each aspect requires a special technique for its investigation.

To carry our biological analogy farther, we must recognize that although biology includes such pure sciences as anatomy, taxonomy, physiology and ecology, its chief value is in its application to human well-being, through the applied biological sciences, such as plant pathology, economic entomology, parasitology, etc. So social science has its application of sociology, social psychology, and other sciences and scientific methods to the problems of social welfare.[6]

Under Sanderson's leadership rural sociology at Cornell University became a magnet for graduate students. By the time of his retirement in

1943, forty-three doctoral degrees had been granted.[7] Many graduate theses were published as experiment station bulletins, a practice which might have been followed to advantage by more institutions.

Other men who made early contributions to the field of rural sociology at Cornell included Warren Simpson Thompson, Bruce L. Melvin, and Walfred Albin Anderson. Thompson's work with Sanderson on primary groups in New York state has been noted in Chapter 4. A native of Nebraska, Thompson received his B.A. and M.A. degrees from the University of Nebraska and his Ph.D. from Columbia University (1915). Although he was destined to spend his career in the field of population studies, he served as professor of rural social organization at Cornell from 1919 to 1922, a period which included the years of his collaboration with Sanderson.

Melvin, a native of Iowa, did all his college work at the University of Missouri, receiving a Ph.D. degree in sociology in 1921. He was associate professor of sociology at Ohio Wesleyan University from 1920 until 1923, when he joined the staff at Cornell. His research there was concerned mainly with population analysis and with the service relations of village and open country.

W. A. Anderson was a pioneer of major importance. Born in Kansas City, Missouri, he was one of the few pioneer rural sociologists who had no farm experience in his background. His early choice of a vocation was the ministry, but after graduating from Garrett Theological Seminary in 1917, he decided to enroll at Iowa State University, where he received an M.S. degree in 1923. Meanwhile in 1922 he had joined Carl Taylor's staff at North Carolina State College as an instructor in rural economics. Here he remained until 1931, when he went to Cornell as professor of rural sociology. The thesis for his doctoral degree, taken at Cornell in 1929, was based on a study of white land-owning farmers in Wake County, North Carolina.

Anderson was a prodigious worker. A partial bibliography of his writings up to 1953 included eighty-four entries; of these, twenty-two were Cornell experiment station publications. His interests covered all phases of rural life, but his most important work was probably his study of rural values and social participation. As one might expect from his seminary training, he was much interested in the church. He visited China in 1930–31 as adviser to a mission sent out under the auspices of the Institute for Social and Religious Research. He also served as adviser to Agricultural

Missions, Incorporated, an agency affiliated with the National Council of Churches whose purpose was to recruit agricultural students for foreign mission service.

Anderson made the first investigation of the relationship between knowledge about, and attitudes toward, cooperatives. This study has been replicated many times by others. He also suggested a classification of the phenomena of sociology which, though it has received little attention, represents one of the few attempts to organize the various areas of the discipline.[8]

Wisconsin Carries On

The seed planted at the University of Wisconsin by Henry C. Taylor and C. J. Galpin grew vigorously under the direction of John Harrison Kolb. The scope of his endeavors has already been suggested, but something remains to be said about his background and his own summary of his work.

Born in Berlin, Wisconsin, in 1888, he received an M.A. degree from the University of Chicago in 1913 and a Ph.D. from the University of Wisconsin in 1921. He held a position in the agricultural extension service of the University of Minnesota from 1913 to 1917. In 1920 he became a professor of rural sociology at the University of Wisconsin; he served as chairman of the department of rural sociology from the time of its creation in 1930 until 1949. He remained a member of the staff until his retirement at the age of seventy in 1958.

On several occasions Kolb took leave from Wisconsin for special service. In 1924 he served with the Institute for Social and Religious Research in collaboration with Edmund deS. Brunner. In 1932 he was associated with Brunner again in the first restudy of 140 villages, and in 1935 he acted as coordinator of the rural research unit of the Federal Emergency Relief Administration in Washington, D.C. His services abroad included a year as research consultant for the New Zealand government in 1938; teaching and research at the University of Oslo in 1949; and teaching and research at the Rural University of Brazil in 1953–54.

Kolb followed his 1921 publication, *Rural Primary Groups*, with a number of studies of village and open-country relationships.[9] The major significance of a bulletin published in 1923 lay in the classification of centers according to the types of services provided. The service centers were described as single; limited and simple; semi-complete or intermediate;

complete and partially specialized; and urban and highly specialized. Kolb also noted the average distance in miles of the various types from the residence of the farm family. A subsequent bulletin reported on educational, library, and hospital services in eight centers in Wisconsin ranging in population from 1,350 to 2,900. In each case the service areas were delineated and the quality of service evaluated. The study sought to establish norms of efficient service for each institution.

Kolb then turned his attention to types of groupings other than those based on area. A study made in Dane County helped to point up some of the problems facing the church.[10] An investigation of interest groups focused attention on various typical community organizations, attempting to chart and explain the origin, rise, and consolidation or failure of such organizations.[11]

Kolb felt keenly his responsibility to bring research results to the attention of the rural public. One effort in this direction was the preparation of a handbook on organization for rural leaders in various situations.[12] A major resource in the early period of extension work in Wisconsin, the book treated the following topics: the meaning of community organization, types of community organizations, the right organization and how to get it, essentials for success, community music, community drama and pageantry, literary work and debate, holidays and festivals, community picnics and field days, community play days, social parties and group games, community athletics, community fairs, community health and welfare, and community buildings and parks. The handbook was followed by another bulletin designed to help its readers translate into action the results of studies in rural social organization.[13]

As far as research is concerned, Kolb's major contribution was undoubtedly his observation and analysis of social change in the rural environment of Wisconsin. Using Galpin's study of Walworth County as one bench mark and his own study of rural primary groups in Dane County as another, he repeated the former every fifteen years and the latter every ten years during his active service at the university. In *Emerging Rural Communities* Kolb summarized the results of nearly fifty years of research in Wisconsin. The monograph was written, he said,

. . . as an exposition of the results of numerous studies and restudies designed to identify and characterize groups and to trace trends in their varying relationships, and also of experiences in social action programs based on research findings. . . . Some comparisons with results of similiar studies in other states are included, mainly those in the four states where early studies of neighborhoods were made, but particularly those in New York State because many of their conclusions forecast what might be expected in Wisconsin one or two decades later.

Within the scope of the review are town-country communities which have emerged relatively recently and are important at present; country neighborhoods, one form of community which in earlier times was the more usual emergent type; village and small-town groups that appeared after frontier settlement on the land; organized interest groups which are increasing in numbers and strength; and now, multiple communities, which are sure to be important in the future, are emerging with an order of interdependence.[14]

The village and small-town groups, Kolb found, usually emerged at crossroads of travel and were differentiated from the neighborhoods. They were more heterogeneous occupationally and this alone tended to set them apart from the countryside, as did their incorporation as governmental units separate from the farm people. Yet forces for integration were at work in education, recreation, communication and electrical services, and religious institutions. Kolb warned: "The processes for these readjustments are often slow and frequently socially painful, filled with conflicts, but they are inevitable. Modified plans for local government will probably be the last to emerge." [15]

After reviewing the Galpin thesis and its emphasis on the town-country community, Kolb pointed out that follow-up studies of Walworth County revealed the emergence of "intercommunity patterns." By this he meant that "these town-country communities, instead of becoming more complete and more nearly self-contained, were actually being differentiated into what could be designated as types with distinguishable characteristics."

Kolb continually stressed the point that "groups as systems of behavior" were not "simply static or existing" but "occurring and changing."

The emphasis is upon people in their interactions, forming groups, not closed systems, upon processes of becoming which revolve about some common concerns, not all of them. This approach escapes any inference that communities are simply localities, or that they must be all inclusive or self-sufficient. The chief concerns as well as the forms of their collective expression vary from time to time and from place to place. The point is, people do do things together and in so doing give meaning and continuity to their group relationships.[16]

Kolb's insistence upon the importance of change and his unflagging determination to measure it by his repeated studies of selected groups constituted a significant contribution to our knowledge of rural society.

Although E. L. Kirkpatrick served at several posts during his career, ten of his most productive years were spent with Kolb at the University of Wisconsin. It is appropriate to make further reference to his work at this point. Born in 1884 on a farm in Iowa, Kirkpatrick received his undergraduate training at Iowa State College (now University) and took postgraduate work at the University of Kansas and Cornell University.

His early interest was horticulture, and in 1918 he became associate professor of horticulture at Colorado Agricultural College (now State University). After receiving a Ph.D. degree in rural sociology at Cornell in 1922, he joined the staff of the Division of Farm Life Studies in Washington. In 1928 he became a professor of rural sociology at the University of Wisconsin. Leaving that position in 1938, he spent five years as codirector of studies of rural youth for the American Council on Education. (Long associated with rural youth activities, Kirkpatrick was the perennial sponsor of the youth section of the American Country Life Association.) During the early 1940s he served as regional representative for New England of the Division of Farm Population. From 1946 until his retirement in 1959 he was a professor of sociology at Marietta College in Ohio.

Kirkpatrick pioneered in the study of the standard of living of farm families. His thesis at Cornell became the first published study in this field. The cooperative study of 2,886 families undertaken in Washington culminated, as has been mentioned, in the publication of *The Farmer's Standard of Living*.[17] Kirkpatrick's years at Wisconsin covered the period of the depression and his research during the thirties reflected that economic crisis as it affected the farm family and community relations.[18]

The Missouri Story

The University of Missouri figured in the careers of a number of distinguished sociologists — Carl Taylor, Zimmerman, Yoder, and Melvin. These men, and others, were influenced by Luther Lee Bernard, and it therefore seems appropriate to begin with him in reviewing the contributions of the Missouri school. Bernard is not regarded as a rural sociologist, but he was one of the first to offer courses in the field at several institutions where he taught; much of his early writing had to do with rural problems; and a number of his students later distinguished themselves as rural sociologists.[19]

Bernard was a native of Kentucky. He earned undergraduate degrees at Pierce City Baptist College in 1900 and the University of Missouri in 1907. His doctoral degree came from the University of Chicago in 1910, where he had served as a fellow from 1907 to 1910. Accepting an appointment at the University of Florida in 1911, he is said to have taught there the first course in rural sociology offered in the South. His course at the University of Missouri, where he taught from 1914 to 1917, may have been the first at that institution. In 1917–18 at the University of Minnesota he gave the first course provided for students in the college of science, literature, and the arts, although, as we have seen, rural sociology had been offered in the college of agriculture in 1915. Bernard spent the year 1926–27 in Argentina as a Social Science Research Council Fellow. In 1929 he went to Washington University in St. Louis and remained on the faculty there for twenty years. From 1949 until his death in 1951, he was visiting professor at Pennsylvania State University. Bernard and his wife, Jessie, a sociologist, collaborated on a number of publications, perhaps the most important of which was the *Origins of American Sociology: The Social Science Movement in the United States.*[20]

At the time when Bernard taught at the University of Missouri, work in rural social life was given under the auspices of the general department. In 1921, however, a separate department of rural sociology was created and E. L. Morgan became chairman, a position he held until 1937.

A native of Illinois, Morgan obtained his B.A. degree from McKendree College at Lebanon, Illinois, in 1904. His master's degree came from the University of Wisconsin in 1912 and his doctorate from Massachusetts Agricultural College in 1932. His career in rural sociology began with his appointment as extension professor in community organization at Massachusetts Agricultural College during the years from 1912 to 1919. The succeeding two years he spent in Washington, D.C., as director of rural service for the American Red Cross.

Among his publications at Massachusetts Agricultural College was a bulletin on community organization that grew out of his experience as community advisor to a small town in New Hampshire. The bulletin contained charts, photographs, and detailed instructions for making a community "survey or inventory," and a selection of references on various aspects of rural community life.[21]

Morgan's initial undertaking after he went to Missouri in 1921 was the study of neighborhoods that has been reviewed in Chapter 4. Early in his years at Missouri, Morgan recruited Henry J. Burt, a capable research man with whom he collaborated on a study of rural youth.[22] In 1937, the year of his sudden death, Morgan initiated another project in the same area and also published a study of the involvement of women in the Works Progress Administration.[23]

The work at Missouri was continued by Charles Elson Lively, Morgan's successor in the department of rural sociology. After a boyhood spent on a farm in West Virginia, Lively studied at the University of Nebraska and the University of Minnesota, where he obtained his Ph.D. degree in 1931. He served for sixteen years as professor of rural sociology at Ohio State University before moving to the University of Missouri in 1938. During the 1930s, in addition to his academic appointments, he acted as state supervisor of rural social research for the Works Progress Administration.

Although Lively's interests ranged over a number of special fields, his published works have been mainly in the areas of population, social organization, and the health and health facilities of rural people. At Ohio, in collaboration with P. G. Beck, he made a pioneer study of rural health with financial support from the Division of Farm Population and Rural Life.[24] He continued his work on health at Missouri.

One of Lively's first publications at Ohio State University — and one of the most interesting — was concerned with social organization. The work is noteworthy for its effective use of maps to indicate the location of various institutions, for example, abandoned churches and churches with and without pastors.[25] But Lively's output of experiment station publications and journal articles at Ohio was heavily weighted on the side of population studies. An important work on population, written with Conrad Taeuber, consisted of a comprehensive analysis of rural migration in the United States during the depression.[26]

Lively shared the interest of other sociologists — especially current during the 1930s — in working on "regions" and "areas." [27] Unwilling to rely exclusively on type-of-farming areas as delineated by the economists, he undertook to determine sub-areas based on cultural factors, in his work both at Ohio and at Missouri.[28] The discovery of state "areas" that tend to be homogeneous is valuable for sampling purposes, as well as for the general understanding of a state's social problems. In states other than

Missouri, such areas have not been delineated; type-of-farming regions are used instead.

Beginnings in North Carolina

The collaboration between Galpin and Carl C. Taylor in the study of name communities in Wake County helped to anchor rural sociology and economics at North Carolina State College. Born in 1884, Taylor had grown up on an Iowa farm and received his early education in a rural environment. He attended Drake University in Des Moines, the University of Texas, and the University of Missouri, where he received his Ph.D. degree in 1917. After spending the years from 1916 to 1920 at the University of Missouri as professor of rural sociology and economics, Taylor went to North Carolina State, where he became professor of rural sociology and economics and later dean of the graduate school and director of the bureau of economic and social research.

Early in 1933 Taylor joined the staff of the newly created subsistence homesteads program in Washington, D.C., under the direction of M. L. Wilson. During 1934–35 he served in the land policy section of the Agricultural Adjustment Administration, and when the Resettlement Administration was set up in 1935, he became assistant administrator and director of the Rural Rehabilitation Division. He served in this capacity for the two years of the agency's existence.

In 1937 Taylor succeeded Galpin as head of the Division of Farm Population, remaining in this position until his retirement in 1953. He then entered upon a second career in the field of community development, serving first as adviser to the community development program of the state department's International Cooperation Administration (a forerunner of AID) and later acting for ten years as a consultant to the Ford Foundation's program in India.

Most of Taylor's career was devoted to administrative work, much of it in government service. The expenditure of time and energy required by that type of work constitutes, of course, a real impediment to scholarly production. In addition, Taylor received many requests to address national and state conferences of various kinds, and his speaking chores took much time and effort. Nevertheless, he has to his credit a substantial body of publications.

In 1926, during his North Carolina years, Taylor wrote one of the two best textbooks on rural sociology available at the time. In the early 1940s

65

Taylor, along with several other rural sociologists, was sent by the Department of State to study rural conditions in Latin America; his year in Argentina resulted in the publication of a book on that country in 1948. Back at his desk in Washington, Taylor mobilized his staff for the preparation of another textbook for college use. The years with the Ford Foundation bore fruit in a collaborative volume on India's economic and social development. The book that will probably stand as his major scholarly contribution, however, is his history of the farmers' movement in the United States.[29]

Taylor's administration of rural research, in which many persons participated, as well as the scholarly work he was able to carry out himself, have made a lasting contribution to the development of the field. Through his wide acquaintance with sociologists, he provided the informal leadership and friendly encouragement so crucial in the development of a new discipline.

Seven years before Taylor joined the staff of North Carolina's agricultural college, another pioneer rural sociologist began his work at the state university. This was Eugene Cunningham Branson, who during the early years exerted an important influence on the development of interest in the rural social sciences, particularly in the South.

Born in North Carolina in 1861, he lived through and helped to guide programs of post-Civil War rural development. He held master's degrees from Trinity College in North Carolina and George Peabody College in Tennessee. His early professional career was spent in the field of rural education — first in the country schools and later as professor of pedagogy and president at Georgia State Normal School. From the latter position he moved in 1913 to the University of North Carolina, where he became professor of rural social economics.

Branson was an effective publicist of facts regarding rural life. Lacking any outlet for publication comparable to that enjoyed by workers in the agricultural colleges, Branson organized the North Carolina Club, which issued an annual yearbook containing facts about the state. He also utilized the newsletter of the university's extension division for biweekly mailings to the press of the state. Many rural sociologists throughout the country also received the newsletter and from it learned something about rural life in North Carolina.

Branson was a member of the North Carolina Commission on Farm Tenancy, an association of state agencies which received funds from C.

J. Galpin. In collaboration with J. S. Dickey, Branson produced a study of tenancy that was one of the commission's most important contributions; his report was certainly one of the most interestingly written. In describing tenant farmers, who constituted more than half the population of the state, Branson commented: "These are the people in North Carolina who own not an inch of the soil they cultivate nor a single shingle in the roofs over their heads. . . . Enduring social structures cannot be built on land ownership by the few and land-orphanage for the many. Civilization is rooted and grounded in the home-owning, home-loving, home-defending instincts." [30]

As founder and head of the department of rural social economics from 1914 to 1933, Branson stimulated widespread interest in the state and throughout the entire South in the problems of tenant farmers, both white and Negro. There is no doubt that his efforts contributed to the development of a program of amelioration during the 1930s. In addition Branson has been credited as the prime mover in developing the University of North Carolina's department of sociology, which was established in 1920 under the chairmanship of Howard W. Odum. [31]

Though Odum was not formally identified with rural sociology, he encouraged rural research and played a not-to-be-overlooked role in the growth of the field. Born and reared on a farm in Georgia, Odum did his undergraduate work at Emory University and took doctoral degrees at both Clark and Columbia universities. The most productive period of his career dates from 1920, when he became chairman at North Carolina. Here he not only organized the department of sociology but also directed the school of social work and the Institute for Research in the Social Sciences. During his tenure at North Carolina, Odum initiated a number of studies in the rural field and many of his students became rural specialists. As sociologist C. Horace Hamilton has pointed out, "Odum's interests and work in the fields of *folk* and *regional* sociology is basic to rural sociology." [32]

One of Odum's colleagues at North Carolina, Rupert Bayless Vance, was to distinguish himself as the author of important works on rural life in the South. Vance graduated from Henderson-Brown College in his native state of Arkansas in 1920 and took his master's degree at Vanderbilt in 1928. After receiving his Ph.D. from the University of North Carolina in 1928, he joined the staff there and began his long professional association with that institution. Primarily interested in problems of cotton culture and the human problems related to it, he is best known to rural sociologists for his *Human Factors in Cotton Culture: A Study in the Social Geography of the American South,* published in 1929.

Sociological Research at Minnesota

Although a course in rural sociology was offered at the University of Minnesota as early as 1915, no established research in the agricultural experiment station was undertaken until 1923. The three community studies mentioned earlier were made by economists; they had many sociological features but were not formally sociological research. Moreover, they were not sponsored directly by the experiment station. Carle C. Zimmerman must therefore be regarded as the pioneer rural sociologist at Minnesota.

A native of Missouri, Zimmerman took his bachelor's degree at the state university. Here he met Carl Taylor, then an instructor in sociology. Zimmerman went with Taylor to North Carolina State College in 1920, where he received his master's degree in 1922. His thesis was a pioneer study of the standard of living of farm families. At Missouri he also did the field work for the study of primary groups which he and Taylor published in 1922. In 1923 Zimmerman joined the sociology faculty at the University of Minnesota, taking his doctoral degree at that institution in 1925.

During a year's leave of absence in 1930–31, Zimmerman served as adviser to the government of Thailand. His was one of the earliest foreign assignments of an American rural sociologist.[33] In 1931 he went to Harvard as associate professor of sociology, a position he held until his retirement in 1962, when he joined the staff of North Dakota State University at Fargo. In late 1967 he became visiting professor at the University of Saskatchewan at Saskatoon, Canada.

Zimmerman's years at Minnesota were productive ones. He did his first studies as a research assistant to John D. Black, chairman of the Division of Agricultural Economics.[34] With the passage of the Purnell Act in 1925, which provided federal grants to the states for research in economics and sociology, Zimmerman's work in sociology was set up on an independent basis as far as research was concerned. There followed an impressive list of experiment station publications and journal articles.

One of his most original investigations focused on trade centers in Minnesota, covering trends over a twenty-five-year period.[35] Zimmerman had accidentally discovered a rich source of information for this study in

Bradstreet's Book of Ratings. In addition to this reference book, he used reports prepared by the League of Minnesota Municipalities. Zimmerman not only described the changes taking place in trade centers, but also proposed a classification of centers as independent, dependent, and elementary types. His classification was based upon the number of business units and the presence of various kinds of communication facilities. This important bulletin became the prototype for several similar studies undertaken by students of Zimmerman in other states.

Zimmerman's most significant contribution to rural sociology during the 1920s was his collaboration with Pitirim A. Sorokin in the writing of *Principles of Rural-Urban Sociology*, a textbook which represented a true milestone in the development of rural sociology.[36] With his vast knowledge of the literature and thought of European scholars, Sorokin opened up broad vistas for the more provincial American students. Zimmerman's general intellectual competence and his thorough knowledge of American research made him an ideal associate for the senior author.

The book brought scientific objectivity to the examination of rural phenomena. At that time most American students considered rural sociology to be an applied science; that is, they believed that any "principles" that were developed should be applicable to the solution of rural problems. Sorokin and Zimmerman, on the other hand, were not concerned with reform; they set out to write a purely scientific treatise.

An outgrowth of the textbook, in a sense, was the production of a more extensive work. In compressing to feasible limits the mass of information collected for the textbook, the authors necessarily omitted a great deal of documentary material. C. J. Galpin was much interested in making available to students in the United States the results of scholarship in other countries. He was able to realize this ambition by collaborating with Sorokin and Zimmerman and helping to finance the publication of *A Systematic Source Book in Rural Sociology*.[37] The project had in addition the sympathetic support of Walter C. Coffey, dean of the College of Agriculture at the University of Minnesota.

The three-volume work has frequently been characterized as monumental, and indeed it is. Each major section was preceded by an introduction giving the selected papers a theoretical setting. Volume I included comments on rural life by eighty thinkers from the ancient Oriental, Greek, and Roman periods down to modern times on such topics as the origin of rural-urban differences, the ecology of the rural habitat, community types, social stratification, mobility, and the fundamental types of rural aggregates. Volume II dealt basically with social institutions and Volume III emphasized the physical, vital, and psychosocial traits of farmers and peasants as well as rural-urban social relationships. In all, the volumes included 212 readings from authorities around the world, in addition to extensive commentary by the authors. After the publication of this work and the earlier *Principles of Rural-Urban Sociology*, American rural sociology could never be quite the same. It was destined to move in the direction of less provincialism and more objectivity. The research and writing of Zimmerman and Sorokin, together with the group of excellent students trained under their direction, made of the last half of the 1920s truly a golden age at Minnesota.

The vacancy in rural sociology occasioned by the departure of Zimmerman for Harvard University in 1931 was filled by the appointment of Robert W. Murchie. A native of Scotland, Murchie had emigrated to Canada and begun his academic career as an economist at the University of Manitoba. He became acquainted with Zimmerman during a major research project known as the Canadian Pioneer Problems study, for which Zimmerman was engaged as a consultant. Murchie did his work for the Ph.D. degree in agricultural economics at the University of Minnesota. His services in connection with various emergency agencies during the depression made it impossible for him to devote much attention to the research program in the experiment station. After his sudden death in 1937, he was succeeded by Lowry Nelson.

Summary

As the preceding review of men and institutions has indicated, the seedling of rural sociology established its roots during the 1920s, particularly in the early years of the decade. Several of the major land-grant schools provided a hospitable soil and environment. Cornell, Wisconsin, Missouri, North Carolina, and Minnesota became the most important centers for graduate study in the new discipline. From them men with M.A. or Ph.D. degrees went out to other schools to pioneer in teaching, research, and extension service. But these five institutions were not alone; others were also initiating or expanding work. They will be the subject of the next chapter.

7

The Growth and the Spread

THE message of the country life movement carried far beyond the important institutions discussed in the preceding chapter. The work of the Commission on Country Life, the early surveys of the Protestant churches, and the promotional work of the American Country Life Association all made an impact, and it is not surprising that here and there across the country individuals and institutions were stimulated to conduct studies and teach courses in rural sociology. In this chapter we will briefly summarize the spread of the work and the careers of men who made the beginnings. Some of these individuals were recruited by C. J. Galpin and their first projects were modestly subsidized by his office in the Department of Agriculture. Some researchers were able to obtain funds from church organizations or local volunteer groups. Others, after 1925, were financed by the agricultural experiment stations with funds made available by the Purnell Act.[1]

Expansion in the Midwest

The land-grant colleges of the Middle West, other than those already mentioned, were generally what might be called secondary adopters of rural sociology. Iowa made an early start, but its progress was slow. Michigan State, Illinois, South Dakota, and other schools did not develop programs until the later 1920s, yet they too had done important pioneer work earlier in the decade.

Although a number of early rural sociologists were natives of Iowa, they found it necessary to go to other states for training in the social sciences, whether agricultural economics or rural sociology. Nevertheless, there was a stirring of interest at Iowa State College before 1920. At the close of World War I, George H. Von Tungeln undertook a number of social surveys of rural townships in Iowa. The results were published by the agricultural experiment station.

Von Tungeln was born and reared on a farm in Galconda, Illinois. After graduating from Central Wesleyan College in Warrenton, Missouri, he received a master's degree from Northwestern University in 1910 and a doctoral degree from Harvard in 1926. As a professor at Iowa State College, he offered in 1913 that institution's first collegiate courses in rural sociology and applied sociology. He also initiated the first formal research in rural sociology at the Iowa Agricultural Experiment Station with a survey of a rural township in 1915.[2] (It is interesting to note that at the Iowa experiment station rural sociology preceded agricultural economics in achieving sectional status.)

There followed other surveys of Iowa townships and counties.[3] (For one of these surveys, made in the summer of 1920, Von Tungeln had as associate authors three young men who were later to make their names in the field — E. L. Kirkpatrick, C. R. Hoffer, and J. F. Thaden.) Von Tungeln's studies were pioneering efforts and thus subject to the weaknesses and advantages of the survey method. The survey attempts to cover all aspects of social and economic life and as a consequence tends to be superficial. On the other hand, it provides the residents of a local community with a broad picture of their condition and an accumulation of data that can be used as a basis for planning.

In 1930 work in rural sociology at Iowa came under the direction of Ray E. Wakeley. A native of Pennsylvania, he completed his undergraduate work at Pennsylvania State College (now a university) in 1917. After serving as an extension agent from 1918 to 1926, he became a research assistant under Dwight Sanderson at Cornell. Wakeley obtained a Ph.D. degree in rural social organization in 1928 and joined the staff of Iowa State in 1930. Wakeley's research interests included population, rural organization, the migration of high school graduates, and rural leadership.[4]

Michigan State established a department of sociology in 1924, during the presidency of Kenyon Butterfield, that staunch advocate of the importance of establishing rural social science in the land-grant colleges. Eben Mumford became the first chairman of the department.

A native of Ohio, Mumford did his undergraduate work at Buchtel College (now merged with the University of Akron). He earned his Ph.D. in sociology at the University of Chicago in 1906. Mumford's academic qualifications were impressive. He was a student of several pioneer social scientists, including Albion Small, W. I. Thomas, George Vincent, Charles Henderson, Thorstein Veblen, and John Dewey. His postgraduate work also included study at European universities, a year of study at Clark University under the direction of G. Stanley Hall, and a period of intensive work at the New York School of Civics and Philanthropy.

After joining the faculty at Michigan State in 1912, Mumford pioneered in many rural social fields. His first work was the organization of a program of farm management field studies and demonstrations, later to become established as the County Agricultural Extension Service. He began organizing county farm bureaus in 1913 and community farm bureaus in 1915. He was the state leader of county agricultural agents from 1914 to 1921.

In addition to launching the department of sociology in 1924, Mumford also organized the Michigan Country Life Association, the Michigan Collegiate Country Life Association, short courses for ministers, and the Michigan Conference of Social Workers. Although his major work clearly lay in the fields of agricultural organization and extension education, he was author or joint author of a number of publications.[5]

Two colleagues of Mumford who belong to the first generation of rural sociologists are John F. Thaden and Charles R. Hoffer. Thaden was born in Iowa. He obtained his bachelor's degree at the University of Nebraska in 1920, his master's degree at Iowa State College in 1922, and his doctorate at Michigan State College in 1930. In 1925 he joined the staff at Michigan State. Thaden's research reflected his concern with population change and its impact upon educational institutions.[6] Perhaps his most important publication in this field was an investigation of high school communities written jointly with Mumford.[7]

Charles Hoffer was born in Indiana of parents who were farmers. He majored in vocational agricultural education at Purdue University and then took a master's degree at Iowa State College in 1921 and a Ph.D. at the University of Minnesota in 1925. In the summer of 1921, at the University of Minnesota, Hoffer began a survey of the relations of the rural trade center to its community; this study became his doctoral thesis and was later modified for bulletin publication.[8] Hoffer's research work at Michigan State University, where he taught from 1925 to 1961, covered a wide range of topics, including town-country relations, health and educational services, the rural church, and the agricultural extension service. His studies of the effectiveness of extension service made an important contribution to this field.[9] An investigation of the reaction of Dutch immigrant farmers to innovations, published in 1942, was one of the earliest in a field of research that became increasingly important after 1950. This study also threw new light on the process of assimilation of foreign stocks in rural America.

It was not until 1929 that the University of Illinois introduced rural sociology and engaged David Edgar Lindstrom as a rural sociologist. Lindstrom received his M.S. and Ph.D. degrees from the University of Wisconsin in 1928 and 1932 respectively. Even before finishing his undergraduate work, he had served one year as a fieldman in plant pathology for the United States Department of Agriculture and another year as a fieldman in irrigation for the federal Reclamation Service. At Illinois, where Lindstrom remained throughout his professional career, he had charge of research, teaching, and extension service in rural sociology. His research interests were strongly oriented to the field of organizational participation by farm people.[10]

When South Dakota State College organized its department of rural sociology in 1925, Wendell F. Kumlien became the first chairman. A native of Wisconsin, Kumlien had taken master's degrees at South Dakota State College (1921) and the University of Wisconsin (1923). The Ph.D. degree was awarded him by Wisconsin in 1941. He began his career as principal of Parker High School in Moradabad, India, from 1911 to 1915. On his return to the United States, he served as a county agricultural agent, state leader of county agents, and finally director of the agricultural extension service in South Dakota before he became the first professor of rural sociology at the state college. His best-known research consisted of a series of studies of what he called "basic trends of social change in South Dakota." After analyzing population trends, the series continued with an examination of the basic social institutions involved in education, religion, local government, and health. The research was supported mainly by Purnell funds, and the results were published by the agricultural experiment station of South Dakota.

One of the most prolific of the Galpin collaborators was J. O. Rankin of the University of Nebraska. In the ten-year period from 1922 to 1932 he published at least thirteen experiment station bulletins dealing with land ownership and tenancy and with family living. Then he suddenly left professional life to become a farmer.

Experiment station studies in the state of North Dakota were not extensive, perhaps because the college of agriculture decided not to move into a field that had already been preempted by John Gillette at the university. The record of research output from the agricultural college includes two studies made by E. A. Willson, at least one of them with aid from Galpin. Willson also participated in a study with Harold C. Hoffsommer that was financed with Purnell Act funds.[11]

Institutions in the South

Although North Carolina State College must be regarded as the bellwether in the march of rural sociology in the South, other institutions were active. In Virginia both the university and the land-grant college (Virginia Polytechnic Institute) sponsored sociological research in the 1920s. At the university leadership was provided by Wilson Gee, who in 1923 became head of what was called the department of rural social economics. William E. Garnett became in 1925 the first chairman of rural sociology at the Polytechnic Institute.

Gee belongs to the list of early cooperators with Galpin. His study, *Some of the Best Things in Rural Virginia*, was published by the university in 1926 in cooperation with the United States Department of Agriculture.[12] This rare instance of U.S.D.A. cooperation with a university in a state where there was a separate agricultural college undoubtedly occurred because the latter institution did not introduce rural sociology until 1925. The flyleaf of Gee's bulletin contained a quotation from Galpin's *Rural Social Problems*, but there is no specific credit otherwise. The content of the bulletin, however, betrayed a major interest of Galpin, who encouraged students in several other states to find some of the "best things" in rural areas — the most successful families, outstanding schools, noteworthy churches, and the like.

Gee was born in South Carolina and did his undergraduate work at Clemson Agricultural College, majoring in zoology and entomology. After obtaining a Ph.D. degree from the University of California in 1913, he began his professional career as an entomologist. Then, like Dwight Sanderson and J. L. Hypes, he decided to leave that field in favor of economics and sociology. He held a professorship in rural economics and rural sociology at the University of South Carolina from 1919 until 1923, when he accepted an appointment at the University of Virginia. In 1926 Gee became director of the Institute of Research in the Social Sciences, a position which he held for thirty-three years. The work of the institute involved research in history, political science, and economics, as well as sociology. Gee's chief interest, however, was in the rural social sciences, and a number of monographs came from his research in this field.[13]

As was the case with E. C. Branson at North Carolina, Gee was attached to the state university rather than the agricultural college, yet his interest lay in the rural social sciences. Like Branson, Gee founded his own department, calling it rural social economics, and published a newsletter for the dissemination of information about his research. Gee, as the younger of the two, may well have taken his lead in some respects from Branson.

Garnett was born in Virginia. He received a bachelor's degree in agricultural science from Cornell University in 1912, a master's degree from Peabody College in 1915, and a doctorate from Wisconsin in 1920. He began his career in sociology as head of the department of rural sociology at Texas Agricultural and Mechanical College in 1921. In 1925 he went to Virginia Polytechnic Institute as professor of rural sociology and sociologist of the experiment station. It appears that only one of the published bulletins of which Garnett was author or joint author received support from Galpin; Garnett's later research was probably supported largely by Purnell funds. Among his earliest publications were two bulletins on the rural church written jointly with C. Horace Hamilton.[14] Subsequent studies, made during the depression and war years, dealt with population, particularly the younger age groups, and with the problem of rural poverty in Virginia, including rural housing.

Louisiana State University began a vast expansion in the field of sociology and rural sociology in the early 1930s under the leadership of Fred C. Frey and T. Lynn Smith. A native of Louisiana, Frey graduated from the state university in 1921 and obtained his Ph.D. degree from the University of Minnesota in 1929. He served at Louisiana State as professor of sociology, dean of students, dean of the college of arts and sciences, and dean of the university. In addition to his leadership in administration, his great importance for rural sociology lay in the role he played in launching the journal *Rural Sociology*, which was published at Louisiana State for its first five years. (See Chapter 10, below.) Because of Frey's absorption in administrative duties, the actual organization of research and instruction at Louisiana became the responsibility of Lynn Smith, whose major research at Louisiana dealt with farm trade centers from 1901 to 1931 and the growth of population in the state between 1890 and 1930. While he was at Louisiana, he also published his widely used textbook, *The Sociology of Rural Life*.[15]

Augustus W. Hayes, a professor of sociology at Tulane University in New Orleans from 1920 to 1925, was one of the early researchers in rural sociology who received subsidies from the Division of Farm Life. Hayes's work consisted of case studies of several communities and a study of town-country relationships.[16] Some further work of his will be considered later in this volume.

Otis Durant Duncan pioneered in rural sociology at Oklahoma State. Born in Texas, Duncan received a master's degree from the Agricultural and Mechanical College and a Ph.D. from Louisiana State University in 1941. For many years he was head of the department of sociology and rural life at Oklahoma's college of agriculture. His fields of research were population movement, rural health, and the social aspects of tenancy.[17]

In West Virginia Nat T. Frame did pioneer work in the application of sociology to agricultural extension work. A native of New York, Frame graduated from Colgate University in 1899. He engaged in farming during the period from 1902 to 1913 and then became a county agricultural agent in Louisville, Kentucky. In 1914 he held the position of state agent in the University of West Virginia and from 1919 to 1933 he was director of agricultural extension. A pioneer in organizing rural communities for self-help, Frame placed primary emphasis on town-country cooperation. During the 1930s and 1940s he held various government positions, including that of regional representative in the Milwaukee office of the Division of Farm Population. Frame was a founder and one-time executive secretary of the American Country Life Association.

A history of the development of rural sociology in the South would be incomplete without mention of Charles Spurgeon Johnson. Born in Virginia, he received bachelor's degrees from Virginia Union University in 1917 and the University of Chicago in 1918. Honorary doctorates were granted by Howard (1941), Columbia (1947), Harvard (1948), and the University of Glasgow (1952). Johnson became director of the Institute for Sociological Research at Fisk University in 1928, and from 1946 to 1956 he was president of that institution. Johnson ranks as one of the most distinguished sociologists of his time; he served on numerous commissions and boards of public agencies, including the President's Commission on Farm Tenancy (1936), the Julius Rosenwald Foundation, and the John Hay Whitney Foundation.

Johnson's work as a scholar was limited by the fact that early in his career he was drawn into administrative work. He is well known among rural sociologists, however, for his great study of Negro farm life, published under the title *The Shadow of the Plantation*.[18] This work was an eloquent description of the Negro's struggle for survival under the semi-slavery of the sharecropping system.

Rural Sociology in the West

Through Galpin's initiative, recruitment, and financial support, research in rural sociology began in Montana, Utah, and Washington in the early 1920s. A study made by J. Wheeler Barger was probably the first rural social study undertaken in Montana. Barger was an employee of Galpin who did his work without direct aid but with the approval of Montana State College. Subsequently, rural sociology became well established at that institution under the direction of Carl F. Kraenzel.

No research in rural sociology was undertaken in Utah until 1923, although the subject had been taught at the agricultural college (now Utah State University) and at Brigham Young University as early as 1915. In 1923 Lowry Nelson, then a member of the Brigham Young faculty, made a study of the farm village of Escalante, located in a remote section of the state. The study held special interest because the Mormons were the only major group of farmers who settled in villages instead of on scattered farmsteads. All the families of Escalante lived in the village, going back and forth to their work in the fields. Besides its importance as a description of a unique form of settlement, the study sought to show the advantages and disadvantages of the village way of life for farm people. Two other villages, less isolated geographically than Escalante, were studied: Ephraim in 1925 and American Fork in 1927–28. The results of all three studies were published by Brigham Young University.[19] The communities of Escalante and Ephraim were restudied in 1950; these results, together with the original findings and other studies of Canadian Mormon settlements, were later brought together and published as a book.[20]

With the coming of the New Deal agencies in the early 1930s, Nelson's research emphasis shifted. He was designated supervisor for the Utah segment of a nationwide study of rural families on relief, conducted under the auspices of the Federal Emergency Relief Administration. In 1934 he joined the Rural Rehabilitation Division as adviser for the four states of California, Arizona, Nevada, and Utah. When the federal Resettlement Administration was created in 1935, Nelson went to Washington as assistant director of the Rural Resettlement Division, under the directorship of Carl C. Taylor. In 1936–37 Nelson served as director of the Utah Agricultural Experiment Station, leaving that post in 1937 to become professor of sociology at the University of Minnesota. During the years from 1937 to 1958, Nelson directed his research toward population analysis with special attention to trends, migration selectivity, ethnic group persistence, farm labor, health facilities, and rural social institutions.[21]

Sociological research began at Utah State University when Joseph A. Geddes joined the staff in 1927. The department of sociology was created in 1928 and Geddes became the first chairman, a position he held until his retirement in 1950. A native of the state, he did his undergraduate work at Brigham Young College in Logan (later discontinued). His graduate work was done at Columbia University, where he received the M.A. degree in 1913 and the Ph.D. in 1924. He served as supervisor of rural research for the Works Progress Administration in Utah from 1934 to 1937. His initial research project, begun in 1927, was a study of life in his native village of Plain City, Utah, and involved a comparison of three categories of residents: village, edge-of-town, and farm. In contrast to the villagers studied by Lowry Nelson, Plain City farm people were not exclusively dwellers in the village itself.[22]

Fred R. Yoder opened up the field of rural sociological research in the state of Washington. A native of North Carolina, Yoder received a master's degree from the state university in 1915 and a doctorate from the University of Wisconsin in 1923. He taught courses in economics, sociology, agricultural economics, and rural sociology at several institutions, becoming in 1923 professor of sociology and later department chairman at the State College of Washington (now the State University), where he remained until his retirement.

During the late 1920s Yoder initiated investigations of social organization in three Washington counties under cooperative arrangements with the Division of Farm Population. All three studies emphasized the identification of rural neighborhoods and communities. In accordance with the Galpin technique, service areas were mapped for such institutions as banks, newspapers, high schools, and churches.[23]

Pioneering in rural sociology at the University of Arizona was Elzer DesJardins Tetreau. He was born in Ontario, Canada, of French Huguenot stock. After undergraduate work at Hamline University in St. Paul, Minnesota, he studied at the University of Wisconsin, receiving an M.A. degree in 1920 and a Ph.D. in 1930. Tetreau taught sociology at Ohio Wesleyan University from 1925 to 1930 and at Ohio State University from 1930 until 1933. During the following two years he acted as analyst and senior research supervisor in the rural research unit of the Federal Emergency Relief Administration. In 1935 he became the first rural sociologist in the Arizona Agricultural Experiment Station, holding as well a part-time teaching position at the university. He took a strong interest in rural social organization, farm organizations, farm labor, and the social aspects of land tenure. One of his most important and original contributions was a study of the migration of wealth from rural areas through inheritance.[24]

Other Work in Rural Sociology

In New England, Massachusetts Agricultural College introduced and fostered teaching and extension work in rural sociology during the presidency of Kenyon Butterfield. Research work, however, was not established as a regular function of the experiment station. The only other institution which undertook work in this field in the 1920s was Storrs Agricultural College (now the University of Connecticut). The work there was inaugurated by James L. Hypes, who made an interesting contribution to the rural sociology of New England and was the only Galpin-aided worker in that region. Hypes's study of Lebanon, Connecticut, documented the change in the town's population from its original old-American stock to various immigrant stocks and the consequent transition in values, sentiments, and loyalties.[25] In 1932 Nathan L. Whetten joined the staff and undertook his very significant studies of suburbanization in Connecticut; he continued his rural sociological research until he was made dean of the graduate school in 1940. (See also Chapter 11.)

A number of individuals made contributions to the discipline in the early period of its development but later went into other special fields. Among these were Ernest Rutherford Groves, Manuel Conrad Elmer, and Thomas Carson McCormick.

Groves exercised considerable influence on the developing discipline of rural sociology before he shifted his interest to the sociology of the family. A native of Massachusetts, he received bachelor's degrees from Yale Divinity School in 1901 and from Dartmouth College in 1903. From 1903 to 1920 he held positions at the University of New Hampshire in the departments of English, philosophy, psychology, and sociology. In 1927 he joined the faculty of the University of North Carolina, where he remained until his death in 1946. His first three books, published between 1917 and 1922, dealt with rural problems.[26] He was a founder of, and an active participant in, the American Country Life Association. At the second meeting of the association in 1919, he served as chairman of a committee on the teaching of "rural social problems:" besides his report, noted earlier, on ways of improving instruction in rural sociology, he also urged the Department of Agriculture to include a section on rural sociology in its *Experiment Station Record*. This action, he believed, would provide a "useful assistance to the teacher and student of rural sociology and also further the interests of rural social life." [27]

Manuel Elmer, a native of Wisconsin, earned his Ph.D. degree at the University of Chicago in 1914. His first position was that of professor of sociology and economics at North Dakota State in Fargo. John M. Gillette, who was teaching at the university in Grand Forks, some fifty miles away, provided guidance and counsel. "He came down to help me get started," Elmer has recalled, "and had me teach in the Summer Session at Grand Forks in 1915. It was from Gillette that I got my real start in Rural Sociology." [28]

In 1916 Elmer became professor of rural and applied sociology at the

81

University of Kansas. Here he initiated studies of several farm trade centers in an attempt "to trace the boundaries of influence of interests and services from the center." After moving to the University of Minnesota in 1919 as professor of sociology and social work, Elmer organized and carried through a number of neighborhood surveys in Minneapolis. He undertook these projects in cooperation with local groups and agencies; the findings were published privately. Perhaps more important than the Minneapolis surveys, from the standpoint of rural sociology, was a study of Stillwater, Minnesota.[29]

In 1924–26 Elmer studied several small communities to the northwest of Minneapolis.[30] He completed a remarkable number of community surveys in a short period of time, with no other financing than that provided by organized groups of citizens. After 1926, when he became chairman of the department of sociology at the University of Pittsburgh, his interests shifted somewhat from rural sociology to research in the areas of family life, urban sociology, and general sociology.

Thomas McCormick was born in Alabama and graduated from the state university in 1911. The next twenty years found him teaching high school and, after he had earned an M.A. degree, offering courses in agriculture and sociology at East Central Teachers (now State) College in Oklahoma. Following a year's graduate work in sociology at the University of Chicago, he was granted a Ph.D. degree in 1929. From 1931 to 1934 he was a professor of rural sociology at the University of Arkansas. It was here that he did his first rural study.[31] An unusually prescient observer in the social sciences, McCormick foresaw as early as 1931 the important changes that were taking place, or were destined to take place, in rural society.[32] In 1934 he moved to Washington, D.C., to serve as research supervisor and acting coordinator of rural research for the Federal Emergency Relief Administration and the Works Progress Administration. He was author or joint author of several reports and monographs during his Washington tenure. In 1934 he became professor of sociology at the University of Wisconsin, acting as department chairman from 1941 to 1952. In this period he concentrated his attention on statistics and gave courses and seminars in research methods.

Some scholars from disciplines other than sociology devoted much time and effort to the task of improving the welfare of the rural population. Among them were Thomas Nixon Carver, professor of economics at Harvard University; Paul Schuster Taylor, professor of economics at the University of California; and Oliver Edward Baker, a long-time employee of the Department of Agriculture.

Carver was particularly interested in the social problems of rural people. He obtained a Ph.D. degree from Cornell University in 1894 and then became professor of economics and sociology at Oberlin College. In 1900 he received an appointment as professor of economics at Harvard University. He took a year's leave of absence in 1913 to serve as director of the rural organization service in the U.S.D.A. Carver became widely known in rural circles through his book *Principles of Rural Economy,* first published in 1911 and revised in 1932. To rural sociologists he is known also for his joint authorship with G. A. Lundquist of a textbook, *Principles of Rural Sociology* (1927). In the final chapter of that book Carver placed great stress on the importance of maintaining the "quality" of the rural population, by which he apparently meant the genetic quality. "Nor should any country," he wrote, "however excellent in its educational system, expect to maintain the capacity and productive efficiency of its people if the most capable and efficient of them multiply least rapidly, and the least capable and efficient multiply most rapidly."

Paul Taylor, like Carver a native of Iowa, took his undergraduate work at the University of Wisconsin. He received a master's degree from the University of California in 1920 and a Ph.D. from Wisconsin in 1922. Joining the department of economics at the University of California in 1922, he remained there until his retirement in 1962. His major research concerns were farm labor in California and other states and the retention of the 160-acre limitation on federal reclamation projects. Taylor's early investigations of the conditions of immigrant farm laborers in California helped to focus national attention on the social problems of these workers, particularly migrants from Mexico. During the depression, his studies — often poignantly documented with photographs taken by his wife, Dorothea Lange — culminated in the creation of the first migratory labor camps in 1935. Although Taylor's major teaching responsibility lay in economics, he found time to teach a course in rural sociology, the only one given on the Berkeley campus.[33]

A man of broad interests and training, Oliver E. Baker can be classified as a geographer, land economist, and demographer. He obtained an M.A. degree from Columbia University in 1905, studied for a year at the Yale Forestry School, and earned doctoral degrees from the University of Wisconsin in 1921 and the University of Göttingen in 1937. After thirty years of service with the Department of Agriculture — many of them spent in the Division of Farm Population — Baker became a professor of geography at the University of Maryland in 1942. He edited the *Atlas of American Agriculture* from 1914 to 1936 and (with V. C. Finch) *The Geography of World Agriculture*. His studies of farm population and rural youth made him well known to rural sociologists, and he visited many campuses to present his data on trends in population change. In 1939 he published jointly with M. L. Wilson and Ralph Borsodi a book entitled *Agriculture and Modern Life*, which discussed current rural problems in informal style.

Summary

The men whose work has been noted in this and the preceding chapters must be considered the founders of the discipline. Most of them originated instruction, research, or extension work in rural sociology at their respective institutions, or were associated with other persons with major responsibility for doing so. Some of them had little if any formal instruction in sociology, either at the undergraduate or graduate levels. Frequently, their undergraduate work was in technical agriculture or in social sciences other than sociology. The methods of study in the early phases of their work did not reach much beyond the social survey and elementary statistical stages. However, most of them knew rural life at firsthand, having been born and reared on farms or in small towns. While this kind of knowledge was no substitute for technical proficiency in the developing field of methodology, it gave them a useful perspective in the interpretation of results of their own studies as well as those of their younger colleagues.

8

Federal Subsidies for Rural Research

IT WAS only gradually that rural social research achieved equality with other types of agricultural research as an enterprise supportable by public funds. In the early days of rural sociology, financial support was extremely limited, as we have seen. Galpin's early work at the University of Wisconsin was supported by funds which came through the department of agricultural economics, probably from state sources. The three pioneer community studies published at the University of Minnesota in 1913–15 were funded by state money. About the same time George H. Von Tungeln produced two bulletins in Iowa that were apparently financed by the agricultural experiment station, very likely from state funds. Some research supported by state money was carried on at the University of North Carolina by E. C. Branson and at North Carolina State by Carl C. Taylor. Other research activity received sponsorship from church organizations and private agencies.

With rare exceptions, the experiment stations did not regard social research as one of their appropriate functions. The Hatch Act of 1886, which authorized the establishment of the stations and provided an annual federal grant of $15,000 for each one, spelled out the purposes for which the funds could be used. Most of the purposes related in some way to plant and animal production, although one clause of the act authorized expenditures for "such other researches or experiments bearing directly on the agricultural industry . . . as may in each case be deemed advisable . . ." Under the terms of this clause, a director conceivably could authorize projects in the social sciences. The Hatch Act appropriations, however, came to be used for administrative expenses, printing, and "experimental effort ranging from thoroughly scientific work to simplified demonstrations." [1]

A second piece of federal legislation, the Adams Act of 1906, increased the annual grant to experiment stations by $15,000 a year but was more restrictive than the Hatch Act in specifying the types of projects that could be undertaken. In general, the appropriated funds were to be devoted to "fundamental problems of agriculture," that is, to technical agriculture and not to social science.

Galpin's administration of the Division of Farm Life Studies provided some stimulation to sociological research. Still, the reaction of college administrators and experiment station directors, with rare exceptions, was sluggish. Throughout the 1920s the directors were men trained in the biological and physical sciences, and it was difficult to convince them of the value of research in economics, let alone in sociology. Furthermore, they could claim that under the provisions of the Hatch and Adams acts they had no authority to use federal grants for research in the social sciences.

The Purnell Act

A breakthrough for the support of social research at the experiment stations came with the passage of the Purnell Act in 1925. This law supplemented the $30,000 annual payments provided by the earlier acts with another $60,000 per year. The increase in appropriations was important, but for social scientists the most significant feature of the new law was a clause authorizing the expenditure of funds for "such economic and sociological investigations as have for their purpose the development and improvement of the rural home and rural life . . ." The Purnell Act thus gave directors of the experiment stations explicit authority to approve research in economics and sociology and to support it with federal funds.

The impact of the new law was assessed in a report on the status of rural sociological research made by Galpin for 1926–27, the first full year of operations under the Purnell Act.[2] Because this survey reflects conditions in what was something of a landmark year, it merits review at some length.

A total of 27 states reported studies in progress during the fiscal year beginning July 1, 1926, and ending June 30, 1927. Of the 40 institutions and agencies conducting research, 27 were agricultural colleges and state experiment stations. Five nonagricultural schools also reported projects, as did three government agencies.

All together, 86 different research projects were under way. Some 25 were devoted to the study of rural organizations; 16 others concentrated on rural population, and another 16 were concerned with the standard of living of rural families. The remaining 18 focused on a variety of problems, such as rural health, local government, the psychology of rural participants in group endeavors, and so forth. Galpin summarized the most significant findings as follows:

The studies of rural, village and farm populations have added to the current knowledge of the composition and characteristics of the village population and farm population in contrast with each other and with urban populations. The subject of migration of population to and from farms has taken on a serious aspect not hitherto attaching to the rather commonplace theme. The progressive loss of farm population for the last seventeen years has been connected up naturally with the growth of industry, the efficiency of agriculture, and the political and economic struggle of the agricultural class; and a new meaning has come into rural mobility.

The standard of living studies have succeeded in bringing to the forefront the hitherto neglected fact that the purpose of income from farms is not fulfilled until income has been exchanged into economic goods of living. . . . The history of farm life has shown that in the past the farmers who have appreciated a balanced variety of the economic goods of life have left farming for cities in order to exchange their financial profits for goods not obtainable in farming communities, especially such goods and services as are furnished by modern institutions.

The studies of rural organizations are struggling to understand the principle of primary group life; the high mortality of farm organizations; the competitive character of many rural associated efforts; the saturation point for efficient organization in rural communities. The facts point in general to limited competition among rural organizations as a requisite to efficient organized life. The beginnings of study on the psychological aspect of farm life bid fair to form an increasing percentage of rural studies in the future, — depending upon the development of a valid technique.

Turning to methodology, the report found the survey to be the prevailing type of study. Of the 86 projects under way in 1926–27, 56 were enumeration surveys. The remainder were classified as statistical analyses, records or accounts, and historical studies. In summarizing research techniques, the report made these comments:

It is worth noting that virtually all the studies reported are based upon data, i.e. facts or assumed facts, obtained by questioning a participant or a near-participant . . . i.e., the scientist relies upon testimony rather than upon the observation of his own senses. This dependence upon secondary data is the result, undoubtedly, of the comparative ease and cheapness of getting information from participants or those presumably acquainted at first hand with the situation involved . . . It is to be noted, furthermore, that the method by testimony necessarily limits the scientist to asking questions in terms of categories lying within the participant's experience. . . .
In the scientific advance in science as a whole, the significant concepts frequently lie outside the ordinary experience of the participant. The very pertinent question is therefore raised at this point whether rural social research is prepared to utilize methods of direct observation and experiment which have proved so successful in the physical sciences.

In an effort to measure the caliber of the personnel engaged in research work, the report cited academic degrees as a measure of ability. Of the 141 persons involved, 39 were undergraduates, 34 held bachelor's degrees, 37 possessed master's degrees, and 31 had received doctor's degrees. In this connection, the report made the following observations:

It is to be hoped that more time in actual field work can be given by the persons possessing the higher degrees. This is especially needed for the sake of perfecting the various techniques of fact-gathering. As soon as the observational and experimental methods come into use, it will be necessary for the matured and highly trained persons to engage in the actual fact-gathering process.

The fact that 27 states reported sociological research in 1926–27 seemed to indicate an auspicious beginning. However, a close examination of the projects listed reveals that only 17 of the 27 agricultural experiment stations reporting projects had supplied their researchers with Purnell funds.[3] Since no projects at all were reported from 21 states, one can assume that a total of 31 experiment station directors had not provided Purnell funds for rural sociology. It is possible, of course, that in these stations no requests had been made; the available personnel was still very limited. Clearly, the first year of Purnell appropriations, while encouraging as a beginning, did not bring a great expansion in research. The new funds were, nevertheless, a great boon to certain institutions already committed to rural sociology, particularly Cornell, Wisconsin, and Missouri.

The resources of Galpin's division were soon to diminish and, indeed, to disappear entirely, with the onset of the depression. In this respect, the Purnell Act came at a critical time to take up the slack. It also provided a basis for the establishment of regular research in a number of institutions already supplied with personnel but without financial resources, such as Arkansas, Connecticut, Minnesota, North Carolina, Ohio, Oklahoma, South Dakota, Utah, and West Virginia. All these schools used Purnell funds in the first year of their availability, and in practically all of them it was the first time the agricultural experiment stations had provided funds for rural studies from any source.

The passage of the Purnell Act, therefore, was a development of considerable significance. First, and most important, it established the legitimacy of rural sociology as a research discipline in the agricultural experiment stations. The directors of these institutions still held the power to decide how the available funds were to be spent, but they could no longer say that it was illegal to spend federal grants for rural sociology. Secondly, in those states where the administration was favorable to social research, the act provided a stable source of federal support, permitting the planning of projects over a longer period of time than a single year. Finally, as already indicated, Purnell funds made it possible for some of the more poorly financed agricultural experiment stations to inaugurate rural social research.

Additional Federal Support and Its Impact

The Bankhead-Jones Act of 1935 and the Agricultural Research and Marketing Act of 1946 greatly increased subsidies to the experiment stations and state extension services. Both acts apportioned funds on the basis of rural population, rather than providing fixed grants in equal amounts to all states regardless of size, as had the earlier legislation. This provision corrected the inequity of flat grants and permitted states with large rural populations to serve their citizens more adequately.

By the mid-1940s Congress had passed five different acts supporting agricultural research and extension — Hatch, Adams, Purnell, Bankhead-Jones, and the research and marketing law of 1946. In 1955 the national legislature amended the Hatch Act to combine all these separate authorizations into one statute. The resultant Public Law 352 retained much of the language of the Purnell Act in providing for experiment station research devoted to the "development and improvement of the rural home and rural life." The authorization of the use of federal funds for research in the social sciences is now clear and broad. There is today virtually universal acceptance of research in economics by the experiment stations, but support for rural sociology is still far from unanimous. The current state of affairs is clearly revealed in a recent analysis of personnel at land-grant colleges and experiment stations.[4]

For the year 1964–65 only twenty-six states and the territory of Puerto Rico reported personnel in rural sociology on the staffs of their experiment stations. A number of states that at one time or another had supported rural social research — notably Oklahoma, North Dakota, and Virginia — listed no rural sociologists in 1964–65. Twenty-five states reported sociology personnel on the staffs of the extension service. In most cases these were states that also reported research workers.

One of the most remarkable aspects of this report is the number of personnel listed as working in the field of family life. Some 29 states, including 14 that had no rural sociologists on their experiment station staffs, listed about 145 workers in the area of family life, usually in departments of home economics. Most of them were teachers, but in 7 states they were also on experiment station staffs. In 21 of the 29 states the extension service staffs included family life personnel. The size of the staff in some institutions was also remarkable. Connecticut reported 7 persons; Oklahoma, 15; and Oregon, 17. In these places nearly all the staff members possessed master's or doctor's degrees.

Galpin, in his report on the status of research in 1926–27, had observed, "it is fair to assume that within two or three years virtually every agricultural experiment station will be carrying on studies." This optimistic outlook, it has become apparent, was based on wishful thinking. Rural sociology will be fortunate if it can hold its present position, with a foothold in only about half the experiment stations. This discussion of research personnel, of course, should not be taken to mean that the teaching of rural sociology has been equally restricted. While no survey has been made recently, it is quite likely that the subject is taught in practically all the land-grant institutions, either in their colleges of agriculture or in departments of sociology in the liberal arts division.

Rural Studies in the Depression Years

The Galpin subventions, followed by or concurrent with the Purnell appropriations, gave the emerging discipline a substantial beachhead in the colleges and universities during the 1920s. But the chronic depression in American agriculture that began after World War I tended to concentrate attention on the prices of farm products and on demands for legislative reform. Rural research suffered a further setback in the early 1930s, when there was pressure on Congress to reduce governmental expenses. Galpin's funds for subventions disappeared and his Washington staff was cut in half. Franklin D. Roosevelt in his 1932 presidential campaign promised to reduce the federal budget by one-fourth, and after the election there was talk of cutting the annual federal grants to the state colleges of agriculture in order to make good on the campaign promises. As it turned out, however, by the spring of 1933 the situation of the country was so critical that campaign oratory was soon forgotten.

In May of that year President Roosevelt signed into law a bill which created the Federal Emergency Relief Administration (FERA). During the following summer, the agency was rapidly organized by Harry L. Hopkins, a former New York social worker. One of the important sections of the new organization was the Division of Research and Statistics. This division immediately undertook a census of unemployment which revealed, among other facts, that there were more than a million rural families receiving relief. When the figure rose to nearly 1,500,000 by July 1934, the myth that people on the land could take care of themselves was delivered a mortal stroke.

Early in the organization of the FERA, Hopkins called in E. L. Kirkpatrick, then at the University of Wisconsin, to advise him on rural problems. A rural research unit was set up in the Division of Research and Statistics and Dwight Sanderson was invited to become its head. Sanderson immediately undertook to recruit rural sociologists to act as state supervisors of rural research. Each supervisor received $25 per month and travel expenses. An assistant state supervisor was selected from the list of unemployed and paid from the work-relief funds. The supervisors proceeded to recruit research workers from the rolls of the Civil Works Administration, the early New Deal work-relief program. By December 1934 there existed state supervisors with organized staffs in twenty-three states. "In one year," Sanderson reported, "expenditures for rural sociology equalled the amount spent by all state agricultural colleges over the past 5 years, and more than the Division of Farm Population and Rural Welfare had spent through its existence of 15 years." [5]

The first project put into operation by the rural research unit was a survey of rural families on relief. The entire project was planned in Washington, including the selection of sample counties and the construction of the questionnaire. The state supervisors had only to organize staffs of interviewers, train them, and send them into the selected counties. Under this and succeeding programs, however, state supervisors were free to undertake other studies on their own account, as long as they were able to perform the duties requested by the Washington office. During the winter of 1934, Sanderson returned to his duties at Cornell. He was succeeded during 1935 by John H. Kolb of the University of Wisconsin. T. J. Woofter, Jr., then took over the direction of rural research until the work was terminated in 1939.

With the passage of the Social Security Act in 1935 and the accompanying reorganization of the relief program, work-relief projects became the sole responsibility of a new agency, the Works Progress Administration (WPA). Rural research was continued under this agency. There is no way of knowing how much WPA money was used by rural sociologists in various states for projects organized on their own initiative and carried out with the use of labor supplied from the WPA lists. The aggregate amount probably equaled that spent by the Washington staff and may have greatly exceeded it. While the workers were not always as well qualified for scientific research as they might have been, it was possible to use them effectively on well-selected projects. Never before had such resources been available.

FERA-WPA Research Publications

Twenty research monographs were published between 1935 and 1940, all but five dealing with rural problems and conditions incident to the depression. Some of them were especially noteworthy for their contributions to understanding and to methodology. *Six Rural Problem Areas: Relief — Resources — Rehabilitation* by P. G. Beck and M. C. Forster was published as FERA Monograph No. 1 in November 1935.[6] The six areas included in the study represented agricultural production patterns particularly vulnerable to climate changes and market fluctuations. Surveys of families were made in 65 counties of these areas, where almost half of all rural relief families lived. In view of new programs for relief and rehabilitation instituted in these same areas during the 1960s — thirty years after the report was written — some of its conclusions are pertinent. For example, the authors concluded that the "lack of schooling of a large portion of the heads of relief families appears to be one reason for their being on relief, inasmuch as the least trained tend to be the first to be dropped and the last to be employed whether for wages in industry or as farm tenants or laborers." Though other conditions contributed to the relief status of the families, including the drought and the condition of the market, the report placed emphasis on the social factors.

Beck and Forster's monograph constituted one of the first attempts by rural sociologists to define rural regions. A more extensive effort to delineate rural sociocultural regions was undertaken by A. R. Mangus.[7] C. E. Lively, then at Ohio State, was also interested in establishing boundaries of rural social areas on a state basis. Perhaps the economists' use of type-of-farming areas was responsible for the rural sociologists' belief that they could delineate homogeneous areas based upon social factors. However, the work of a sociologist, Howard W. Odum, also stimulated interest in this line of research, even before the publication of his first book in 1936.[8]

Mangus took as his point of departure the type-of-farming areas which had been mapped for the United States by F. F. Elliott.[9] However, for the final delineation of cultural areas he used these indexes: plane-of-living index, ratio of children under 5 years of age to 1,000 women aged 20-44 years, percentage of tenancy in 1935, percentage of farms producing less than $1,000 in 1929, per capita value of land, and percentage of rural families residing on farms. With some other factors, including Negroes in the population of the South and wage laborers in the Far West, he delineated 32 major cultural regions, and 218 subregions.

The only WPA rural project in which all the state supervisors participated was the survey of rural families on relief, made as of June 1935. The findings showed that in 1930 rural families constituted 42 per cent of all American families; 6.6 million of them were farm and 5.9 million nonfarm. Between 1930 and 1935 one out of four of these families had sought public or private assistance. The sample included 128 counties in nine agricultural areas and 116 townships in New England. The agricultural areas were: eastern cotton, western cotton, Appalachian-Ozark, lake states cut-over, hay and dairy, corn belt, spring wheat, winter wheat, and ranching. The entire area of the sample had been declared drought disaster counties in 1934, in 1935, or in both years.[10]

Weather and business cycles were known to be factors operating in the early thirties to produce dependency in rural areas, but it was also found that the heads of these families were more poorly educated and had larger families to support than nonrelief families. This study was one of the most effective presentations of rural distress published by the WPA. The text was effectively augmented with a selection of excellent illustrations by such photographers as Dorothea Lange and Ben Shahn.

Beck and Forster's monograph, *Six Rural Problem Areas*, dramatically exposed the entire cotton South as a problem region, one of the most serious in the entire nation. Of course, farm tenancy and the discussion of it was not new. As we have pointed out, E. C. Branson and Carl C. Taylor in North Carolina had published reports on the conditions of tenant farmers in the early 1920s. Yet a careful description of the plantation had never been made. This was the subject to which T. J. Woofter, Jr., and a staff of collaborators devoted themselves.[11] The results were based upon a study of 646 plantations of medium or large size located in the eastern cotton belt. A tract with five or more resident families including the landlord was defined as a plantation. The study concentrated on the "human elements associated with the land tenure system in the Eastern Cotton Belt," rather than on technical agriculture or farm economics. The plantation, as the authors pointed out, "constitutes a community within which the tenants and laborers have definite relationships, both with the landlord and among themselves." [12]

After an analysis and description of practically all phases of plantation life — its organization and management, labor conditions and tenure classes, credit system, income, living conditions, mobility, education — the authors discussed remedial measures. They concluded that long-range programs were "hampered by the tenant system to the extent that the landlord-tenant relationship hinges on a money crop agreement." The most fundamental reform suggested was to promote the ownership of family-sized farms.[13]

The crises of depression and drought inevitably increased movement of the rural population, particularly that on farms. While observers had been aware of the rural exodus for more than a generation, and many prominent spokesman had deplored it, there was little accurate information about its volume or direction. The usual assumption that it was a movement only from the farms to towns and cities lacked any statistical basis; indeed, during the crises of the thirties this belief became particularly questionable, since employment opportunities in cities did not exist. One of the WPA projects sought to find out more about rural migration.[14]

The migration study was based largely on the census, which provided historical background up to 1930. This part of the work was facilitated by the separate enumeration of rural farm and rural nonfarm population by states, provided for the first time by the 1920 census. The census analysis was supplemented with a field study of the migration history of 22,000 families, obtained through interviews in Iowa, Kentucky, Maryland, North Carolina, North Dakota, Ohio, and South Dakota. Also utilized were the results of the estimates of farm population movement gathered annually by the Division of Farm Population. Of particular importance in this volume were a chapter on the social significance of rural migration and a discussion of methodology in the appendix. Five aspects of migration were discussed: effects upon rural life, effects upon the cities of rural-to-urban migration, mobility within agriculture, migration and opportunity in agriculture, and the relation of migration to relief and rehabilitation. Methodologically, the calculation of net migration from counties represented a major undertaking, as did the calculation of survival rates as a measure of the absorptive power of agriculture for those born into the farm population. This volume was illustrated with photographs taken by Dorothea Lange and others.

The FERA-WPA monographs were largely descriptive and were aimed at providing policy-makers with facts on which to base their decisions. It should be noted too that they constituted a valuable body of reliable material for teaching and that they were widely quoted by the textbook writers. The monographs were supplemented by a number of smaller research bulletins and by miscellaneous reports on trends issued at more frequent intervals.[15]

Resettlement-Farm Security Research

After 1936 there were apparently no further nationwide or regional field surveys sponsored by the WPA. At the federal level major attention was given to analyzing the vast amount of data already collected and publishing the monographs discussed above. Research activity with WPA support was carried out at the state level by local supervisors in the waning years of the decade. As war clouds began to cast their shadows, however, the preparedness program initiated in 1940 immediately opened up private employment and the WPA lists of unemployed began to shorten.

As far as developments in Washington were concerned, the attention of rural sociologists came to focus again on the Division of Farm Population. The regular budget of the division was extremely limited, but it was possible to use personnel paid by the Resettlement Administration and its successor in 1937, the Farm Security Administration, to inaugurate and carry out some projects. Carl Taylor, who had been assistant administrator in charge of the Division of Rural Resettlement, began his tenure as chief of the Division of Farm Population in 1937.

The programs which were developed to meet the crisis of the depression became objects of analysis because of their impact upon rural people. Notable among the special programs were the rural rehabilitation efforts of the federal government. Under the Federal Emergency Relief Administration and later the Resettlement Administration, the government established cooperative farm projects to take rural people off the relief rolls and restore them to productive life in agriculture. Since these resettlement projects meant the creation of communities *de novo*, they represented an excellent opportunity to observe community formation and development in process. Charles P. Loomis, after receiving his Ph.D. from Harvard University and spending a year at the University of Heidelberg, joined the staff of the Division of Farm Population in 1934. He immediately outlined studies of the level of living and of the relations of families in seven new communities.[16] Studies were also conducted of some Reclamation Service projects to ascertain the methods of selecting settlers and to evaluate the experience. It was assumed the results might be of value to the resettlement program as far as selection of settlers was concerned.[17]

The Division of Farm Population gave attention to other problems of the depression years. Notable were two major studies of what can be classified as rural social stratification.[18] A total of eighteen projects were completed and reported during the 1930s; they were sponsored by the division but financed in large measure by the Resettlement Administration and the Farm Security Administration.

The early 1940s saw the completion of studies of six communities, first projected in 1939 and published under the series title, Culture of a Contemporary Rural Community. The communities were chosen to represent

points on a presumed continuum from "stability" to "instability." While
the project has been criticized because of the inadequate definition of the
concepts of stability and instability, each monograph in the series stands
as a contribution in its own right to our knowledge of community life in
America.[19]

Following the war, the division's major undertaking was a series of
cooperative studies with the various states on the general topic of social
organization. The project was designed on the basis of careful sampling
of 24 counties from various types-of-farming regions of the nation. It was
hoped that from this sampling it would be possible to acquire data which
would add up to a national rural sociology.[20] These cooperative investigations, like the six studies of rural communities, revealed again the diversity of conditions and problems in rural America.

The Bureau of Agricultural Economics

Meanwhile, as the emergency agencies gave less and less support to
rural research, the Bureau of Agricultural Economics experienced some
expansion. In the reorganization of the Department of Agriculture in
1938, the bureau became the "arm of the Secretary" for program formulation; as a staff agency its responsibility was policy-making rather than research.[21] This change in function was to bring about an unfortunate conflict with Congress. In the Agricultural Appropriation Act of 1939, Congress gave the bureau very broad authority. The formulation of policy,
however, was a delicate matter, inasmuch as other powerful bureaus — the
Agricultural Adjustment Administration, the Soil Conservation Service,
the Farm Security Administration, and the Extension Service — as well as
organized groups outside the government, such as the Farm Bureau, were
not ready to yield any of their influence. In consequence the BAE suffered from a process of attrition. One of the critical points of attack was
the land-use planning work inaugurated in 1937. Under this program the
BAE provided for each state involved in the program a specialist who
would help to organize and advise planning committees at the state and
county levels. Regional offices were also established for purposes of supervision and technical assistance. Opposition of the Farm Bureau and
other agencies finally forced the cancellation of the program.

Of greater importance to the history of rural research was the fate of a
project of the Division of Farm Population. By way of background, it is

necessary to review the trend in the BAE's appropriations from 1940 to 1947. The bureau's work was divided between "economic investigations" and "crop and livestock estimates." In 1941 the respective appropriations were $3,908,602 and $1,122,200. By 1947, after a steady decline of the one and an increase of the other, the figures were $1,994,607 and $2,037,-000. It was from the "economic investigations" that the Division of Farm Population derived its funds. During the division's more prosperous period in the early 1940s, Taylor planned to study social problems in some 71 counties, carefully chosen to represent a cross-section of the rural life of the nation. There were to be some "reconnaissance cultural surveys" before the project proper went into the field. One of the areas involved in the reconnaissance was Coahoma County, Mississippi, which was surveyed in the summer of 1944 by Frank D. Alexander.

Alexander's report was entitled "Cultural Reconnaissance of Coahoma County, Mississippi." A number of copies were distributed, mainly within the bureau, for criticism and suggestions. One copy went to a bureau worker in Texas and by a circuitous route fell into the hands of a congressman from Mississippi. Other congressmen from that state then asked for and received copies. The report aroused tremendous antagonism on their part. One of them spoke of "secret documents" and "ulterior motives." Another said: ". . . I have not put these matters in the record because I did not want to spread an indictment of fine folks, regardless of the types and character of folks that may have made it, or the motives they may have behind them in this report."[22] The "fine folks" were the white citizens of Coahoma County.

The charge of secrecy grew out of the fact that the document was a preliminary one, meant only for staff use and criticism. As far as motives were concerned, the report was, from the point of view of its author and others interested in social research, an informative and straightforward piece of investigation.[23] Among other observations, Alexander reported that "militant Negro leadership in urban centers of the North is making its opinions felt on the rural Negroes of Coahoma County." He also noted that the city of Clarksdale had a highly rated school system and a junior high school for Negroes. In addition, he observed: "The municipal swimming pool for whites is located on the campus of the white high school. The school system maintains a free kindergarten for white children of preschool age. The superintendent of the white school is strongly opposed to employing Negro teachers who come from the North or who have been educated in northern schools." [24] These remarks were interpreted by the congressmen as a "vicious attack" on the "fine folks" of Coahoma County.

As a result of the furor, agricultural appropriation acts after 1946 bore a rider that none of the funds could be used to support land-use planning or social surveys. In the Division of Farm Population, however, a readjustment was made. The original 71-county sample was reduced to 24, and work went forward with the assistance of field staff members attached to the state agricultural experiment stations where the studies were made. Although the phrase "social surveys" was not used, the studies were conducted and published under the general concept of "social organization." [25]

Summary

In historical perspective, it would be difficult to show that any basic principles or generalizations resulted from the vast outpouring of funds for research in the sociology of rural life during the 1930s and early 1940s. Nor could such an outcome have been expected. All the research was devoted to the solution of problems, with the possible exception of the studies of stability-instability communities and of the county social organization reports. It was research born of crisis and oriented to practical matters of policy formation. Nevertheless there were certain noteworthy achievements.

In the first place, the myth that farming and economic security went hand in hand, as far as it still retained vitality in the public mind, was given its deathblow. Over a million rural families were on relief in the depression years. The anatomy of rural poverty in all its grimness was fully exposed, along with its causes and consequences. Second, the existence of extreme diversity in rural conditions, ways of life, and levels of culture was dramatically revealed, as was the variety of types of strata in the rural population. No longer could one speak — as Butterfield had — of the "farming class." The study of the structure of rural society had an effective beginning in the depression years.

A third achievement was that patterns of migration, both rural-urban and intra-rural, along with all their social consequences were brought fully to public attention for the first time. And finally, the studies of New Deal resettlement projects contributed an imaginative beginning to the under-standing of how new communal life emerges. The monographs, bulletins, and reports of the thirties and forties were largely descriptive. Practically all of them lacked a stated hypothesis; none produced any profound gen-eralizations. Yet the store of knowledge of American rural life was greatly enriched.

9

Defining Scope and Content

IN ANY emerging discipline there must be a decision as to what areas of knowledge and inquiry are to be included and what are to be excluded. The scope of a field depends to a large extent on a deliberately formulated definition of its extent and purpose. Moreover, no matter how dogmatically a field of knowledge may be defined at a given time, it is subject to redefinition later. In the social sciences, as in other disciplines, the question of definition is a continuing one and becomes increasingly important and difficult as the sciences proliferate into subdivisions or tend to merge. Thus sociology in its early period had to distinguish itself from economics, politics, psychology, and anthropology; in later years it was to give rise to such interdisciplinary fields as social psychology, political sociology, and medical sociology.

In the end, any discipline must define itself in terms of the problems with which it is concerned. Rural sociology was concerned with the problems, or maladjustments, of rural people, but this was also true of rural economics. The pioneers in rural sociology were confronted with a hybrid question. What was the discipline's relation to general sociology? And how could the field be defined so as to distinguish it from rural economics? In the nature of things, the sociologist was concerned with social problems and the economist with economic problems. This distinction seems simple enough, but problems do not come in neatly labeled bundles. Is poverty an economic or a social problem? Are people ill educated because they are poor, or poor because they are uneducated? Or, to take the case of land tenure, is this a social or an economic problem? The answer, of course, is that it is both. Yet the nature of academic disciplines seems to demand a division of labor and knowledge.

One approach to evaluating the scope and content of a particular discipline is a chronological examination of the textbooks produced and used by members of the field. This chapter is devoted to a review of the efforts of pioneer textbook writers to come to grips with the questions raised above, and an assessment of the ways in which subsequent authors modified scope and content with the passage of time and the proliferation of dependable information about rural life. Other approaches and a more general analysis of the field will be taken up in Chapter 12.

Books by Educators and Clergymen

The earliest writers who attempted to define the field were concerned with rural institutions which presented recognizable problems, notably the school and the church. L. H. Bailey, as we have seen, constantly preached the need to improve rural education, though he was short on specifics. The education professionals who worked in rural areas, on the other hand, were not only aware of the deficiencies but also saw ways in which reforms could be made. One of the earliest to write on this subject was O. J. Kern.[1] Born in 1861 and reared on a farm in Illinois, he began his career as a teacher and administrator in rural public schools. His book on the country school was published in 1906. In 1913 he became assistant professor of agricultural education in the University of California and was probably the first person in the United States to hold that title. Kern's courses at California, according to his syllabi, actually covered the whole area of rural life insofar as the available literature allowed him to present it.

About the same time Mabel Carney published her pioneer textbook in rural education.[2] Indicative of the book's scope is its subtitle: *A Study of the Agencies of Rural Progress and of the Social Relationships of the School to the Country Community*. The cause of the "farm problem," she

102

declared in her first chapter, was the "isolation of country life." The "agencies of rural progress" were discussed in chapters dealing with the farm home, the country church, the Grange, farmers' institutes and the agricultural press, and the problem of rural roads. Five chapters dealt with technical aspects of rural education, including such matters as the training of teachers and school consolidation. In an appendix the author presented an "outline of a course in rural sociology for country teachers," which closely resembled the curriculum suggested by Butterfield.

A somewhat more analytical treatment appeared in a book on education and the community edited by Joseph K. Hart.[3] Hart himself wrote four chapters covering the community as educator, the human resources of the community, the political life of the community, and the general social life of the community. Only two chapters of the book dealt with education proper, one on community life as the curriculum of the school and another on community life and the administration of education. Hart's volume was, in effect, a textbook on the rural community, although it was oriented to the field of education. It represented a real step forward in the literature of rural life. Mabel Carney's book was largely descriptive and technical, yet she showed an awareness (as Kern had not) of the broader community context in which the school functioned. It remained for Hart to produce the first analysis of the educational institution as it functioned in the rural milieu.

Of the early works on rural education, the one which most resembled a text in rural sociology was Ellwood Patterson Cubberley's *Rural Life and Education*, published in 1914.[4] Cubberley opened his book with a historical survey, dividing the changes in rural life into four phases: "early pioneer," up to 1830; "transformation," 1830–60; "the home-building farmer," 1860–90; and the "new rural life," after 1890. About half the book consisted of a description of these changes and their effects on social life, local government, the church, and the school. The remainder of the book was devoted to the problems of the school.

Although by the turn of the century members of the clergy had become aware of the impact upon the church of the changes taking place in rural society, it was rare for anyone to present the church as an institution in the broad context of the rural community. One of the earliest to do this was Wilbert L. Anderson.[5] In his preface Anderson stated: "This book endeavors to set forth rural changes in their historical, scientific, and social aspects. Incidentally a wide consensus of opinion in disparagement of rural communities is challenged, and the pessimist who haunts the country towns that he regards gloomily is confronted." But Anderson was no Pollyanna. He dug for facts, although the information available to him was inevitably limited and his generalizations were colored by the ideology of his time.

The first half of the book traced the effects of the industrial revolution on the countryside, including outmigration to the cities and the increase of population in the suburbs, which the author designated as the "zone of rural growth." The "facts" demonstrated that rural depletion was inevitable, not only quantitatively but also qualitatively. However, he found some satisfaction in his conviction that industrial development had driven not only the most desirable elements but also the lowest stratum of society from the country to the city. In short, though conditions were bad and the outlook gloomy, Anderson believed that the rural community could be saved by improvements in the environment: education, evangelization, and wider participation in the "great movements of the age." This book was a thorough analysis from the perspective of social Darwinism and of the moral agrarianism which saw the country as fundamentally superior to the city.

By far the most important book to come from the clergy was a work by Warren H. Wilson.[6] His pioneer study of *Quaker Hill* as a doctoral thesis under F. H. Giddings, has been mentioned earlier. As a Ph.D. in sociology, as well as an ordained minister, Wilson brought to his book on the country community a higher level of sophistication in respect to the sociology of rural life than any of the books previously mentioned. Like Anderson, Wilson felt it necessary to explain the historical background of the situation in which the church and the rural community found themselves, and to propose solutions. But he took a more realistic approach than Anderson had to the rural community, recognizing the importance not only of the town, but also of the people on the farms tributary to it. Hence he attempted to explain and define the community, using Willett M. Hays's concept of the "team haul."[7] On the other hand, Wilson accepted the prevalent notion that the community was "sometimes corrupted by vicious principles in its construction" and that its members were "in proportion defective." The community, Wilson believed, "produced in excessive degree idiots, blind, deformed, neurotic, insane or criminal individuals."[8] The book was used as a textbook in some places and a reference in many more, although by later standards it was, of course, far from adequate.

Another small book that deserves mention in this history of early attempts to systematize the field is Edwin L. Earp's *Rural Social Organization*.[9] Earp, like Wilson, was a sociologist, and held a professorship at Drew Theological Seminary. Publishing his book in 1921, Earp was able to draw upon earlier writers for guidance and material. The book contained twenty chapters covering such topics as the nature and methodology of social organization, the larger social values of rural life, principles of rural economic organization, and the purposes and methods of rural community organization. Chapters on specific institutions and agencies — the home, the school, the church, farmers' organizations, cooperation, welfare, tenancy, roads, and marketing — were followed in each case by a discussion of the meliorative role that the church could play.

It is interesting that the town or village was so often the subject of these early writers. Generally members of the country life school were concerned with farm people, though it was usual to make little distinction between town and country in speaking of country life. They seemed to agree that the town was in a bad way. In the preface to his book on the small town, Harlan Paul Douglass noted the existence of a "new wealth of impulse and inspiration for the dweller in the open country. Most of it is equally applicable to the little town." [10] But, as he complained, "Country-life evangelists do not ordinarily regard it as any part of their business to address the town directly — unless to scold it."

Douglass' little book represented a further advance toward the writing of a usable textbook. The author made use of such literature as represented objective research, including Galpin's "rurban" concept. Although a professional in the field of religious organization, he refrained from drawing a "lesson for the church" at the end of each chapter. It was the best study yet of the rural town.

Early Textbooks by Sociologists

None of the books thus far reviewed were adequate to meet the requirements of a course in rural sociology. They were helpful reference works for the pioneer teacher, but they fell short of what was needed. Rural society had yet to be presented in its broader aspects without regard to serving a special audience such as that of education or religion. The first textbook to attempt this goal, and the first with "rural sociology" in its title, was John Gillette's *Constructive Rural Sociology*.[11] Gillette no doubt felt constrained to use the adjective "constructive" in his title because at that time rural sociology was supposedly concerned with "improvement" or "betterment" or "rural progress." [12] In future editions Gillette dropped the adjective.

This historic textbook was only a tentative beginning, but it served better than any book before it. The titles of its chapters indicate its scope: Meaning and Importance of Rural Sociology; Distinction between Rural and Urban Community; Types of Communities as Results of the Differentiating Effects of Environment (one type was the "backward community"); Rural and Urban Increase (mainly a discussion of migration); The Social Nature of the Rural Problem; Advantages and Disadvantages of Farm Life; Improvement of Agricultural Production; Improvement of the Business Side of Farming; Improvement of Transportation and Communication; Social Aspects of Land and Labor in the United States; Rural Health and Sanitation; Making Farm Life More Attractive; Socialization of Country Life; Rural Social Institutions and Their Improvement; Rural Charity and Corrections; and Rural Social Surveys.

Gillette anticipated criticism of the chapters dealing with economics. "It may be alleged," he wrote, "that matters are treated which belong to economics, agriculture, and to sanitary and mechanical engineering. Technically such a criticism is just. It is lessened by the practical consideration, however, for many institutions in which instruction in rural matters is desired may not offer separate courses which develop those subjects . . ." He further justified his inclusion of the matter of economics by citing the example of T. N. Carver, who had used in his *Principles of Rural Economics* "considerable material of a sociological nature." This first textbook thus posed a problem with which all subsequent writers have had to deal: where to draw the boundary between economics and sociology.

As the chapter headings show, the entire book was oriented to the goal of improving rural life. The author had little scientific information on which to rely, and much of the text was obviously based on his personal observations in country areas, with consequent untested generalizations. The book was widely used at the time, however, and was translated into Japanese and Czechoslovakian.

Gillette attempted no concise definition of rural sociology. In a paragraph devoted to "scope and meaning" he wrote: "Rural sociology has as its particular task to take a full inventory of the conditions of life in rural communities. It must discover their tendencies and deficiencies, map out

106

the special problems and indicate ways of betterment according to the best ideals of social life." In short, Gillette's point of view was that of the rural reformer, who studied the countryside to discover its problems and then made recommendations for solving them.

In 1923 Gillette brought out another and much larger textbook.[13] As he was careful to point out in the preface, this was not a revision of the earlier work, but a wholly new book. He emphasized his reliance on factual information: "I have preferred to keep closely to the facts rather than to make easy and sweeping statements. . . . I have not found it possible to suggest improvement in farm life at all points, but wherever remedies could appropriately be given, they have been presented." This book clearly shows a weakening of the urge for reform and a determination to generalize only on the basis of facts.

Although he devoted an entire chapter to "Rural Sociology as a Science," he still refrained from a concise definition. He came closest to the mark when he described rural sociology as "that branch of sociology which systematically studies rural communities to discover their conditions and tendencies, and to formulate principles of progress." [14] He also spoke of it as "an applied science while general sociology is a theoretical science."

The 1923 textbook gave far more space to economic problems. Rural sociology, Gillette now wrote without apology, "accepts the findings of the economist" and has an "imperative duty to ascertain the bearing of these matters on rural welfare in its various phases and to arrive at an evaluation of them as agencies in the determination of vital conditions." [15]

A third and greatly enlarged edition, appearing in 1936, continued the trend of placing more emphasis on facts and less on "advice and methodology of rural improvement." [16] "I regard this course inevitable," he wrote in the preface to the new book, "because information about rural life has become much more abundant and because advice and directions are apt to be poorly founded and, anyway, are usually ignored by those who need them."

Gillette had now come to the conclusion that the "trend in rural sociology is away from being a strictly applied science." [17] In fact, it was no more to be called an applied science than was general sociology. The latter, like rural sociology, evaluates "social conditions and treats of methods of controlling and improving them."

It has seemed appropriate to include this somewhat extended consideration of Gillette because he was the first to write a textbook in rural sociology and because his three books manifested an interesting and important evolution in the concept of the field and of the subject material it should incorporate. Rural sociology was destined to retain something of its practical orientation, but writers of textbooks became less and less inclined to tell people what they should do.

In 1917, four years after Gillette's first book appeared, Paul L. Vogt of Ohio State University published his textbook.[18] Like the early Gillette, Vogt was under the spell of reform ideology. His definition of rural sociology revealed this bias: "Rural sociology is the study of the forces and conditions of rural life as a basis for constructive action in developing and maintaining a scientifically efficient civilization in the country." He regarded the discipline as an applied science, whose goal was not so much to discover new principles as to "understand conditions for the purpose of applying principles of sociology, already discovered, to their maintenance or improvement."[19]

Vogt was somewhat optimistic about the "principles of sociology" that had already been discovered and especially about how they might be applied to achieve a "scientifically efficient civilization." But such utopian hope was common to the period. Like Gillette, Vogt included chapters on the economic problems of agriculture, on social institutions — the church, the school, and farmers' social organizations — and on population movements; an interesting innovation was the inclusion of six chapters on the village. The book represented an advance over Gillette's first book because Vogt had already completed a number of social surveys in Ohio and thus had a body of facts and tested observations on which to base much of his discussion. Curiously, Vogt made no reference to Gillette's book nor to Galpin's bulletins.[20]

A Decade of Progress

Although only two textbooks designed for courses in rural sociology had appeared before 1920 — three if Galpin's *Rural Life* is included — authors and books proliferated during the twenties. The period, characterized by T. Lynn Smith as one of "growing pains in a decade of progress," saw the appearance of no less than fifteen textbooks.[21] In reviewing the contribution made by the most significant of these new books, we shall consider not only definitions of the field and the scope of subject matter,

108

but also various definitions of community, because about half the volumes used that concept as their central consideration.

Walter Burr published his *Rural Organization* in 1921. His conception of the rural community was essentially the same as Galpin's "rurban" approach, although Burr made no reference to it — nor to the works of anyone else for that matter. "A rural community," Burr stated, "may be defined as a population group in an agricultural area of such size and unity as to permit its citizens to readily cooperate in group activities . . . It is not to be concluded from this statement that the citizens of the Rural Community are all directly engaged in farming. The proper conduct of the business affairs of an agricultural area depends quite largely upon the maintenance of an efficient business center." [22]

Writing in the same year as Burr, A. W. Hayes defined rural sociology as a "social discipline which has for its specific functions the study and understanding of the social phenomena growing out of rural life affairs." Amplifying this statement, Hayes continued: "A knowledge of the origins, developments and manifestations of these phenomena gives the rural sociologist a working-base upon which to assist in the interpretation and direction of rural society." [23] Here, despite the vagueness of the phrase "social phenomena," we have something more nearly approaching a sociological definition. It would appear that the rural sociologist, though charged with the "direction" of rural society, was spared the responsibility for seeing to its "betterment" or "progress."

A third textbook to come off the presses in 1921 was a book on the community by E. C. Lindeman. Like Burr, Lindeman thought of the rural community as including both farm and village. A community, according to his definition, "must be capable of satisfying the major economic wants of the population . . ." Therefore, he wrote, in a "strictly scientific sense, it is doubtful if there are any open country population groups that can be called true communities." [24] Lindeman devoted a chapter to "neighborhood and community," quoting the definitions of a number of writers, including Butterfield, Sanderson, C. C. North, and Mabel Carney.

In 1924, the year that saw the publication of Galpin's *Rural Social Problems*, John T. Phelan edited a book of readings. Phelan himself essayed no definitions, but one of the contributors, A. R. Mann, wrote as follows: "The sociology of rural life is, roughly, then, the study of associated or group activities of the people who live in the country viewed from the standpoint of the effect of these activities on the character of the farm people themselves." [25] This definition was more specific than the formulation proposed earlier by Hayes, whose "social phenomena" was replaced by "associated or group activities."

Horace Boies Hawthorn, in a textbook published in 1926, described rural sociology as the "scientific study of rural socialization" and made this pertinent observation on its earlier development:

In the past, rural sociology has lacked singleness of aim. . . . Actuated by the philanthropic desire to do missionary work in rebuilding a presumably "decadent" rural life, rural welfare enthusiasts mobilized every science or art that might have a bearing on better community life . . . [including] hygiene, ethics, highway economics, farm management, home economics, education, and religion. Certainly there was an urgent need in interpreting these various sciences and arts in terms of rural welfare, and it can be said, to the credit of earlier rural sociology, that it did this task in such a way as to give the nation a clearer vision of rural development. It is quite probable that if rural sociology had advanced by the purely sociological method, it would not have its present prestige, for sociology has been very immature.[26]

Hawthorn felt, however, that rural sociology, like other sciences, was growing toward maturity and would "tend to limit itself to the more closely sociological analysis of socialization problems."

It must be granted that Hawthorn took an important step forward in placing emphasis upon the field as sociology rather than as a mere survey of rural problems. His "process of socialization," however, was so broad a concept, and, as the author himself admitted, so difficult to define, that it had a limited scientific utility. Nevertheless, the author persisted with the concept — "the spinal cord of Rural Sociology," as E. A. Ross called it — and attempted to interpret all the conventional subject matter of the field in terms of it. Moreover, Hawthorn proposed a system for its measurement. His method was based upon social contact, or "exposure events," reduced to the unit of person-hour contact. In a survey of high school students in Iowa, the instrument was divided into "impressional" and "expressional" events, and the subjects were asked to indicate how often and for how long they participated in such events. Similarly, Hawthorn believed, a community could be measured by the social-exposure test. This method, he held, could "determine quantitatively the size of the socialization stream which annually flows through a rural community" by discovering the "number and type of group events to which audiences are exposed." [27] Hawthorn's book was, and continues to be, an important work.

Many other students of rural society have placed great emphasis on social participation and on instruments for its measurement.[28]

In a textbook appearing the same year as Hawthorn's, Carl C. Taylor made a careful distinction between rural sociology and general sociology. The latter, he stated, "must analyze and describe the structure and functioning of all human relationships," whereas the former specializes in

those human groups which live by the occupation of agriculture or by occupations immediately dependent upon agriculture. Rural sociology is concerned with the relations of rural people to each other, the relations of rural people to other sections of national and world populations, with rural institutions, with the rural standard of living, and with the social problems which attach themselves to life and labor on the farm and in farm communities. Under this broad classification all sociology may be divided into rural sociology and urban sociology.[29]

Taylor also attempted to distinguish between rural sociology and rural economics — a difficult task, as he pointed out, because "every rural social fact has an economic corollary and vice versa." Agricultural economics, Taylor wrote, "deals specifically with agricultural wealth, credit, cost, income, management, and marketing factors. Rural sociology is concerned with these factors only as they condition social organization or social well being." The chapters devoted to economics — one each on farm labor, land and society, and tenancy and ownership — treated the "sociological aspects" of these topics.

In a revised edition that appeared in 1933, Taylor omitted his definitions of rural sociology. Rather he devoted the first chapter to the "rise and nature of the rural problem in the United States." Here he departed from virtually all earlier writers by pointing out that there was not one but several "rural problems." The revision gave much more attention to the historical background of America's rural society and utilized new data, including some material made available by Sorokin, Zimmerman, and Galpin's *Systematic Source Book for Rural Sociology*. Significantly, the title of chapter ten in the first edition, "The Problem of Rural Isolation," was expanded in the revision by the addition of the words, "and Socialization." The influence of Hawthorn was evident. Although Taylor praised Hawthorn's attempt to measure socialization, he considered that "any such measurement obviously cannot be accurate, since it is impossible to determine how much of the world's culture and ideas one individual carries about with him."

Another venture in the search for a theoretical orientation appeared in Newell L. Sims's *Elements of Rural Sociology* (1926). It was based upon a mechanistic theory of society. "Briefly stated," the author wrote in the preface, "society is thought of in terms of energy manifest organically, materially, and culturally in a unity which we call the human group. Sociology thus becomes the study of the behavior of the energy of such groups." In conformance with this concept of society, clearly borrowed from physics, the author organized the book around four elements: the structural element (including community, village, functional organization, and principles and practice of rural organization); the vital element (population analysis); the cultural element (traditions, attitudes, the family and other social institutions); and the material element (including wealth, income, and standard of living).

Sims's definition of rural sociology was similar to Taylor's; it is, he said, the "study of association among people living by or immediately dependent upon agriculture." Sims noted the existence of two approaches to the subject, the particularistic and the pluralistic. The first approach, characteristic of early writers, attempted to include everything under one problem — the rural problem. The second approach comprehended many problems rather than one. Sims preferred what he called the unitary approach: "We call it unitary because it tries to summarize the whole situation without ignoring a multiplicity of causes and phases. According to this view, the rural problem arises from social instability and its solution lies in a process of stabilization . . ." In a third edition (1940) Sims called Hawthorn's concept of socialization the "one attempt to produce a rural sociology from a unitary standpoint"; "unitary approaches of this sort are correct and the outcome is true sociology." But he added, "It would seem that rural sociology must eventually comprehend the total behavior of rural locality and interest groups. This will involve something more than the process of socialization, even though that be made to include ever so much." He seemed to doubt that "socialization" could be stretched that far.[30]

In his third edition Sims introduced a final chapter on the techniques of achieving rural change. The techniques included the "persuasive method," the "demonstration method," the "morphological method" (the changing of social organization), and "deterministic change," by which he meant social change that takes place automatically or "mechanically." Other varieties were the "contact," "compulsory," "genetic," and "educational" methods. This addition to his book doubtless resulted from the thinking that went into a volume on the subject of social change which he published in 1939 and which was the first textbook to give serious analytical consideration to social change.[31] After 1950 this topic became one of primary interest and concern to sociologists, rural and other.

The chronological and literary climax of the period of growing pains was Sorokin and Zimmerman's *Principles of Rural-Urban Sociology*.[32] The contents were arranged in five parts: (1) The Rural World and the Position of the Farmer-Peasant Class in the "Great Society"; (2) Bodily and Vital Traits of the Rural-Urban Population; (3) Rural-Urban Intelligence, Experience, and Psychological Processes; (4) A Cross-Section of Rural-Urban Behavior, Institutions, and Culture; and (5) Rural-Urban Migration. The approach was comparative. Rural and urban populations and behavior were continually set off against each other, and generalizations drawn from these comparisons.

In the first chapter, Sorokin defined rural sociology as a special branch of general sociology, with similar purposes in its own field. Its fundamental task was to describe the "relatively constant and universal traits or relations of the rural social world as distinct from the non-rural or urban social universe . . ." An additional function was that of explaining the causes of the differences between rural and urban traits. Sorokin denied the common belief that "practical advice regarding the improvement or reconstruction of 'rural life'" was the chief purpose of rural sociology. This task, he said, belonged not to the theoretical science, but to an *"applied rural social technology."* [33] His and Zimmerman's book, along with those of Sims and Hawthorn, practically ended the reign of the Country Life-ers and their preoccupation with "problems" to be described and solved.

Principles of Rural-Urban Sociology introduced American students to a vast amount of European, and indeed of world, scholarship and commentary. True, Vogt had written a chapter on the medieval village community, and Sims in a book of readings published in 1920 had presented an elaborate treatment of foreign literature from the community point of view. But Sorokin and Zimmerman were the first to bring the literature of many countries to bear upon all aspects of their central theme. The impact of their book, however, was less than overwhelming at the time of its publication.

Unfortunately not many teachers of rural sociology had the necessary background to use it as a text. Although every sociologist recognized the work as a major achievement, the provincialism of American rural sociologists was not to be greatly modified overnight. Even in the long run the influence of this work has not been pronounced. Sorokin complained about excessive fact-gathering without synthesis, but that process continues nevertheless.[34] Studies in sociology are still oriented to the need for understanding contemporary society because of the rapidity of change. It is difficult, if not impossible, for American students to keep informed about current trends in the United States, let alone attempt the building of systems based upon the past and involving the literature of the entire world.

The limitation of the Sorokin-Zimmerman volume, viewed from the vantage point of the 1960s, lay in its assumption of "relatively constant and universal traits" of rural peoples as compared with non-rural society. There would seem to be no constancy in these traits or in the relations of rural and urban groups. The differences between them as described in this book have greatly diminished during the past generation and in some cases disappeared as far as the United States is concerned. Change is continuous, as these authors well knew; indeed, it is the supreme constant, and its study is the mandate of the sociologist.

Emphasis on Groups and Social Organization

In contrast with the sudden flowering of books in the 1920s, the following decade saw the appearance of only three new textbooks of a general character.[35]

Charles R. Hoffer, whose *Introduction to Rural Sociology* appeared in 1930, considered rural sociology to be essentially an applied science. "Practical problems come within its purview. These problems are integrated and explained, however, by use of the principles and concepts developed in abstract social science whenever possible. Thus it would seem that rural sociology is an applied science, because . . . an applied science is a classification of knowledge in a manner which makes it useful for purposes of technology." [36] Calling the field an applied science did not, in his view, imply a dedication to social reform, which he thought of as a quite different field, although one to which rural sociology, along with other sciences, might make a contribution. A revision of the book in 1934 contained new chapters on children, youth, and rural leaders, but the content was otherwise unchanged and followed conventional lines, Sorokin and Zimmerman notwithstanding.

"Rural sociology," wrote Roy H. Holmes in a book published in 1932, "is the sociology of family-farm life." But he also placed the discipline in the larger context of general sociology: "rural sociology is a field of specialization within the more comprehensive science [of sociology] which considers rural man from the standpoint of his group relationships." Holmes did not define the phrase "family-farm," but he seemed to have in mind the farm family living on the land, regardless of the type of farm. As a student and colleague of C. H. Cooley, he naturally stressed Cooley's concept of the primary group and recognized the secondary group type of society. The main emphasis was upon social institutions.[37]

Holmes's conceptual framework came close to being "sociology," but the book was open to criticism for its provincialism. Despite the prevalence of the family farm in American rural society, it has not been the only type of people-land relationship. Holmes recognized this by inserting a chapter on the corporation farm, noting the possibility that all farming might eventually be conducted on the factory system. In that case, however, he thought there could be no rural sociology. The book was deliberately limited to America and, indeed, to the Middle West. Moreover, the rural nonfarm population and the trade-center villagers were given practically no attention.

The most important book to make its appearance in the thirties was Kolb and Brunner's *Study of Rural Society* (1935). Both authors had had much experience in their field — Kolb at the University of Wisconsin for the previous fifteen years, and Brunner at Teachers College and the Institute for Social and Religious Research during the same period. Both had a significant list of research publications to their credit.

The authors did not define rural sociology as such. The book was presented as "a study of rural society, its organization and changes, from the point of view of important backgrounds, recent developments, and significant trends."

Rural society [they wrote in the preface] is considered as a unit made up of both farmers and villagers and the modern rural community as a town-country community. The rural and urban elements in general society are regarded throughout as inter-dependent parts of the larger whole. At the same time, a number of neglected aspects of rural life are discussed, such as the social influences of school curricula, the institutions of rural retail trade, local government, and national policies affecting agricultural life. While problems are not treated as such, many troublesome problems of rural life do emerge from these pages; nor are economic factors considered as separate from rural social life. Rather, the myriad activities and institutions associated with making a living are regarded as an essential part of rural society and of the social behavior of its people.

Two aspects of this book stand out. The first is the extended treatment of what Sims referred to as the morphology of rural society, and the second, the emphasis placed on social change. It was to be expected that these authors would give much attention to spatial aggregates in the rural population. Both of them had undertaken a great amount of research in this field. Material on the family, the neighborhood, the village, and the rural community, together with chapters on rural-urban relations and special interest groups, constituted nearly a third of the text. In addition, the book emphasized the rapid alterations of the rural scene during the twentieth century. The discussion of change occurred throughout at the appropriate places, and a final chapter dealt with "trends in social relationships." The scope of the book otherwise covered the conventional rural social institutions and their operation in rural society.[38] It should be noted, however, that this was the first textbook to carry a bibliography of the rural sociology of foreign areas.

The book received some unfavorable comment because there was no clear theoretical framework. The authors responded to this criticism in the preface to the second edition (1946):

While there is no chapter or section devoted exclusively to social theory as such, there is a definite frame of reference within which the materials are organized and there is a conscious plan and theory implicit in the discussion throughout . . . Much use is made of the studies of the 140 village-centered communities because they make possible comparisons over time and indicate changes under way. Similarly, many of the materials on neighborhoods, communities and the various social institutions are drawn from studies made in these particular localities.

It was still not clear just what constituted the theoretical framework, unless it was, by implication, the observation of changes over time. This at least was the major approach. The second edition, reflecting the concerns of the depression years, added fresh material on rural youth, the agricultural laborer, and tenancy.

Toward Scientific Maturity

The output of the thirties added little to the topical subject matter of rural sociology. By this time the discipline had developed a wide consensus on content, if not on theoretical orientation. All the authors discussed thus far agreed on the following general divisions of subject matter: population (growth and composition, migration); spatial groups (neighborhood, village, community); organizations (informal and formal); institutions (family, church, school, government, economic). The period did not, however, produce any attempts to find a unifying principle around which to polarize subject matter, comparable to the efforts of Hawthorn, Sims, and Sorokin and Zimmerman. The discipline still lacked any uniformly acceptable theory.

Indeed, much sociology of rural life still remained to be developed. The sociopsychological aspects, which played an important part in early textbooks, decreased in importance because of the paucity of reliable data. The shifting patterns of farm-village-city relationships, on the other hand, demanded new analysis from time to time and required new formulations of principles. Textbooks, therefore, continued to come from the presses in the 1940s. As the decade opened, several of the books we have noted were in current revisions or at least not yet out of date. The works of Gillette, Sims, Taylor, and Kolb and Brunner were still widely used. Nevertheless, a number of new competitors showed up.[39]

The beginning of the decade saw the appearance of T. Lynn Smith's *Sociology of Rural Life*. Smith was influenced more than any of the other textbook writers by the works of Sorokin and Zimmerman, under whom he had studied.[40] Like his mentors, he conceived of rural sociology as a scientific discipline, the sociology of rural society. His approach, however, was not exclusively that of the rural-urban dichotomy treated comparatively. Although he compared the two entities in terms of environment, population characteristics, and behavior, as did practically all the writers, he refused to follow the concept slavishly.

Smith's organization and treatment of subject matter diverged somewhat from the work of earlier writers and incorporated some important additions. In the first place, he gave much more attention to the analysis of population. Second, he placed more emphasis on the relations of people to the land, including such matters as the form of settlement, land division, land tenure, and size of holdings. These relationships he considered to be part of the general subject of "rural social organization," which also embraced social differentiation and stratification, along with the institutions of the family, school, church, and local government. A noteworthy innovation in Smith's book was the treatment of social processes in rural society. He was the first textbook writer to discuss competition and conflict, cooperation, accommodation, assimilation, acculturation, and mobility.

This was one of the most scholarly texts yet to appear. Another characteristic of his book deserves mention. Smith spent his professional life in the South, although he was born in Colorado and educated in the North. As he grew acquainted with conditions in the South, he came to feel that the available texts failed to pay sufficient attention to southern society. As he pointed out, the bulk of the nation's rural population lived in the South. His book was as regionally oriented to the South as practically all other texts were oriented to the North.

A third edition of Smith's work, published in 1953, contained an important new chapter on "systems of agriculture." Five systems, classified according to a sequence from primitive to modern, were illustrated from historical documents or from the writer's own observations in Latin America and other places.

The emphasis on social process was central in Paul Landis' *Rural Life in Process*, also published in 1940.[41] Landis explained his approach as follows:

The phrase "in process" used in the title implies primarily the view maintained throughout that rural life is in a state of rapid transition. . . . Experience, institutions, and problems, every important aspect of personal and institutional life, are being modified by new social forces. Secondarily, but in a more specific sense, the phrase "in process" is used to suggest the emphasis on the social processes operative in rural life. The rural sociologist, like sociologists in other fields, begins his study with man and the environment. The purpose of his science is to show how raw human nature is formed by forces within the environment. Social processes are the interactive forces that shape and reshape the person in the environment and that also lead to the continual modification of the environment itself.

Landis stressed the point that the environment of the rural dweller had been greatly enlarged by the development of "material devices that multiply contact and broaden experience."

Rural society can be understood only when considered as a part of the total design of American life. . . . In such an approach social facts and statistical findings, analyses of structure, and descriptions of organizational frameworks are used as data to reveal the more active, dynamic, living elements of rural association. Interest centers in the personality formation and adjustment of the individual, in alignments and realignments of social relationships within the rural group, in functioning of institutions, in their lags and readjustments, and in the emergence of new problems as they are manifest in the new cultural scheme.

Landis noted the emphasis of earlier writers on the "anatomy of the rural community," but stressed the need for treating both structure and function. He considered the discussion of structure as the stage "on which the social drama is set."

In accordance with his dynamic approach he viewed population "as a factor in social organization." The emphasis was not on population analysis as regards composition, but rather on the movement of peoples. Thus he devoted four chapters to migration, which was treated as one of the "interaction processes of a dynamic society." Other aspects of this topic were "isolation, contact, and the interactive process," "social differentiation and the process of stratification, " "cultural change," and "social control." It should be noted that Landis differed from Smith in considering differentiation and stratification as processes rather than as part of structure. The church, the school, the farm family, government, and "economic values in the standard of living" — the institutional framework — were considered in relation to changes affecting them. A final section of the book treated "emerging problems" — farm youth, farm tenure, farm labor, pathology and welfare problems, rural health, and the "implication of the social trend."

More than any of the previous writers, Landis emphasized changes occurring in rural life and the organic relationship to the larger society brought about by increased communication facilities. Along with Smith he established social processes as an important part of the subject matter of rural sociology.

In a textbook published in 1942, Dwight Sanderson, like Landis, devoted part of his space to sociological analysis and part to a discussion of problems. The title, *Rural Sociology and Rural Social Organization,* suggested this dichotomy. But the two authors differed greatly in their approach. Whereas Landis stressed process, Sanderson emphasized structure, because, as he wrote, "the student must have a knowledge of the nature of the phenomena before he can think intelligently concerning their processes or qualities." Moreover, where Landis dealt so largely with personality formation and with the general subject of what could be called the social psychology of rural life, Sanderson deliberately omitted extended discussion of the sociopsychological aspects for the reason that "we do not, as yet, have a great quantity of empirical data in this field and because the principles involved apply to all the social structures of rural life and really require a separate treatment . . ." [42]

Sanderson's book received criticism for the inclusion of a disproportionate amount of information on the economic aspects of agriculture — tenure, credit, soil conservation, and the McNary-Haugen bill and other farm relief proposals. Nor did the author always make clear the significance of this information for sociological analysis. In contrast with Smith and especially with Landis, Sanderson's treatment of social processes was brief. His chapter on social change was important, as was his discussion of social groups, but in general the book made little contribution in terms of theory or approach.

Four books of the late 1940s also deserve consideration. David E. Lindstrom's *American Rural Life*, more than other textbooks of the period, was oriented to the "betterment" mood of earlier years. As he put it, "I have tried to balance academic objectivity with guidance and help to the student and professional worker. I have in each chapter, selected problems for discussion which are typical, have set them in their natural social settings, and have offered suggestions for their solution." [43] The chapters covered the now fairly conventional subject matter, using a descriptive method.

A textbook by Lowry Nelson, appearing in 1948, bore some resemblance to the volume published by Smith earlier in the decade. However, in Nelson's book population analysis as such received much less attention; there was one chapter on composition and one on migration. The subjects of population fertility and mortality were reserved for brief consideration under the topics of the family and health respectively. The social processes were given more emphasis, as were social institutions. Rural sociology was defined as the "description and analysis of groups of various kinds as they exist in the rural environment." [44] The difference between sociology and other disciplines lay not in method but in subject matter. Most topics in this book were discussed in historical perspective, in the belief that many contemporary phenomena could be understood only in terms of historical backgrounds.

In 1950 Carl Taylor and his colleagues in the Division of Farm Population produced a work that was distinctive in its emphasis on the regions of the United States. Nine chapters were devoted to seven type-of-farming regions and their cultural features. The senior author set the orientation of the book in two opening chapters on rural life and rural sociology, and the evolution of American rural society. "Rural sociology," wrote Taylor, "is the study of rural people and their social relationships with one another and with nonrural people." [45] The concluding chapter, "Significant Trends and the Direction of Change," was still a reliable projection in the late 1960s, nearly twenty years after it was written.

Just as Sorokin and Zimmerman's *Principles of Rural-Urban Sociology* represented the climactic achievement of the 1920s, so, it is fair to say, Loomis and Beegle's *Rural Social Systems* topped the work of the 1940s. [46] It was the most ambitious effort in more than two decades to design a theoretical system which would accommodate the mountainous accumulation of facts laboriously compiled by hundreds of workers. In setting forth their theoretical framework, the authors described social systems as being of two kinds, concrete and abstract. The first type was the "cooperative social structure," such as a football team, a Farm Bureau local, or a family. The abstract system was one in which "patterns of relationships prevail from generation to generation and from region to region." An example of this type was the Roman Catholic Church. [47]

"According to our conceptual scheme," the authors declared, "the subject matter for sociology and cultural anthropology is human culture and interaction. Although such subject matter may be viewed in many ways, we choose to make the various types of social systems our chief concern." In defining the significant unit of social systems, Loomis and Beegle continued, "we accept Sorokin's 'meaningful interaction of two or more individuals,' and his requirement that interaction be an event 'by which one party tangibly influences the overt actions or the state of mind of the other.' " Social systems consisted of social interactions and the cultural factors which structured these interactions.

The authors listed seven "elements" which composed a system: roles, status, authority, rights, ends and objectives, norms, and territoriality. Recognizing that systems differed in social structure and value orientation, the writers devised a continuum to measure these variations. The continuum employed was the Gemeinschaft-Gesellschaft poles as described by Ferdinand Toennies. [48] One of the problems involved in the use of such measures as continua is the underlying assumption of linearity, whereas the phenomena involved are in reality extremely complex.

Following their introductory material, Loomis and Beegle proceeded to discuss, as social systems, seven aspects of rural life: family and informal groups, locality groups, social strata, religious groups, educational groups, political and occupational groups, and rural service agencies.

The book represented a definite landmark in the effort to find a theoretical system by which factual information about rural society could be summarized and made meaningful. It suffered from the deficiency of other unitary approaches in its failure to fit all situations. For example, to treat regions as social systems seems to be a contradiction in terms. Regions are neither social nor systems, but more complex congeries. The same difficulty appears when social strata are considered as social systems. By definition the word "system" implies unity and organization.[49]

Nevertheless, one can agree with Otis Durant Duncan that the book represented a welcome addition to sociological theory. As Duncan wrote, "the time has come when treatment of 'fundamental principles,' so often eschewed by the older sociologists, are [sic] needed for students with only preliminary exposure to rural sociology to project them beyond the intellectual level necessary for counting screened porches, electric lights, and outdoor privies." [50]

The authors followed their first book with a shorter one, *Rural Sociology: The Strategy of Change*, published in 1957. The new book presented an attractive emphasis on change and the mechanism of inducing it. In summary, the theory visualized two social systems, one of which was the "target" of the other (for example, the United States and an underdeveloped country). The nexus in the process was the "change agent" (agricultural expert or health officer) who brought new technology to the target system and tried to induce its adoption. The extension agent was thus viewed as playing the role of the change agent, with farmers as the target. The new book presented some modifications in the seven basic "elements" composing a system; it also introduced several new concepts, including, among others, "systemic linkage," "boundary maintenance," and "equilibrium."

The two books by Loomis and Beegle, particularly the later one, have had a pronounced impact on rural sociology. Their influence is manifest in several textbooks published in the late 1950s and early 1960s. Noteworthy are Bertrand, *Rural Sociology*; Sanders, *The Community* (in which the community is treated as a social system); Rogers, *Social Change in Rural Society*; Slocum, *Agricultural Sociology*; Taylor and Jones, *Rural Life and Urbanized Society*; and Copp, *Our Changing Rural Society*.[51] These books were all influenced more or less by the concept of the social system and by social change and its meaning and methods of study. In addition, all reflected more or less the impact of the revolution in rural society resulting from the new technology, mass communication, and the urbanization of the population.

Summary

In considering the evolution in the scope and content of rural sociology, it seemed logical to examine some of the textbooks that have appeared since the beginning of the discipline. The early years of the century saw the appearance of a few books by persons concerned professionally with the problems associated with rural education and the rural church. The writers viewed these problems in the broader social context of the rural community and rural life and sought to describe the interrelationships. The important systematizers were, however, the professional rural sociologists, and the works we have examined may be grouped into three broad and sometimes overlapping categories: the reform period, the rurban community period, and the scientific period.

The discipline had its origin in the period of reform dating roughly from 1870 to the beginning of World War I. The first usable textbook bearing the name rural sociology appeared in 1913. Its author, John Gillette, offers an interesting example of the evolution in subject matter and in concepts of the field which was taking place. His first book emphasized the sociologist's responsibility to give advice on the solution of problems. In three subsequent books the emphasis on science increased and that on problem-solving declined. The subject matter was essentially a description of population trends, the rural community, the social economics of agriculture, and rural institutions. There was little attention given to finding a theoretical design for the steadily mounting accumulation of empirical data.

The role of C. J. Galpin became central in the rurban community period. Galpin's invention of a method for delimiting boundaries of the rurban complex and his strategic position after 1920 for recruiting workers and subsidizing studies in various parts of the United States gave impetus to the concept. It became standard practice for textbook writers to consider neighborhood, village, and community. Factual material from the numerous studies sponsored or inspired by Galpin rapidly increased in volume. Hawthorn in 1926 was the first to design a thesis around which this material could be polarized. The central idea was socialization, and its unit of measurement was the person-hour contact in "expressional" or "impressional" events. Two years later Sims devised a different but also unitary approach in the concept of "social energy," including the "instability" which creates problems and the "stabilization" which solves them. Neither of these theoretical schemes was adopted by other writers.

The year after the appearance of Sims's first book, Sorokin and Zimmerman published their *Principles of Rural-Urban Sociology*. Although their concept of "rural-urban" was not the same as Galpin's "rurban," the work signaled the introduction of the idea of rural-urban relations on a grand scale into rural sociology. Even though the treatment was more contrast than comparison, and certainly far from Galpin's notion of integration of town and country, the comparative approach was widely employed in other books. At any rate, urban society as a factor in the lives of rural people was now part of the content of rural sociology and was destined to become increasingly important. By defining rural sociology as a theoretical science, Sorokin and Zimmerman removed it still further from the fields of welfare and amelioration. That latter responsibility was to be left to other professional fields.

In spite of the preoccupation of rural sociologists with problems of relief during the 1930s, the trend toward the development of a scientific discipline was not impeded. Some texts in succeeding years paid special attention to such conspicuous problems as youth, migratory labor, and tenancy, but they utilized the mass of empirical data produced by the special studies made during the depression. The Purnell Act of 1925, by giving recognition to rural social science as a proper field of research for state agricultural experiment stations, provided an additional spur to the development of the science. Textbooks became more and more loaded with the empirical data now available from all parts of the United States. The treatment of regions grew increasingly important as authors sought to break from their provincial and regional bounds to produce a national sociology.

The topical subject matter underwent little change, but there was a more rigid discipline in the use and interpretation of facts. Textbooks differed from each other mainly in the emphasis they placed on the various aspects of society. Some authors chose to give greater importance to population as a force in, and a measure of, change. Others stressed social processes or social institutions and organizations. Some focused on the social aspects of the economic life of farm people, particularly their relations to the land. The one attempt after the 1920s to provide a general theoretical system was that of Loomis and Beegle. Their social system theory, drawn especially from Sorokin but also from the development of the concept by Talcott Parsons, George C. Homans, and others, has influenced the textbooks which followed more than has any of the other theories mentioned.

10

The Profession

THE growth of the professional organization of rural sociologists, like the development of rural society itself, has involved a movement from informal to formal groups and structures.[1] Today's professional association had its beginnings more than fifty years ago when, at the annual sessions of the American Sociological Society, a few members who took a special interest in rural life problems gathered at informal and unscheduled meetings to discuss their common concerns.

The first such gathering, according to the recollection of E. deS. Brunner, occurred in 1912. For that year's program the sociological society had selected the theme of "Rural Life," chiefly as a result of the widespread interest in rural problems stimulated by the report of the Country Life Commission. During the sessions, Brunner recalled, twelve men who were "interested primarily in rural sociology assembled in a hotel room. From this meeting grew annual informal gatherings, which eventually expanded into the rural section of the society and then into the Rural Sociological Society."[2] Among those present in 1912 were Kenyon Butterfield, Warren Wilson, C. J. Galpin, Newell Sims, Edwin Earp, Paul Vogt, and two young graduate students, one of whom was Brunner.

Manuel C. Elmer has recalled a similar meeting when the society assembled in 1915. "John M. Gillette," Elmer wrote, "rounded up a small group of men who gathered in a sample room of the hotel to discuss the teaching of rural sociology and the problems of rural sociology . . ." [3] Besides Gillette, that year's gathering included Wilson, Vogt, Galpin, Elmer, George H. Von Tungeln, E. L. Morgan, and A. R. Mann. It is worth noting that the names of only twelve individuals appear in the two accounts. At the time there were not many other practicing rural sociologists in the country. Perhaps a dozen additional names could be added to the list, but only by a liberal definition of the term rural sociologist.

According to Elmer, the 1915 meeting resulted in action on two proposals. The first was a successful request to the society's newly elected president, George Vincent, to choose rural sociology as the theme of the 1916 program. The second was the appointment of a committee to recommend cooperative research projects which could be carried on simultaneously by a number of persons, and to formulate definitions of some fundamental concepts as a basis for that research. The committee, made up of Galpin, Vogt, and Walter J. Campbell, developed careful definitions of such key terms as rural, village, neighborhood, community, farm population, and so on. Their report was later published in the *American Journal of Sociology*.[4]

Organization of the Rural Sociology Section

Rural sociologists continued to participate in the general programs of the American Sociological Society for the next seven years. During this period only three papers on rural topics were read — one by John Phelan in 1918, one by Dwight Sanderson in 1919, and one by Kenyon Butterfield in 1920.

In 1921 rural sociologists held an informal gathering prior to the opening of the general sessions of the society. This meeting was apparently devoted to the problem of organization, for the following year the Rural Sociology Section was organized. Dwight Sanderson served as the first chairman, although the section as such did not appear in the program for 1922. In 1923, under the chairmanship of Carl Taylor, an official section meeting was held before the opening of the official sessions. Section chairmen for the succeeding fourteen years were J. H. Kolb, C. E. Lively, E. L. Morgan, E. L. Kirkpatrick, Eben Mumford, B. F. Coen, W. A. Anderson,

Theodore B. Manny, Edmund Brunner, C. C. Zimmerman, Fred C. Frey, B. L. Hummel, Lowry Nelson, and George H. Von Tungeln.

Before presenting the further history of the professional organization, it seems appropriate to discuss the establishment of the journal, since this event preceded the creation of the Rural Sociological Society.

The Story of the Journal

The problem of publication outlets for rural sociologists became an early concern of the rural section. In 1929 a committee composed of Dwight Sanderson, Carl Taylor, and E. L. Kirkpatrick recommended that the section publish a yearbook which would contain papers to be discussed in the annual meeting and which would be sent in advance to the membership of the section. In accordance with this recommendation, the yearbook appeared as Volume 24, No. 4, of the *Publications* of the American Sociological Society. Apparently, this first edition was financed jointly by the section and the society.[5]

The publication of the yearbook was, however, no solution to the larger problem of the publication of papers by research workers. At that time rural sociologists contributed to the *American Journal of Sociology*, which from 1906 to 1936 served as the organ of the American Sociological Society; to the *Journal of Applied Sociology*, established in 1921 by Emory S. Bogardus at the University of Southern California; and to the *Journal of Social Forces*, established by Howard W. Odum at the University of North Carolina in 1922. Some sociologists also wrote fairly regularly for *Rural America*, published by the American Country Life Association, but contributions to this magazine were popular rather than scientific papers. As the number of workers in sociology expanded, the demand for additional outlets increased, not only among the rural group, but among other sociologists as well.

The *American Journal of Sociology*, while it served as the organ of the society, was in fact a publication of the University of Chicago. It was edited by that institution's department of sociology and was in no real sense an official organ of the society. For several years during the early 1930s the society held discussions on the desirability of publishing its own journal and finally in 1935 the membership agreed to establish the *American Sociological Review*. The momentum of this decision carried over into the rural section. Meeting in December 1935, rural sociologists first thought of capitalizing on the publication of the forthcoming journal for their own purposes.[6] Bruce Melvin urged the rural section to request that some issues of the new review be devoted entirely to the "presentation of rural material." In the ensuing debate on the need for better publication outlets, the discussion turned to the possibility of establishing a separate journal of rural sociology. At one point Fred C. Frey of Louisiana State University informed the group that his university would be willing to underwrite such a project for the first few years. After several hours of earnest discussion, Carl Taylor introduced, and Frey seconded, a motion calling upon the "incoming chairman of the Section . . . to appoint a committee to assume the responsibility of discovering and creating channels by which the maximum amount of space could be obtained for rural sociology articles in some standard publication." The committee, meeting soon after, unanimously recommended the establishment of *Rural Sociology*. The first issue appeared in March 1936.

Louisiana State University served as financial guarantor of the journal but assumed no responsibility for content. The Rural Sociological Society, after its organization, became the publisher and copyright holder, and a board of editors, acting for the society, determined policies and approved manuscripts. A managing editor handled correspondence and business matters, received and circulated manuscripts, and looked after details of the physical form of the journal. (After the first year, the chairman of the editorial board held the title of editor. In 1963 the functions of editor and managing editor were combined.[7])

' The new organ's first editorial board consisted of J. H. Kolb, C. E. Lively, Dwight Sanderson, C. C. Zimmerman, and Lowry Nelson, chairman. In a statement of policy, the board made the following affirmations:

The purpose of the journal is to afford an additional medium of expression for scholars in the field of Rural Sociology. The pages will not be confined exclusively to Rural Sociologists as a professional group; articles are invited from workers in related fields of social science, from teachers, and from rural workers who may contribute to the sociology of rural life. Moreover, it will be the policy to solicit manuscripts from workers in foreign countries, although it is intended that all such papers shall deal with some phase of rural social life. . . .

Rural Sociology stands for no special school of social thought; it is rather a forum in which any individual who has a contribution to make can present his findings. It is intended that the papers shall maintain a high standard of scholarship and logical presentation.[8]

129

The launching of a journal is an enterprise which deters all but the most hardy and courageous. The first years of the new quarterly were inevitably difficult and crucial ones. The editorial staff had to plan the format, prepare and mail announcements to potential subscribers, solicit and edit manuscripts. Much time and energy was devoted to the enterprise by T. Lynn Smith, the first managing editor. During this hectic period Fred Frey was an anchor to windward, as was Marcus M. Wilkerson, the able manager of the Louisiana State University Press, which took on the details of publication.

During its first year the journal netted less than 200 subscriptions at $2.50 each. In 1938, the year of the Rural Sociological Society's organization, there were only 286 member subscriptions. The income from the sale of subscriptions produced merely a fraction of the cost of producing the magazine, and while the guarantor institution made up the deficit, such an arrangement could not result in the permanence that was desired. Fortunately, with the establishment of the society the number of member subscriptions grew, as did the number of nonmember subscriptions from libraries and others. In 1960 the circulation reached 1,196; in 1965 it averaged 2,300 copies per issue, and in 1967, 2,600. By the mid-1960s the society was well established financially, and no further responsibility for meeting deficits rested upon the institutional sponsor. At what point complete financial independence was reached is not a matter of record, but as late as 1951, according to the annual report for that year, North Carolina State College made up a deficit of $250.

From Section to Society

As a professional association, the rural section presented some difficulties. In the first place, its members were required to be members of, and pay dues to, the parent society. This provision automatically eliminated prospective members who had no desire to join the general society. In the second place, rural sociology was not a truly specialized field of interest comparable to the family, population, methodology, or the community. Rural sociology was in fact as broad in its content as sociology itself. The section was thus an enclave in the general society, rather than an organic part of it. A further disadvantage of the sectional organization arose from the fact that a member who wanted to present a paper on a rural topic could not at the same time contribute a paper on some other subject in another section, under the society's general rule, admirable in itself, that a member be limited to one paper during the annual meetings.

The 1935 meeting of the rural section which launched the journal also took up the matter of organizing a separate society. One of the earliest and most persistent advocates of an independent group was Bonney Youngblood. Trained in agricultural economics, Youngblood had served first as economist and then as director at the Texas Agricultural Experiment Station. He was later appointed as an examiner in the Office of Experiment Stations in the Department of Agriculture. A faithful attendant at the annual meetings of the rural section, he seldom failed to make a few remarks urging the formation of a separate society.

Addressing himself to this topic at the 1935 meeting, Youngblood emphasized again the importance of a "strong professional organization through which rural sociologists could promote their own interests." On the motion of Fred Frey, the section accordingly voted that the "incoming executive committee be instructed to study the possibilities of forming an autonomous organization of the Rural Sociology Section . . ." The committee consisted of Dwight Sanderson, chairman, John Kolb, Carl Taylor, B. O. Williams, and O. D. Duncan.

The rural section's response to the idea of an autonomous society did not, however, match in enthusiasm and unanimity the earlier support for the journal. In fact, there was widespread reluctance to separate from the parent society.[9] This disinclination became apparent when the executive committee brought in its report at the end of 1937. A majority of the committee rejected separation, favoring instead an effort to secure revision of the society's constitution in order to provide a larger measure of autonomy for the rural section. A minority report, submitted by O. D. Duncan, recommended the immediate organization of an independent society. It was only after lively and prolonged discussion that the section adopted the minority report and proceeded to organize the Rural Sociological Society.[10] The first officers were Dwight Sanderson, president; John Kolb, vice-president; T. Lynn Smith, secretary-treasurer; and C. E. Lively and Carl Taylor, members of the executive committee.

In the minds of many individuals the most important argument for an independent society concerned the welfare of the journal. Although published by the rural section, the quarterly could not be financed through membership fees. The main society, which already had an official organ, had preempted this possibility. At that time, at least, it was impossible to

131

sell enough subscriptions to make the journal self-supporting. As the official organ of an independent society, on the other hand, the journal would become independent of outside support. This concern for the journal led many otherwise reluctant members to vote for an independent organization.

Membership

The membership of the new society (and subscribers to the journal), it was hoped, would come not only from professional sociologists — that is, those engaged in teaching, research, and extension work in the various states — but also from persons in the closely related disciplines of agricultural economics, home economics, rural education, and the rural clergy. Some members, it was thought, might even be recruited from the professional staffs employed by farm organizations, cooperatives, and the like. By far the largest group of prospects, of course, consisted of teachers of rural sociology in the colleges. In 1936, the year the journal was launched, there were 618 such individuals, according to a survey made by the Division of Farm Population.[11] Although many nonrural sociologists, agricultural economists, and other professionals joined the new society, the hopes for recruitment of large numbers of such people were never realized.

The infant organization inherited a small base of membership from the rural section. Records for the section are not readily available, but the number of members was relatively small. In 1938, the society's first year, the membership was 206. Although the organization's early years coincided with the last part of the depression, membership figures showed a steady rise: 315 in 1939, 367 in 1940, and 386 in 1941.

As the accompanying tabulation indicates, the membership of the society and the journal circulation fluctuated during the years between 1941 and 1965.[12] The effect of World War II is apparent in the figures for the early 1940s, when no gains and some actual losses took place. In the late 1950s there was another decline. This decrease probably resulted from (1) the relatively small number of persons of college age, due to the low birthrate of the 1930s, (2) the decline in enrollment in agricultural colleges at that time, with a related decline of interest in rural sociology, and (3) the consequently smaller number of instructors and graduate students in the field. Moreover, salaries were low during this period and the recession of 1958–59 was a negative influence.

Year	Members	Journal Circulation
1941	386	823
1942	389	851
1943	329	830
1944	358	890
1945	399	968
1946	400	988
1950	507	. . .
1955	575	. . .
1960	544	1,196
1965	747	2,300 (est.)
1966	840	2,900

The growth in both membership and journal circulation after 1960 can be explained by the burgeoning college population, a remarkable rise in professional salaries, and the general feeling of well-being resulting from the steady price levels of the six years subsequent to 1960. Another important factor has been the steady increase over the years of members in foreign countries, from 15 in 1945 to 191 in 1966.

Reports on categories and geographic distribution of membership in more recent years have produced data that are worthy of some comment. (See the accompanying tabulations.) First of all, the number of active members has shown a discouraging tendency to fluctuate from year to year. The substantial increases in 1966 and 1967 were clearly the result of major membership drives during those years. A report of the society's membership committee in 1965, though it noted success in recruiting new

Categories*	1963	1964	1965	1966	1967
Active	368	376	358	394	423
Joint	18	26	28	26	34
Emeritus	25	22	22	20	18
Associate	126	135	155	177	184
Student	149	157	181	213	224
Sponsored	3	3	3	10	6
Total	689	719	747	840	889
U.S. members	547	562	578	649	702
Outside U.S.	142	157	169	191	187
Drop-outs	. . .	110	155	139	154
U.S.	. . .	. . .	. . .	95	98
Foreign	. . .	. . .	. . .	44	56
New members	. . .	140	180	232	140
Libraries	. . .	. . .	1,175	1,375	1,475

* Source: *Rural Sociology*, 32:538 (December 1967).

Geographic Distribution*	1963	1964	1965
U.S. Northeast region	109	115	111
U.S. North Central region	208	192	229
U.S. Southern region	174	204	188
U.S. Western region	56	51	51
Total in U.S.	547	562	579
Canada region	16	25	25
Western Hemisphere region			
(excluding U.S. and Canada)	34	37	36
Europe and Middle East region	39	37	34
Asia and Australia region.................	43	48	52
Africa region	10	10	22
Total outside U.S.	142	157	169
Grand total	689	719	747

* Source: *Rural Sociology*, 30:537 (December 1965).

members, reported for the first time a disquieting loss of old members — 110 in 1964 and 155 in 1965.[13] The drop-out problem continues to be serious. Encouraging, however, is the marked increase in the number of student members, since this group necessarily constitutes the future strength of the organization.

As far as geographical distribution is concerned, only the North Central region of the United States produced a substantial gain in membership during the years from 1963 to 1965, although the Southern region also showed a slight increase. The number of foreign members has showed a rather consistent annual gain in the 1960s, except for a slight decline in 1966-67. Foreign drop-outs also increased in those two years.

One other observation on geographic distribution is appropriate. A directory published by the society for the years 1964–65 showed members in 43 of the 50 states, in the District of Columbia, and in Puerto Rico. States with twenty or more members included New York, Pennsylvania, Wisconsin, Michigan, Iowa, Ohio, Kentucky, the District of Columbia, North Carolina, California, and Missouri. Fifty-two foreign countries were represented.

By the late 1960s the society was in all respects at its highest level of success. Financially, it suffered from such an embarrassment of riches that members had become concerned about the large accumulation of invested funds (more than $41,000 in 1967). One result was the appointment in 1965 of a committee on development, with the important, if not main, purpose of finding projects that would promote the cause and jus-

tify expenditure of some of the money. The membership was at its highest
point and the growth of student and foreign members indicative of future
stability. The maintenance of members through continuous renewal remains a problem for the organization, in view of the heavy rate of de-
linquency.[14]

Rural Sociology in the Academic Structure

It will be recalled that rural sociology experienced a period of uncer-
tainty as to its status in the college and university structure. The field was
sponsored by agricultural economics in some agricultural colleges and by
sociology in other institutions. It was even taught in departments of history, general economics, and education. Not unnaturally, rural sociologists sought to establish independent departments in some places. At Cornell University, where there was no department of sociology with which
rural sociology might have affiliated, the work was established from the
first as a separate unit. At Wisconsin it began as part of the department
of agricultural economics but later became independent. At this institution, as at many others, general sociology was for years a part of the department of economics and thus in no position to sponsor rural sociology.

A rough survey of land-grant institutions for the year 1964–65 shows
that separate departments of rural sociology existed in twelve states: Connecticut, Kentucky, Louisiana, Mississippi, Missouri, New York, North
Carolina, South Dakota, Washington, and Wisconsin. In Kentucky, Missouri, and Louisiana, however, the separation was nominal, since the
chairman of rural sociology also served as chairman of the department of
sociology in the arts college. In several states separate departments existed primarily for the administration of the experiment station and extension activities.

In fourteen states rural sociology was combined with agricultural economics, usually under a joint departmental name. In a few cases persons
doing research or extension work in rural sociology were listed in the department of agricultural economics, without the word sociology in the
department title. In at least seventeen states that the writer knows of, rural
sociology is taught in the department of sociology. Where land-grant agricultural colleges are separate from the state universities, administration
is less difficult. Here rural sociology can simply be a part of the general
department and as such participate in the experiment station and extension activities.

There are advantages and disadvantages in having separate departments. In those institutions where the colleges of agriculture are adjunct to the state universities, separate departments face difficulties in the teaching program. Since rural sociology is sociology, a complete program of instruction requires the teaching of many courses ordinarily considered as general sociology or anthropology. Thus, if rural sociology offers degree programs, it must either supply the general sociology courses with its own staff or depend upon the general department to do so. Almost invariably it does the latter and members of the staffs of the two departments are joint appointees. On the other hand, separation from general sociology has in the past facilitated participation in the research and extension programs of the colleges of agriculture.

Recruitment and Training

One of the functions of a professional association is to recruit and train young men and women for careers in its field. This task is particularly important in rural sociology because of its special situation in the academic structure. As a rule, academic departments offer courses leading to major and minor specialization and are thus able to recruit postgraduate students from among their undergraduate majors. This is not true for rural sociology, even where separate departments exist. There is no incentive for undergraduates to major in rural sociology, since there are no immediate prospects of employment. The tendency is for them to major in sociology, which is a common undergraduate preparation for the field of social work and, with the addition of other social science courses, for teaching social studies in the high schools.

Potential rural sociologists can look forward to a career only by completing graduate work. At the same time, the departments of rural sociology must depend upon attracting general sociology graduates to work for advanced degrees in the rural field. Fortunately, recruitment has not been too difficult because the rural sociologist on the experiment station staff has been able to offer research assistantships. These have permitted many postgraduates to undertake at institutional expense the research necessary for theses. Even so, the graduate student must acquire most of his education in the department of sociology. Rural sociology is a matter of emphasis, with special seminars and the preparation of a thesis in the rural field.

136

From time to time, rural sociologists have concerned themselves in a formal manner with recruitment and training. A major conference on this theme was held at Pine Ridge, North Carolina, in the summer of 1940. Topics discussed included the following: "The Place of Rural Sociology in the Undergraduate Curriculum," by O. D. Duncan; "Undergraduate Preparation of Students Who Expect to do Graduate Work in Rural Sociology," by T. Lynn Smith; "Requirements for the Master's Degree in Rural Sociology," by Howard W. Beers; and "Training to the Doctor's Level in Rural Sociology," by Lowry Nelson. In addition to the discussion of teaching, five papers were presented in the field of research: "An Inventory of Rural Sociological Research Projects in the South During the Past Five Years," by B. O. Williams; "A Critical Review of a Few Representative Rural Sociological Projects Recently Published in the South," by Charles P. Loomis; "Charting Needed Areas for Rural Sociological Research in the South," by C. Horace Hamilton; "Cooperation in Rural Sociological Research on an Interstate and Regional Basis," by Carl Taylor; and "Selection and Recruitment of Personnel in Rural Sociology," by Warner E. Gettys.[15]

In 1944 the present writer — at the time president of the society and concerned about the disruptive effects of World War II on the profession — appointed a committee on postwar recruitment and training of rural sociologists. The members of the committee were John Kolb, C. E. Lively, T. Lynn Smith, Conrad Taeuber, Carl Taylor, and E. deS. Brunner, chairman.

The committee sent a questionnaire to thirty-seven departments of rural sociology in thirty states, asking for information on these points: (1) "Into what sorts of jobs do your majors in rural sociology go in normal times?" (2) "Do you have any definite procedures for recruiting promising majors on the Master's level for advanced study?" (3) "Are you planning any major revisions in your rural sociology graduate program after the war?" [16]

The reporting institutions indicated that from one-third to three-fourths of their graduates took jobs with the Farm Security Administration, the Extension Service, and other agencies in the United States Department of Agriculture, and with the rural social services of state boards of welfare. There appeared to be more positions — and better-paying ones — available in these fields than in teaching and research. Institutions which did not offer work leading to the Ph.D. degree reported that most of their teaching was in the form of service courses for prospective teachers, social workers, public health nurses, and the like. Yet no serious attention was being given, respondents complained, to the training of teachers for such courses.

Only three institutions planned any changes in their work; none of them provided information on the reforms contemplated. Only six of the thirty responding institutions were making any effort to recruit students for graduate work at the master's level. Scholarships and assistantships were reportedly insufficient in number or amount to encourage students to enter the field.[17]

A questionnaire was also sent to graduate students who had not completed their work for the Ph.D. Some forty replies were received, an overwhelming proportion from men serving in the navy. All those in the services reported that they planned to return to the field of rural sociology and that they would need financial aid. About half the replies offered some criticism of training programs. The criticism fell into three main areas. Respondents felt that not enough attention was given to preparation for teaching, which most of them expected to do. They also considered research training to be inadequate, mainly because they had participated only in minor ways without having been involved in the initial planning stages. A third complaint had to do with the language requirement, which was felt to be an unnecessary hurdle.

This report contained implications and recommendations which were given less attention than they deserved. A follow-up survey of the men who responded to the questionnaire would have proved interesting. Never implemented was the committee's suggestion that a summer seminar be provided for demobilized men to ease the transition to civilian life and to act as a refresher course. The committee also recommended that more emphasis be given to the training of teachers of rural sociology and particularly to the orientation of teaching methods to the needs of students from other fields. Since the teaching of the subject matter has probably changed very little in recent years, additional investigation might profitably be undertaken in this area.[18]

Further shortcomings in recruitment and training practices were revealed in a report issued by the Farm Foundation in 1950.[19] A committee investigating the nation's land-grant colleges found that administrators complained of great difficulty in acquiring competent personnel. Among the principal requirements for competence, the administrators listed:

"Understanding and appreciation of rural conditions, peoples and values," "technical competence," "rural background," "practicality and good sense," "research ability and enthusiasm," and "adequate training in sociology."

The 1950 report took note of the great diversity in departmental organization: "Not fewer than 17 different forms of departmental organization for rural sociology are represented in the land-grant colleges . . . from a separate department of rural sociology to an arrangement in which the subject is distributed among several departments." [20]

Interviews with undergraduates turned up several areas of dissatisfaction. Students complained that classes in the subject included persons of mixed preparation and of such heterogeneous backgrounds and interests as to make instruction difficult. They also reported difficulty in arranging to enroll in rural sociology because of other course requirements in agriculture. Students majoring in various fields of agriculture, the investigators found, were sometimes dissuaded by their instructors from registering for courses in sociology. The committee concluded that most students "favor having the subject required of all agricultural students, as it already is in several land-grant colleges. But the students insist . . . that the course be competently taught . . ." [21]

Before leaving the subject of recruitment and training, it is important to cite the 1966 report of the society's committee on development. As a guide to potential student recruits, the committee compiled a *Directory of Universities Offering Graduate Degrees in Rural Sociology*. The directory provided information on the graduate work offered in eighteen institutions. Though clearly incomplete, it indicated something of the substantial resources that now exist for graduate training in the United States. For each institution the report gave data on graduate degrees offered, course offerings, financial aid available, special programs or emphases, the number of graduate students in 1965-66, members of the staff, and the person or persons in charge.

Obviously the attractiveness of a field of learning is enhanced when its opportunities and challenges, as well as its prestige, become known. In an introduction to the pamphlet the committee pointed out that rural sociology is sociology and that rural sociologists deal with much the same general subjects as do other sociologists, the only difference being that they are concerned with people living in rural areas. The committee also observed that while most rural sociologists were employed by the land-grant universities, they were by no means limited to that source of employment or to the rural field. "Many outstanding sociologists whose reputations have been built in other fields of sociology received their training in rural sociology. These include several presidents of the American Sociological Association."

Summary

Beginning as a small, informal gathering of sociologists with a common interest in rural problems, rural sociologists organized first as a simple section within the parent body, the American Sociological Society. While there was autonomy in electing section officers and in arranging programs for the two general sessions devoted to rural problems, there were limitations to this arrangement. Only members of the parent society could belong to the section. Only one paper could be presented by a member at the annual meeting. Publication outlets were limited, and even though the section established a quarterly, the journal could not become an official organ, and its future remained problematical. This situation was a major consideration in bringing about the third phase in the evolution of the organized profession, the establishment of the Rural Sociological Society in 1937.

Then began the gradual process of developing a membership adequate for self-maintenance, both for the society and for the journal. At the very beginning, World War II created difficulties. Later, in the 1950s, membership fell off as a result of diminished enrollments in agricultural colleges, relatively low salaries, and financial recessions in the general economy. After 1960 prosperity shone on the society, as it reached a peak membership of 889 in 1967 and accumulated financial resources of more than $41,000.

Along the way, members of the society sought to improve their performance in teaching, in research, and in the application of principles to the practical problems of rural America. Clearly, as the 1966 report of the committee on development showed, facilities for the training of graduate students had expanded enormously over the years.

11

Rural Sociologists Abroad

THE story of the development of rural sociology in the United States would not be complete without some review, however brief, of the work that has been undertaken by members of the profession in other countries. In view of the great expansion of overseas work in recent years, it is impossible to give a full account in a single chapter. The following discussion, therefore, has been limited largely to pioneer efforts and, with rare exceptions, to the work of rural sociologists proper, although anthropologists, geographers, and economists have contributed impressively to the studies of rural life in foreign countries.

Perhaps the first examination of foreign agricultural life by a rural sociologist was E. C. Branson's *Farm Life Abroad*, published in 1924.[1] The book was a collection of weekly letters written during a year's European travel, mostly in Germany, France, and Denmark. Though not a study in any real sense, it did present the observations of a perceptive individual on the nature of European farm life.

In 1925 Daniel H. Kulp II published what must have been the first description by an American sociologist of a Chinese village; this was a thoroughgoing case study.[2] Another important study of rural China was begun in 1929 by John L. Buck, an American agricultural economist at the University of Nanking.[3] Buck's work deserves mention in the annals of rural sociology because it represented an early effort at an American-style analysis of China's farm economy, population, and family standard of living. According to the preface, the five-year project was undertaken at the suggestion of O. E. Baker and sponsored by the Institute for Pacific Relations. It covered 16,786 farms in 168 localities and 38,256 farm families in 22 provinces.

The late twenties also saw the appearance of E. deS. Brunner's *Rural Korea*, published in 1928 by the International Missionary Council. A decade later, it may be noted, Brunner undertook a similar investigation in Australia and New Zealand for the Carnegie Corporation.[4] Other Asian studies of the late 1920s and early 1930s were initiated by the Layman's Missionary Inquiry Commission, an agency sponsored by the Institute for Social and Religious Research. Under its auspices studies were made by W. A. Anderson in China, J. L. Hypes in India, and Fred Yoder in Japan. Their reports, published for limited circulation within the participating church bodies, were not available for public sale.[5]

In 1930 Carle Zimmerman took a leave of absence from the University of Minnesota to serve as adviser to the government and royal family of Siam. After studying forty villages in various regions of the country, he published a report on family income and expenditures, food and diet, health and medical services, and types of agriculture.[6] Zimmerman's book on rural Siam stands with the works of Kulp and Buck as among the most important studies of the Far East up to that time.

Meanwhile, on the other side of the world, Walter A. Terpenning made a special study of European village and open-country neighborhoods in the late 1920s. During a year abroad he visited villages in Switzerland, England, Germany, France, Italy, Denmark, and Russia, as well as a "neighborhood" in Ireland. A student of Charles H. Cooley, Terpenning had developed a special interest in the effectiveness for social life of the two ecological patterns of village and neighborhood. He was partial to the village as a basis of socialization and his book included designs for the construction or reconstruction of rural villages in the United States.[7]

Latin American Studies

During the 1930s rural sociologists, with few exceptions, concentrated their attention on domestic problems incident to the depression. The out-

142

break of World War II, however, abruptly brought into focus the relationships of the United States with other countries and particularly its neighbors to the south. As the war cut off traditional sources of jute, rubber, quinine, and other badly needed commodities, South America and the Caribbean assumed unprecedented strategic importance. The required products came from rural and often remote areas. Yet North America possessed little reliable information about the rural hinterlands of the capital cities, which had too often engaged the almost exclusive attention of embassy personnel.

In the early years of the war, therefore, the departments of state and agriculture took steps to obtain a better knowledge of rural Latin America. One move was the establishment in the Department of Agriculture of the Office of Foreign Agricultural Relations (OFAR). The agency's sphere of concern was naturally worldwide, but because Latin America was recognized as a crucial area and was besides accessible, OFAR tended to concentrate its efforts there. It recruited rural sociologists to gather desired information and sent them to specified countries. Each man was accredited to the United States embassy of the country to which he was assigned and received cooperation from the foreign service personnel.

Since the investigations of rural sociologists in Latin America have been so intensive, and have also represented something of a pioneer effort in foreign studies, it seems appropriate to present the results of their endeavors in terms of the men involved rather than by a strict chronological or geographical sequence.

T. Lynn Smith. Smith drew an early assignment from the Office of Foreign Agricultural Relations and went to Brazil for a year in 1942–43. Three years after his return to the United States, his sociology of Brazil appeared as the first tangible result of OFAR's investment in Latin America.[8] The volume's five central sections discussed cultural diversity, levels and standards of living, relations of people to the land, and social institutions. The work was outstanding for its detailed population analysis, its treatment of the relationship of people to the land, and its wise use of Brazilian documents and historical works. Smith has been the only author of a book-length study of a Latin American country to continue his observations. Repeated trips to Brazil enabled him to revise the original edition and to publish other material on the country.[9] His work was widely appreciated in Brazil and he was awarded honorary degrees by the University of São Paulo and the University of Brazil.

Meanwhile Smith was busy on other projects as well. A preoccupation with the basic significance of land and the relationship of people to it led him to assemble, translate, and edit important works by Brazilian writers on the subject of agrarian reform.[10] Although Brazil was his original interest, he has by no means limited himself to that country. Colombia claimed his attention as early as 1943, when he obtained the cooperation of the Ministry of National Economy for a study of Tabio, a rural county near Bogotá. This project was undoubtedly the first application in Latin America of survey techniques developed by rural sociologists in the United States. The resulting monograph described the characteristics of the population of the trade center and its hinterland, the relationships of people to the land, social organization, including stratification and mobility, and the levels and standards of living.[11] A valuable feature of this publication was the inclusion of the questionnaire employed in the study, which has since been used by other Latin American students as well as North Americans.

Smith's most important work on Colombia, a projected three-volume study, is still in the process of completion. The first volume, which has already appeared under the title *Social Structure and the Process of Development*, covers the basic features of the land system, patterns of settlement, community and community development, and social stratification and the class structure. A second volume will deal with demography, including urbanization, while the third will cover the basic social institutions of family, school, church, and government. Other works include his *Latin American Population Studies,* based on the general census taken in most Latin American countries about 1950, and more than fifty journal articles dealing with some phase of Latin American society.[12]

Smith's influence on sociology in Latin America, moreover, is not to be measured by his writing alone. Many students from Latin America have received instruction from him at Louisiana State University, at Vanderbilt University, where he directed the Institute of Brazilian Studies, and finally at the University of Florida. Under his direction a number of graduate students from the United States have written Ph.D. dissertations on various countries of Latin America.[13]

Carl C. Taylor. Another sociologist recruited by the Office of Foreign Agricultural Relations was Carl Taylor, who spent a year in 1942–43 studying rural conditions in Argentina and later published a book on that country.[14] Like Smith in his study of Brazil, Taylor depended in part upon the available literature and public documents and in part upon personal observations in the major type-farming areas. Besides interviewing more than 120 farm families and other representatives of the farm population, he conversed with local newspaper editors, leaders of farm organizations, businessmen, schoolteachers, ministers, and government employees.

During the course of his research Taylor suffered a severe handicap in the paucity of population statistics and other census data. Argentina had not conducted a census since 1914, and all population data were merely estimates (which, as the census of 1950 was to show, were extremely inaccurate). In reference to the inadequacy of census data, Taylor noted in his book that he was obliged to fall back on the population censuses of 1895 and 1914, using estimates for later years with caution. Fortunately an agricultural census of 1937, though it was not primarily a population census, proved to be of some value. Taylor's book covered the following topics: various type-farming areas, the people, immigration, farmers and farm people, the history of agriculture and rural life, ownership and distribution of the land, agricultural and cultural regions, rural isolation and communication, locality groups and communities, levels and standards of living, the farm home and family, colonization and resettlement, agricultural reform, farmers' organizations, and the farmer's place in Argentine culture.

Olen E. Leonard. During the 1940s Leonard spent more than two years in Bolivia as an administrator of cooperative agricultural programs and in conducting rural sociological studies in two selected areas. During those years he also made the observations and collected the materials which led to his book-length study of the country.[15] In its principal subdivisions this work discussed regional diversity, population, landholding patterns, social institutions, and levels and standards of living.

Earlier Leonard had made a study of a government-owned hacienda in Ecuador.[16] Like Smith in his study of Tabio, Colombia, Leonard employed the survey methods developed by rural sociologists in the United States. The topics under investigation included the number, distribution, composition, vital processes, and migrations of the population; the relation of the people to the land, with sections treating settlement patterns, land division, land tenure, size of holdings, and levels of farming; the family, religion and the church, education and the schools; social stratification, social differentiation, and mobility; and levels of living, including housing, facilities and utilities, health and sanitation, and food and diet. This study was sponsored by the government of Ecuador and by the Interdepartmental Committee on Scientific and Cultural Cooperation of the United States.

Charles P. Loomis. In 1943 Loomis joined the Office of Foreign Agricultural Relations to serve as assistant chief of the Division of Extension and Training. His interest in Spanish-American affairs was of long standing. Together with Leonard he had made a study of El Cerrito, New Mexico, for the Division of Farm Population in 1941. One of his first studies in Latin America concerned extension work in Peru.[17]

In 1947 Loomis, then chairman of sociology and anthropology at Michigan State, and Ralph Allee, director-general of the Inter-American Institute of Agricultural Sciences in Costa Rica, developed a cooperative arrangement between their respective institutions. Loomis became an associate staff member of the institute, and there followed an extended series of research studies in Costa Rica and an interchange of graduate students and staff members. The major outcome of this cooperation, as far as research was concerned, was a book on the Turrialba area written jointly by several participants in the series of studies.[18]

Among the chapters in the volume are: Social Status and Communication, Informal Social Systems, The Ecological Basis of Social Systems, Demographic Characteristics of the Population, Religious Systems, Educational Systems, Political Systems, Levels of Living on Haciendas and Small Farms, and Study of the Strategy of Change on Large Estates and Small Farms in Latin America. Another paper, not included in this volume, but growing out of the Turrialba research, compared social class structure in a community of small landowners with that in an area where large estates predominated.[19]

Incidentally, the area around Turrialba, which is the seat of the Inter-American Institute of Agricultural Sciences, is the part of Latin America that has been given the most thorough study and analysis by rural sociologists and other social scientists. Perhaps it is the most thoroughly studied rural area in the world.

The work of Loomis in Latin America is characterized by two innovations as far as research is concerned. In the first place, he sought to apply the concept of the social system to the conditions of farm people. Second, he used for the first time various sociometric devices in the study of groups and social structure. One might mention another aspect of his work, namely, the effort to apply the results of his research to the promotion of desirable changes.

Nathan L. Whetten. The author of book-length sociologies of two countries, Mexico and Guatemala,[20] Whetten possessed excellent qualifications for his studies. Born and reared in Mexico, he acquired fluency in the Spanish language and familiarity with Latin American history and culture. Moreover, he was able to obtain leave from his institution for a three-year period (1942–45), rather than the single year available to most of the other men. As a rural sociologist attached to the United States embassy in Mexico, he traveled widely throughout the country and conducted extensive interviews.

Whetten's book on Mexico is divided into four principal parts. The first takes up the subjects of geographic environment and the growth, distribution, and composition of the population. The second part, entitled "The Relation of the People to the Land," is made up of chapters on the landholding village and the hacienda before the revolution of 1910, agrarian aspects of the revolution, the redistribution of land, colonization and the development of the small private holding, and the *ejido* system. Chapters on housing, diet and clothing, health and mortality, and Indianism in relation to standards of living are grouped in part three. The last section, on social institutions, includes chapters on marriage and the family, education and the rural schools, rural cultural missions, religion and the rural church, the Sinarquista movement, and government.

Rural Mexico will long remain an indispensable reference work for the student of Mexican society. Whetten's review of the early history of land distribution and tenure, and of the changes in these relationships after the revolution of 1910, will remain a classic treatment.

Whetten's book on Guatemala was based on visits of several months' duration in 1944, 1952, and 1955. In organization and presentation, the work is similar to the earlier volume on Mexico. In a final section the author made the following observations on changes in the social structure and their impact upon the political stability of the country: "In an effort to maintain order, reversion to conditions that existed during the Ubico dictatorship is certainly within the realm of possibility, although a dictatorship of the extreme right would encounter resistance from a number of groups in Guatemala that are now beginning to exercise a significant influence."[21] Among these groups, Whetten mentioned university students and teachers, returning political exiles, a rising middle class, disappointed agrarians, frustrated labor leaders, and Communist sympathizers.

Lowry Nelson. Although assigned by the Office of Foreign Agricultural

Relations in 1945 to study rural life in the Caribbean area, Nelson soon discovered that one year was scarcely enough time to study a single country, and his work was therefore concentrated on Cuba. He spent the months from September 1945 to September 1946 in that country. The outcome of his stay was another book-length report on a Latin American country.[22]

The author had the full-time collaboration of Casto Ferragút, an intelligent and well-trained young man who had spent nearly a year in the United States familiarizing himself with current work in agricultural economics and rural sociology.[23] This collaboration, along with the full cooperation of the Cuban ministry of agriculture and of the incumbent president, Grau San Martín, permitted Nelson to make surveys in eleven areas representing different types of farming. In all, 742 usable family schedule interviews were obtained, and these constituted valuable basic material. The book covered the following topics: population; the land, climate, and seasonal rhythms; locality groups and the settlement pattern; the evolution of the Cuban land system; land division, measurement, and registration; systems of farming; the social class structure; social stratification; the family; the level of living; education and the schools; and prospects for the future.

In view of the success of the Cuban revolution in 1959, it may not be inappropriate to quote briefly from the final chapter of this book, where the following measures were recommended: the expansion of the field service of the ministry of agriculture, the promotion of farmers' organizations, the establishment of a definite plan for road construction and maintenance, continued research in social and economic problems, and the initiation of agrarian reform. In connection with the last point, the author observed:

Political unrest, arising from the frustration of the desire of peasants to obtain possession of and security on the land, will be chronic in Cuba until more positive action is taken in this respect. Admittedly the problem is a difficult one, with the existing rights of large landholders to consider, but it is not a question that can be continually postponed. It is likely that continued delay in carrying out the law may result in serious political consequence.[24]

George W. Hill. Hill took leave in the 1950s from the University of Wisconsin's department of rural sociology to act as consultant to the Venezuelan government in regard to its colonization program. Although the assignment was expected to be a temporary one, it proved to be otherwise and Hill remained until 1962. In the meantime he also served as a member of a technical-assistance mission to Honduras for the Organization of American States. With Marion T. Loftin he prepared a report on "Characteristics of Rural Life and the Agrarian Reform in Honduras."

Hill's work in Venezuela was that of consultant, researcher, and teacher. He was instrumental in the establishment of a department of sociology in the University of Caracas and trained several sociologists to carry on the work. His research reports were published in the Spanish language.[25] In 1964 Hill took charge of the Central American office of the Land Tenure Center of the University of Wisconsin.

Several other rural sociologists have done work in Latin America, notably Carle Zimmerman, John Kolb, and John and Mavis Biesanz. Zimmerman became in 1935 the first to report on family living in a Latin American country.[26] Kolb, as has been mentioned earlier, spent a year teaching at the Rural University of Brazil in 1953–54; in 1960 he served as a consultant on the organization of rural social sciences in Brazilian colleges. John and Mavis Biesanz are the authors of books on Costa Rica and Panama; both works were the result of observation and study over a period of time.[27] Most of the writers discussed here also contributed to a massive work on the middle class in Latin America, published in 1950–51.[28]

In summary, it is fair to say that rural sociologists have produced sociologies on the following Latin American countries: Argentina, Bolivia, Brazil, Colombia, Costa Rica, Cuba, Guatemala, Mexico, Panama, Peru, and Venezuela.

Work in Europe and Asia

The postwar Fulbright awards, together with the government's Agency for International Development (AID) programs in various countries and the foreign programs of private American foundations, have greatly facilitated international contacts for American scholars generally, and for rural sociologists in particular. For the most part, assignments to European countries involved teaching in universities rather than research, and as a consequence only a limited number of publications resulted. Two Fulbright research grants to Italy and one teaching grant to Sweden, however, produced reports in the 1950s and 1960s.[29]

The work of Irvin T. Sanders in the Balkans has been important and continuous. His investigations in Bulgaria and Greece were pioneer efforts.[30] Sanders taught at the American College in Sofia, Bulgaria, from 1929 to 1932. During most of this period he intensively observed and studied a village near the capital city. After revisiting the area in 1945–46, he published his book-length study of Balkan village life.

In his later work on Greece, Sanders employed a different method. Rather than making a study in depth of a single village, he chose to turn to the "more vulnerable area of personal interpretation." "Throughout this work," he wrote, "I have tried to show how the world looks to the Greek villager . . . Whenever possible I have let him speak for himself." The whole work is presented in readable style. The chapter headings indicate the content: The People of Greece; Mountains, Plains and the Sea; The Village Setting; Land and Birthright; The Peasant at Work; The Changing Life of the Shepherd; Woman's Work is Never Done; Local Government; The Village School; Religion and the Greek Peasant; The Village Community; Social Change in Rural Greece; and Social Consequences of Foreign Aid. The last chapter deserves to be read by all technical assistance workers in underdeveloped countries.

While major studies have apparently not been made recently in the countries of the Near East by American rural sociologists, many contacts have been made through the technical-assistance program. The most important study of life in a Near East village was produced in the early 1940s by Afif I. Tannous.[31]

Because of the disruption caused by World War II and the unsettling effects of postwar developments, the United States has had to give much attention to the Pacific area for purposes of reconstruction and rehabilitation. The occupation of Japan resulted in revolutionary changes in that country, and in order to study the impact of land reform on local villages, Arthur Raper and three assistants undertook a comprehensive investigation. Their book-length study included thirteen villages and analyzed seven phases of village life: agrarian reform, problems of the farmers, village and community organization, leadership and political participation, the changing family, religion, and educational media.[32] Other research in Japan was carried out a few years later by David Lindstrom.[33]

During the 1950s Raper also studied Formosa and produced a book-length report on that country.[34] His study, undertaken at the request of the Joint Commission on Rural Reconstruction, used information secured from township records, conversations with local leaders, and lengthy interviews with heads of families in selected areas of the country.

The foreign-aid program holds contracts with a number of universities to provide assistance to various countries. One such contract has resulted in a cooperative arrangement with Michigan State University (financed by AID), the Ford Foundation, and the government of Pakistan. Both Raper and Edgar A. Schuler have been associated with this Pakistan program.[35] Cornell University has served for a number of years as the contact with the Philippines. Several staff members of the university have served in the islands, and many Philippine students and officials have been brought to Cornell for a year of study. Robert A. Polson has had major responsibility for this program.

Robert T. McMillan was stationed in the Philippines for several years as a member of another foreign-aid mission. In this capacity he helped to organize and implement a project undertaken cooperatively by the Philippine Council for United States Aid and the Mutual Security Agency of the United States (a forerunner of AID). The field work was begun in 1951. The resulting report, the authors said, presented a "cross-section of rural life in the Philippines from a sociological point of view." [36]

Aside from Latin America the most concentrated study of rural life by American social scientists has been made in India. Although scholars from the United States have made studies under various auspices, the work of the Ford Foundation has been followed through with the most consistency. In 1952 sociologist Douglas Ensminger left his positions in the Division of Farm Population and the Cooperative Extension Service of the Department of Agriculture to administer the Ford program in India. During his years of service there, he has had the benefit of consultation with a number of other rural sociologists. Especially important in this capacity was Carl Taylor, who, after his retirement from the Division of Farm Population in 1953, spent the better part of ten years as adviser to the project. The outcome of this cooperative arrangement was the publication of a book on India's economic and social development.[37] The book included several chapters of critical evaluation written mainly by Taylor. In the preface the authors summarized their work as follows:

The first eight chapters of this book describe the setting with which Indian planned development began, that is, the major conditioning factors and identifiable situations, inherited from the past which would inevitably condition the process of planned change. The next ten chapters discuss the various rural development programmes and give the authors' critical assessment of the trials, errors, and successes of those programmes. The last nine chapters present analyses of observed experiences in the operation of India's rural development programme which we trust will make some contribution to what might be called the sociology of development.

The neighboring country of Ceylon has been studied by Bryce Ryan, who spent a number of years there during the 1950s and published several articles and a small volume based on his investigations.[38]

While it is impossible to mention everyone who has served abroad, it is important to record the contributions of Howard W. Beers, who has served with several agencies in an administrative and advisory capacity, mainly in Asia. Beers, along with Sanders, Ensminger, Taylor, Loomis, Brunner, and others, has long been interested in translating the findings of research into action programs. Even before the war ended, much thought was given to the problem, and indeed the major emphasis in foreign work has been on inducing change in developing countries. An early outcome of this concern was a collection of essays on agricultural extension throughout the world written by a number of well-known scholars, most of them drawn from the ranks of rural sociologists in the United States.[39]

The underlying theme of the volume is stated in the following sentences: "Science, wherever it has gone around the world, is responsible for progress in agriculture and rural welfare. Bringing that science to more and more rural people is the job of extension." The introduction, "What Extension Is," was written by Ensminger and Sanders. Two chapters on nonliterate societies were prepared by Solon T. Kimball and Felix M. Keesing. Six chapters grouped under the heading of "Peasant Societies" make up the bulk of the volume. These include a general chapter by Sanders, one on China by Hsin-Pao Yang, one on India by D. Spencer Hatch, one on the Arab fellahin by Afif Tannous, one on the Balkans by Clayton E. Whipple, and one dealing with Latin America by Charles Loomis. There are also chapters covering Euro-American rural society by Carle Zimmerman, extension work in the United Kingdom by Robert Rae, extension services in northwest Europe by P. Lamartine Yates and L. A. H. Pieters, extension work in the United States by E. deS. Brunner and C. B. Smith, and the "role of extension in world reconstruction" by M. L. Wilson and Brunner.

Other Overseas Developments

The individuals mentioned in this hurried review are almost exclusively those who published books or other reports on their work abroad. Equally important but more difficult to evaluate is the work of numerous rural sociologists who have served overseas under the auspices of the technical-aid programs of the United States government, the United Nations and its specialized agencies, and the various private foundations. These men have usually served as consultants on community development and extension education projects. Their work has been no less significant, and may be even more so, than the work of those who produce publications.

The influence of rural sociologists abroad has been manifested in research and writing, in teaching, and in consultation services, chiefly with governments introducing programs for rural development. In China and the Far East research and teaching were initiated mainly by church missionary agencies, while in Latin America these activities were first sponsored by the United States government through the departments of state and agriculture. Since World War II the work has proliferated far beyond what could possibly have been foreseen. This was chiefly the result of the federal government's role in the promotion of reconstruction and rehabilitations in war-ravaged countries and in the establishment under President Harry S. Truman of the so-called Point Four, or technical aid, program. The Fulbright Act also facilitated service abroad by a large number of rural sociologists. Some members of the profession have made important contributions as administrators and supervisors of programs sponsored by private foundations.

In addition it is important to note the expansion of rural sociology as a college discipline in a number of foreign countries. By the 1960s there was sufficient interest and enough personnel to make possible the establishment of a professional organization in Europe and the publication of a journal.[40] In August 1965 three hundred delegates from fifty countries attended the First World Congress of Rural Sociology in Dijon, France. The central theme of the meeting was the impact of changes in agriculture on the developed and modernizing countries. A second world congress met in 1968 at the Agricultural University in Wageningen, The Netherlands.

While it would be fatuous for American rural sociologists to claim full credit for the organized development of the discipline in other lands, there can be little doubt that they have had an influence. Postwar developments in countries of Europe — the emphasis on economic growth, the rising tide of population increase, and the basic importance of food production — have brought rural conditions into sharper relief. Moreover, the techno-

153

logical developments in communication that have broken down the old isolation of rural people have brought new emphasis to the study of rural society. During the postwar years also many students from Europe have studied rural sociology in American universities and increasingly they have come to realize the important role which this field of study can play in their own countries.

12

Progress, Problems, Perspectives

IN CONTEMPLATING the growth of rural sociology as a scholarly discipline since 1902, when Kenyon Butterfield received his appointment as instructor at the University of Michigan, one is led to certain conclusions. In the first place, the discipline in its rather amorphous beginnings was the response of a few perceptive individuals to the crises and disorganization of American society, particularly in respect to the rural and agricultural population. A second conclusion is that rural sociology was the offspring of two late-nineteenth century movements: the urge to reform society and the growth of the scientific disciplines.

It should not be surprising that the pioneers in rural sociology were predominantly reformers. When they began their work, there was an urgent need to ameliorate the conditions of life on the farm — particularly to improve communication, raise the level of education, and strengthen the rural church as ways of facilitating the spread of information to the countryside and lessening the isolation of the farmer from the rest of society. Thus the evangelists of the reform period undertook the task of centering the nation's attention on the critical problems of the American countryside.[1]

Thoughtful individuals very early perceived, however, that more was needed than mere polemics against the evils and shortcomings of rural life. Although the need for facts was apparent to any astute observer, scientific methods for obtaining data about society were not well developed. Nevertheless scientific influence was at work even in the earliest stages of the development of the discipline. Warren H. Wilson, a trained scientist with a Ph.D degree in sociology from Columbia University, was also a reformer, concerned with the welfare of the church. In his position at his denomination's national headquarters, Wilson was able to undertake many social surveys that revealed facts about the social environment in which the church had to function. In Wilson, as in his contemporary, Paul Vogt, the two ideals of reform and science were synthesized.

Progress in Methodology and Theory

The scatter-gun type of social survey prevailed only briefly. Rural researchers soon felt the need to focus on more specific problems. Even while the great church-sponsored boom of the second decade of the century was under way, Galpin at Wisconsin had begun to concentrate on the problem of defining the boundaries of the rural community. The method he invented to achieve his objective had a profound influence on rural social research, especially in the 1920s. Other ecological units — neighborhoods, villages, hamlets — were studied and mapped. It was obvious, of course, that the geographically isolated farm family was also an ecological unit related to and part of neighborhoods and communities. It was further obvious that other groups existed, groups based upon interests or needs and including larger formal organizations and social institutions. So the projects for study proliferated.

Meanwhile, thanks to the general development of scientific methodology, the sociologist had an expanded range of research tools. Among these were many instruments for measuring behavior and attitudes. For example, while studies of the standard of living of farm families made during the 1920s and 1930s provided a basis for the investigation of social stratification based on income and expenditures, the method was cumbersome. The demand for simpler tools was met in part by the level of living index developed by the Division of Farm Population and based on census data. A more important instrument was a device to measure socioeconomic status. Such a tool was developed and standardized by F. Stuart Chapin

156

at the University of Minnesota for urban family studies and one was developed for farm families by William H. Sewell.[2] Meanwhile, the instruments available for the measurement of other aspects of social behavior have multiplied.

Other important developments included the steady improvement in sampling techniques, which resulted in much greater economy in effort and money and the consequent enlargement of the range of problems studied. Present-day research workers are more likely than their predecessors to formulate specific hypotheses for testing, to define their concepts, and to make sophisticated analyses of data, including the application of tests of significance.

Rural sociology need not apologize for its early reliance on purely descriptive study. As John Madge has pointed out, this emphasis is characteristic of a young science. Descriptive studies, Madge has written, produce material of "immediate administrative utility" and contribute to a "better understanding of social life." Such studies also serve as a "necessary stage not only in building a language but also in providing opportunities needed to develop sophisticated techniques of investigation." Nevertheless, as he concludes, "what is needed at all levels of generality is the formulation and testing of significant hypotheses. Ultimately, the power of sociology rests in its accumulation of probable and applicable ideas, not merely of facts." [3]

As well as changes in methodology, there have been shifts in the topical interests of rural sociological researchers over the past thirty years. The trends from 1936 to 1965 have been summarized by William H. Sewell, who read and classified 1,025 articles in the journal *Rural Sociology*.[4] The distribution of articles by percentages according to major topics is shown in the accompanying table.

Social organization, including groups, institutions, and other aspects

Major Topics	1936–45	1946–55	1956–65	1936–65
Social organization	29.4%	35.1%	28.1%	30.8%
Social change	2.0	8.6	14.9	8.3
Social psychology	6.8	10.3	22.8	13.1
Population	11.5	7.7	8.3	9.2
Social welfare and policy	33.5	16.8	7.9	20.0
Methodology	8.7	10.8	12.6	10.6
The discipline	8.1	10.7	5.4	8.2
Total	100.0%	100.0%	100.0%	100.0%
Number of articles	(358)	(339)	(328)	(1025)

157

of social structure, has consistently attracted more attention than any other topic. Over the total period, social welfare and policy rank second, but it is the emphasis in the first ten years (those of depression and war) that brings up the average. Interest in this field flagged in subsequent decades. Social psychology — including personality, attitudes, aspirations, communication, participation, and leadership — has risen markedly to give this category an overall rank of number three. Even more marked, relatively, has been the increased concern with social change, due in part to the multiplication of studies dealing with the diffusion of farm practices and associated factors. Methodology too has shown a steady rise in treatment through the years. Although not indicated in Sewell's tabulation, another interest which has caught the attention of rural sociologists is community development in the United States and in foreign countries.

Sewell also subjected the articles published in the year 1936, 1950, and 1964 to tests of scientific adequacy as measured by twenty-two selected criteria organized as follows: orientation of study (objectives, hypotheses, theoretical orientation, concepts defined, oriented to past research); data collection (universe defined, sampling used and described, interview data, questionnaires, standardized instruments, documentary sources, observation); data analysis (tabular presentation, correlation, tests of significance, control of associated variables); and conclusions (statement of conclusions, limits of generalization indicated, weaknesses of study indicated, suggestions for future research, findings oriented to problem area, findings oriented to general theory).

"The research articles published in 1936," Sewell observes, "clearly reflect the relatively unsophisticated theoretical and methodological orientation common in the rural sociology of that period." Only four of the seventeen articles appearing in *Rural Sociology* in 1936 would meet today's minimum criteria of adequacy, he concludes. By contrast, almost half of those published in 1950 would measure up, as would practically all the nineteen articles that appeared in 1964.

In spite of the industrious fact-gathering in which rural sociologists have engaged, no grand theoretical design has yet emerged. It is fair to say that this has been true of all phases of sociology in the United States. American sociology, from its beginning, has been empirically oriented. And while one might expect that from the vast accumulation of data there would emerge a synthesis and a body of theory around which facts could be polarized and made more meaningful, such has not been the case. The theoretical formulations which presently characterize the field are largely the work of such foreign scholars as Max Weber, E. Durkheim, and Ferdinand Toennies. The question of whether theory arises from empirical research has not been convincingly answered by American sociologists, unless it be in the negative.

In an earlier chapter we described some attempts at theoretical orientation by the writers of textbooks in rural sociology. Sims sought to orient the available data on rural life around the concept of social energy and its behavior. Hawthorn developed the theory of isolation-socialization and the measurement of the latter by the person-hour-contact unit. Sorokin and Zimmerman marshaled their data according to the rural-urban comparative scheme. Loomis and Beegle introduced the social system as the centralizing, synthesizing concept. Among these overall attempts at synthesis only the social system theory now claims much attention, although the rural-urban schema still serves in presenting contrasting situations in the major segments of society.[5]

Sewell notes the lack of theoretical orientation in the works of rural sociologists,[6] a criticism he has leveled against his fellow workers for many years. Rural sociologists, he believes, tend to focus attention on limited groups in small localities, a practice giving rise to what he calls "parochialism." By the nature of things this approach precludes any generalizations relevant to broader segments of society. Sewell sees hope, however, in the growing tendency for research to be conducted on regional bases. The restricted field in which the rural sociologist operates is a problem to which we will return.

Problems of the Discipline

At once the major advantage which rural sociologists have enjoyed, and one of their most difficult relationships, is their connection with the agricultural colleges. We have noted earlier the fact that Bailey and Butterfield, the most outspoken and effective evangelists for rural reform in the early period, were officials of land-grant colleges. It went almost without saying that the place for the rural social sciences to become established was in the agricultural colleges. Here the subject would not only be taught, but would also share in the research appropriations of the agricultural experiment stations. After the passage of the Purnell Act in 1925 had made it clear that federal funds could be used for research in rural sociology and agricultural economics, sociologists hoped that every state college of agriculture would in future give a place to these disciplines. But no more than two-thirds ever adopted rural sociology, and over the years the average number has been little more than half.

It was difficult at first for directors and deans to see where sociology could fit into the existing disciplines in technical agriculture. While many administrators were aware of the social and economic problems of rural people, they were unsure of either the feasibility or the desirability of making those problems the object of scientific investigation.

In those institutions where the discipline of rural sociology gained acceptance, its position in the organizational structure was often ambiguous. As far as teaching was concerned, the Farm Foundation's investigation of 1950 found seventeen types of departmental organization in the forty-eight land-grant colleges.[7] There were only five separate departments and the most common arrangement was for courses to be offered in departments of sociology. No research was carried on in nineteen institutions. The investigating committee gave no information about the structural relations of the discipline in the experiment stations which did support research. It is clear, however, that except where there are separate departments of rural sociology the research budget must be derived through various other arrangements, most often perhaps by association with agricultural economics. Sewell's criticism regarding the parochialism of rural sociological research is a just one. This narrowness results, paradoxically, from the fact that rural sociology covers a broad spectrum of subject matter — almost as broad as sociology in general. This situation, coupled with the usual small staffs in experiment stations, places research workers in the dilemma of deciding whether to investigate a variety of problems or whether to concentrate on one or two. If a researcher chooses the former alternative, his work will often prove to be superficial and to have little relevance beyond the local area. If he chooses the second course, he stands a better chance of digging deeply enough to produce significant results.[8]

Another factor related to parochialism is that until the 1950s — when federal appropriations provided for regional committees — the research carried on by sociologists in experiment stations was perforce limited to the state at most, and more often to a local area within the state. Still, where intense specialization is made possible by adequate staff, the concentration on a local area can produce significant results. Witness the work of J. H. Kolb on Walworth and Dane counties in Wisconsin.

Another criticism of rural sociological research is that the rural sociologist is limited in the kind of studies he may undertake by his interpretation, consciously or unconsciously, of the mood or temper of the rural people of the state. In a critique of rural community studies, Philip Olson has charged that rural sociologists are "limited to the level of analysis at which residents themselves are limited," that they must focus on "factual details and their theoretical significance is unspecified and their meanings are unclear." He concludes that the types of community studies sponsored by agricultural institutions, in comparison with other community studies, "provide only the most limited understanding of communities and American society." [9]

One need not agree entirely with this criticism to recognize its justice. Certainly the rural sociologist, whether supported by state funds or federal money, must realize that the results of his studies may affect future appropriations. If he produces conclusions that reflect unfavorably on a community, regardless of their factual basis, his efforts will not be regarded sympathetically.[10] Economists no less than sociologists have had to reckon with public opinion, or the "public ideology" of the rural constituency. Fortified margarine may be as nutritious as butter, but in a dairy farming state it is impolitic to say so.

The fact of being part of a land-grant college staff also imposes on rural sociologists a strong sense of the need to be useful. Colleagues in the technical fields are constantly finding answers to farmers' problems, answers which can be translated into values measurable in dollars. This type of research provides administrators with effective arguments for appropriations from state legislatures and Congress. Rural sociologists rarely produce results that can be so translated. Economists are only a little more successful on this score. Yet administrators are coming to see the value of sociological research as it begins to show meaningful generalizations. Among the more notable achievements in this regard are the studies of the diffusion of farm and home practices, undoubtedly the best example to date of the concentration on a single research problem by a number of sociologists in different states.[11] This cooperative attack was stimulated by a regional committee initially sponsored by the Farm Foundation and later supported by regional funds from the experiment stations.

The diffusion studies led to further intensive studies on the nature and theory of social change, representing another recent achievement of importance.[12] Social change has been a recurrent theme in the literature of rural sociology. For the most part, however, it has been a matter of simply recording what has taken place. For example, one may mention again the work of J. H. Kolb, as well as Brunner's restudies of 140 villages. Lately, however, the emphasis has been on the process and technique of inducing and directing change. The impulse has come not only from a desire to improve the techniques of agricultural extension education, but also from the need to accelerate the process of change in developing countries.

Such disadvantages to rural sociology as resulted from its existence within the structure of the agricultural colleges were offset to some extent by certain compensations. First of all, in those institutions which adopted the discipline the sociologists had a fairly consistent source of funds for research. Second, in the enjoyment of experiment station funds, they were usually released from some of their teaching duties to work on their projects. That is to say, they received part of their salaries as research workers and part as teachers. This is a benefit which very few sociologists could claim until recent years. The research funds were also used to employ graduate students as assistants, which not only gave them experience in that activity, but increased the amount of research that could be carried forward. A third advantage lay in the access of sociologists to publication outlets. Every agricultural experiment station operates on the wise assumption that the results of research should be published if they meet minimum standards of scientific adequacy. There is provision for publishing bulletins, circulars, and research papers, as well as funds to purchase reprints from scientific journals.

Perspectives

Having surveyed, however inadequately, the rise and growth of rural sociology during the twentieth century, one is naturally tempted to speculate on future trends. While such speculation must of course depend largely on extrapolation from the past, one is irresistibly tempted to express some personal judgments too.

It scarcely needs to be said that research will continue along the lines indicated by the Sewell survey. Studies will be made of the various social groups and institutions and of social processes. It is also safe to assume that future developments will be conditioned by changes taking place not only in the science itself, but also in those areas of rural society which have been of particular interest to the discipline.

We have already indicated the marked growth in the adequacy of the science itself, the greater range of tools available to the investigator, and the improved caliber of the workers. The changes in rural society itself are equally familiar: the transformations in communication and agricultural technology; the remarkable rise in the standard of living of farm families; the steady increase in the level of education; the integration of rural and urban segments, accompanied by the sharing of social institutions formerly distinguishable as farm or nonfarm. These points have all been discussed in books and journal articles and require no further treatment here. What we need to ask is the meaning of these trends for future research by rural sociologists.

In the past much attention has been given to the differences between rural and urban groups, with the farm population treated very much as an isolated or segregated unit. These differences have disappeared or are disappearing. The cityward drift from the farm and the countryward drift from the city present the student with a new situation. While the anatomy of the rural community may show a skeleton little changed since 1915, the physiology is vastly different. This would seem to suggest the need for a new emphasis in the study of the community, which is an entity no longer limited by its so-called anatomy. Specifically, its parts — its groups and institutions — are now more closely integrated.

It is too much to speak of this process as homogenization, because differences have not been entirely eliminated, even though farm, village, and city are now part of what we call mass society. All its members are exposed to the same media of mass communication. All hear and read the same news and watch the same television programs. Yet we know that differences in reaction to these stimuli exist and that they range over a wide spectrum. Intensive study will be necessary to discover the factors conditioning these responses.

One factor, surely, is the kind of work in which a person is engaged. The study of occupation and its effects on individuals and groups is already a subject of study. To take only one example, the influence of various occupational groups on local and national power groups has become a matter of interest with the implementation of the one-man-one-vote principle of representation in government. Nevertheless, much more investigation of occupation is needed.

It would seem logical therefore for rural sociologists to emphasize the study of community and of occupation. In addition to these areas, con-

163

tinued study of social change is vitally important. Here the focus has been on induced, or directed, change, with the object of discovering how a novel idea, practice, or invention can be introduced to, and accepted by, a target group. In this area fall the various diffusion studies. Moreover, it is the hope that this procedure can be applied to the developing countries.

One would like to see the studies of change go beyond their present limited objectives. Such studies represent a brief segment of time and, as Bryce Ryan, a pioneer in this kind of study, has suggested, a longer view of development is needed.[13] The economists are well on their way to evolving an economics of development. Sociologists are challenged to work out a comparable sociology of development and, because the developing countries are primarily rural, a large share of the responsibility will rest with rural sociologists.

It seems only fair to remark that since 1950 sociologists have shown a particular fascination with statistical manipulation. Admirable as the results of their efforts have been, they cannot contribute much to the sociology of development; much more than statistical proficiency is required. Something akin to the generalizing capacity of a Spencer, a Sorokin, or a Toynbee will be necessary. An awareness of the past is essential for a perceptive analysis of the present and a rational projection for the future.

Finally, professional rural sociologists should continue the tendency to integrate their field with sociology in general. The profession and the field should no longer be regarded as something apart from general sociology. As Harold Hoffsommer has pointed out, rural sociology is as broad as sociology itself and is related "to the discipline as a whole and to its several component areas." [14] And, as John Gillette suggested fifty years ago, the adjective "rural" might well be discontinued.

MEMOIRS

MEMOIRS

How They Became Rural Sociologists

IT IS inevitable that pioneers in a new field of thought have to make their way without the benefit of formal instruction in their specialty. For most of the early rural sociologists, indeed, there was not much instruction to be had even in general sociology. Many of them drifted in from other fields. Several attended seminaries in preparation for the ministry and a few were ordained clergymen. Some did their undergraduate or graduate work in economics. Others moved into rural sociology from secondary school education, the extension service, or such technical fields of agriculture as entomology and horticulture.

With this diversity of background in mind, it occurred to me that it would be interesting to assemble personal statements from as many of the pioneers as possible. They were asked to respond to the questions: "How did you happen to become a rural sociologist?" "What experiences, persons, and events were most responsible in influencing your career in this respect?" Some of the following accounts were obtained many years ago by members of my seminar; others were personally solicited by me. The collection is not as complete as it might have been, partly because I began it too late to obtain the recollections of some persons, and partly because the pioneer generation was arbitrarily defined as those men who were born in the nineteenth century.

In the interests of readability, the accounts have been somewhat condensed, and spelling, punctuation, and paragraphing have been adjusted. Editorial comments have been supplied in brackets and in the footnotes.

James Mickel Williams

Williams was born in 1876 in Waterville, New York, the son of a rural merchant. In 1898 he received a B.A. degree from Brown University. The president of Brown at that time was E. Benjamin Andrews, an outstanding administrator whom Williams credits as one "to whom I owe my original interest in sociology." [1] Williams graduated from Union Theological Seminary in New York with a B.D. in 1901. From 1899 to 1902 he was a graduate student at Columbia University and he held the University Fellowship in Sociology in the academic year 1902–3. During the years 1903–6 he was engaged in the community study that became his Ph.D. thesis. After a year as lecturer in economics at Vassar, he went to Hobart College in Geneva, New York, where he remained until his retirement as the only teacher of sociology. The following statements are excerpted from letters written in 1957 and 1965.

I wrote *An American Town* because I was born and grew up there and was in a position to know the people because my father ran a dry goods store in Waterville during all my school and college life, had customers from seven miles around, and "trusted" them all. So when the first bicycle with wheels the same size (the "Columbia" about 1890) came on the market, he bought me one and started me riding over the hills around Sangerfield [a small center near Waterville] "collecting bills." So everybody knew "Jimmy," as they called me, and I knew everybody. I liked people and they liked me. For instance, one summer day I started out with bills for people up in the southeast hills, and about noon arrived at a farm house and turned into the driveway. A woman called, "Here comes Jimmy — come on, Jimmy — dinner is about ready." The men came in from the field and we had a good dinner. After that it was difficult to pull out the bill and she did not give me any help. But finally I did pull out the bill and apologetically asked her if she could pay. (I was really a poor collector.) "Can't you pay a dollar?" "No, we haven't a cent in the house." After a pause, "When can you pay a dollar?" She named the date when she would have the egg money. So I rode home, fourteen miles there and back, and on the day she set I rode back and got the dollar and another dinner and back home. Twenty-eight miles for a dollar! So, you see, I knew the people of Sangerfield. Father once said: "Jim, if you ever run for office you'll get every vote in town."

Father had to do a credit business. You see, if a woman came in to buy dress goods, she would select a certain cloth and father would cut off. Then braid and he'd cut that off. Then lace and he'd cut that off. Then buttons and he'd cut the card. Then, she'd say, "Mr. Williams, I can't pay for this today." Well, a piece of goods cut off was no use to him, so he'd let her take it all and "trust" her and that would be another bill for me to collect. It was the same in the millinery department which mother had charge of. We had stiff competition.

Women could take the train and go to Utica, twenty-two miles, to buy, if they had the cash.

But we had two big advantages. Many women wanted *advice* as to what to buy and trusted father and mother to advise them. Then, too, father knew the financial standing of every man for seven miles around and, if a woman's eye was caught by a bolt of cloth which father thought was too expensive for her, he'd pull down a cheaper cloth and say something that would make her like it better. So his business continued good until he retired. One reason for *An American Town*, then, was that I knew the people.

Another was that we could see that the price of hops affected not only business, but every activity in Sangerfield. The rural people raised hops or worked for those who did. In Waterville lived the hop dealers. I was naturally curious and my mind dwelt on all these relationships. So, when I went to Columbia for graduate work in sociology and my turn came to give a seminar paper, it was on the town of Sangerfield. It was natural to take a subject about which you knew more than anybody, including Giddings himself. After the seminar he suggested that I take Sangerfield for my doctor's dissertation, which I did. I went home, searched all written records on the town, and came to know every family.

If I ever had any method I never thought of it. It was all just common sense. I never wrote out my method of investigation, or published anything on it. I simply searched until I found the Town of Sangerfield census records of 1845 and 1875, and then took my own census in 1900. Rode over the whole town on my bicycle, so I knew the name and location of every family in those three years. In 1900 I knew them all by visiting with and talking with them about the neighborhood and themselves. I did not take any courses in statistics from anybody. All the statistics I used was just common sense.

The fact is, however, that Williams really did have a method, one similar to that of the cultural anthropologist. His interviews were informal and open-ended. In *An American Town* Williams made the following comments on his procedure: "The method of study has been simply to record what significant mental traits were observed in chance conversations. The conversation usually was allowed to take any course as it happened, that there might be perfect frankness in expression. Very often the significance of certain expressions did not strike the author until some moment of casual reflection, perhaps days afterward." [2]

Such a method places great emphasis on observation. Williams was in fact what we would now call a participant observer. In *An American Town* (pp. 9, 10) he also made these pertinent remarks: "There will be no such thing as sociology until we have begun at the A, B, C of method — observation" and "What we need is statistical data furnished by many skillful field workers."

Williams was the first American social psychologist of rural life. His work was full of significant insights, though his method was not one that others felt confident in using. His work has not received the full critical examination it deserves, partly because he was not active in professional societies and had little dialogue with other members of the profession.

Newell L. Sims

Born in Indiana in 1878, Sims had bachelor degrees from Tri-State College in his native state and from the University of Kentucky. He later attended Columbia University, taking his M.A. degree in 1910 and his Ph.D., under F. H. Giddings, in 1912. As he recounts below, his first teaching positions were at the University of Florida and Massachusetts Agricultural College. From 1924 until his retirement, he was head of the department of sociology at Oberlin College. He died in 1965. The following account was written at my request in 1957.

It would not be far wrong to say that I chose rural sociology as a major interest because it seemed to be the line of least resistance. After some years in the Christian ministry in which I found myself in conflict with many accepted practices and viewpoints of the church to which I belonged and, having been tried and found guilty of heresy by this denomination, I decided to demit the ministry and turn to teaching. Sociology was the subject in which I had developed considerable interest as a pastor, hence I decided to specialize in that subject as a candidate for the doctorate at Columbia University.

Back of all this there were factors that had prepared and inclined me quite unconsciously for the study of rural life.

In the first place I was born and reared on a farm in the Northeast corner county of Indiana. My ancestors on both sides of the house had all been farmers from time immemorial. Until I was eighteen years old, the rural neighborhood was my only world. Our community in my childhood and youth was a relatively isolated and primitive one, whose sole outlet on the wider world was through two small village marketing centers. The neighborhood in which I grew up was known as Hell's Point, in part because of its hilly and swampy topography, but particularly because of its moral and religious behavior, which was of low tone. That environment in its physical aspects, though not so much in its moral phases, was a significant influence in shaping my character and outlook, producing a youth of the soil deeply ingrained with the habits and preferences of country folks of the last quarter of the nineteenth century in the American Midwest.

When I left the farm to go to college, my objective soon became the Christian ministry, and my college course was directed to that end. The curriculum offered only one course in sociology. A text by Henderson was used. I took this course, which left no lasting impression on me with the exception of the fact that a term paper was required. I wrote my paper about a small country village which I knew fairly well. In preparing the paper I made a cursory survey of the village institutions and activities. As I recall, this subject was chosen because it seemed to be the easiest one I could think of, requiring the least work in preparation. That was in 1900. At the time I had no special leaning toward sociology nor did this course awaken any. Least of all did I have any notion of ever teaching this or any other subject.

A second phase of my background concerns my early pastorates. Immediately after graduating from college, I became the pastor of a church in a small village in central Michigan. I was the only resident minister there. The village was a decadent one, having survived its lumber camp days as a farm trading center. Two years later I entered the College of the Bible of Transylvania University at Lexington, Kentucky, for theological training. While a student there, I preached for village and open country churches in Kentucky, southern Indiana, and especially in Brown County, Ohio. I was quite in my element ministering to these rural parishes. They provided a diversified experience and initiated me into many of the sociological realities of the rural community.

From this seminary I was called to a city pastorate in Missouri where I served for three years. Resigning this Carthage, Missouri, pastorate, I went to New York City and enrolled for post graduate work in the Union Theological Seminary and Columbia University. I had decided to turn to college teaching and chose sociology for my field of specialization at Columbia.

It is interesting to note that we three men (Williams, Wilson, Sims), writing on rural villages at Columbia, had somewhat similar backgrounds, experience, and training. Rural-born and reared, Wilson and I had held country pastorates. All three of us were graduates of the Union Theological Seminary in New York and had come under Giddings' influence while students in the seminary and Columbia University. Williams' *An American Town* appeared in 1906; Wilson's *Quaker Hill* in 1908; and my work, *A Hoosier Village*, in 1912.[3] However, the first draft of my study had been submitted to the Columbia faculty as a master's thesis in 1910, but was not published. Thus within the space of four years these three field studies had been made. I had read Williams' and Wilson's dissertations before deciding to follow in their footsteps with another community analysis. That line seemed to lead right up the rural alleys that I had trod and in which I felt wholly at home. So I made choice of old and familiar ground to cultivate for my doctor's thesis.

These three field studies of rural communities differed greatly from each other as regards the type of community surveyed and the specific methods employed in gathering and interpreting the data. Sociologists regarded them when they appeared as pioneer works. They were cordially welcomed as original contributions to sociological literature both from the standpoints of method and content.

My first teaching was at the University of Florida in Gainesville from 1915 to 1920. There I gave a course in rural sociology which was required of all students in the agricultural college. The library facilities of the university were almost nil in this field at that time. I felt the need of extensive reading material to supplement the textbook we used. I wanted the students to get a comprehensive picture of the rural community and its development, activities and types of organization. This led me to gather, organize, and write the stuff included in *The Rural Community: Ancient and Modern*, which was designed as a source book of readings for courses in rural sociology.

The book was well received and widely used among rural sociologists. When I wrote my textbook, *Elements of Rural Sociology* [1928], it was planned to fit the two works together and thus put into the hands of students an extensive and fairly comprehensive body of material on country life. However, on the appearance of the text from the T. Y. Crowell Company, Scribner [publisher of *The Rural Community*] notified me that they had destroyed the plates of my book and that no more copies would be available. This was a great disappointment, for there was an increased demand for the source book among those who adopted my textbook. Scribner regretted their haste in discontinuing a work which they thought was too slow in moving and too limited in its appeal.

When I went to Amherst, Massachusetts, to join the faculty of Massachusetts Agricultural College in 1920, it was to teach rural sociology exclusively. The introductory course was required of all sophomores. Thus I came to know the entire student body through this class. Many of them took other courses with me after the sophomore year. President Kenyon Butterfield, whose interests were primarily sociological, also gave a course in rural organizations. I assisted him. His course, like much that he did, was superficial, lacking any systematic organization and strangely devoid of all scientific methods.

Massachusetts Aggie at that time drew the bulk of its student body from urban or semi-urban areas of the state. The greater part of them came to Aggie because it was inexpensive. They had very little and often no essential rural background or experience of country life. At Aggie they got highly specialized training in a number of more or less tangential fields to agriculture, rather than in the more basic aspects of farming, and after college entered upon careers in their various specialities. Quickly discovering this peculiar condition and the great lack among the students of what I considered an adequate rural background and their very limited outlook on the rural scene, I proceeded to give them as broad and as full a view of American country life as I could. It was quite natural to begin with the old New England towns which were right there all about us in the Connecticut Valley. From firsthand studies of these communities I proceeded next to trace the development of divergent forms of community settlement in the hinterland of America. Thus I built up my course in the elements of rural sociology from this New England foundation.

My text appeared four years after I came to Oberlin College to head the department of sociology of this institution. However, the material for the textbook had all been assembled while at Massachusetts Aggie and should have been published long before it was, for I had only to write it up. This I did not find time to do until I had my Oberlin courses and the department well in hand. It was natural for me to introduce rural sociology into the Oberlin curriculum. I gave the first course that had ever been offered in the institution in rural sociology and continued to require it of all the majors in the department for the twenty years I taught in the college. I emphasized the fact that rural sociology should really form the basis of, and the introduction to, all other sociological knowledge for American students, since it was from a rural background that American society arose and in which its primary institutions and mores were formed.

Unfortunately few present-day sociologists have the rural background that many of the earlier ones had, and they are strangers to the significance of this subject for sociology as a whole.

John M. Gillette

Gillette was born in Missouri in 1866. His B.A. came from Park College, Missouri, in 1892. After graduating from Princeton Theological

Seminary in 1895, he was ordained a Presbyterian minister. He took his Ph.D. degree from the University of Chicago in 1901. After a pastorate in Dodge City, Kansas, and a series of positions at Bible Normal College in Springfield, Massachusetts; Chadron Academy in Nebraska; the Academy for Young Women in Jacksonville, Illinois; and the State Normal School in Valley City, North Dakota; Gillette became head of the department of sociology at the University of North Dakota in 1907, where he remained until his retirement. He died in 1949.

My first acquaintance with anything like rural sociology, a term which had not then been invented, was in the University of Chicago, academic year 1899–1900, where I took a course with Professor C. R. Henderson entitled "Rural Communities." I had been raised on a farm and had lived more or less all over the United States and observed farming processes; a good deal of the information stuck to me because of my previous farm experience. I took "Rural Communities" because it seemed to reflect rural life.

Professor Henderson's work in that field was very formal and seemed to me quite remote from actual farming living conditions, but I worked out a project in the field of rural community change in which I organized and interpreted quite a lot of material which probably did more to crystalize my interest in the rural field than the course given by Professor Henderson.

Some years later in developing the department of sociology in this institution, about 1910 I think, I put in a course which I called rural sociology.[4] The text I used as a basis of discussion was Butterfield's *Chapters in Rural Progress* and the report of the President's Country Life Commission. I soon began to sit at my desk and write out material on the rural situation in which I was interested and which seemed to be worth putting down. By 1913 I had quite a considerable manuscript. This was published in 1913 as *Constructive Rural Sociology* by the Sturgis and Walton Company.

This was, I believe, the first systematic treatise of rural sociology published. The reception of this beginning work was a great surprise to me. It was widely and well received in this country and abroad; especially in France, it attracted the attention of students of sociology. René Worms, secretary of l'Institut International de Sociologie, requested my consent to review it for the organ of that organization, *Revue Internationale de Sociologie*, and also to review it before the French Academy of Agriculture. My later work, *Rural Sociology*, also received consideration in this country and abroad and has been translated into Czech, Japanese, Portuguese, and some of it into the Chinese languages.

I received and enlarged *Constructive Rural Sociology* and the second edition came out in 1915. Later on I tried to forget that I had written anything on rural sociology and projected and wrote *Rural Sociology*, a much larger work published by the Macmillan Company in 1922. This was revised as the 1928 edition. The rural scene and rural conditions had shifted so much that I felt the book was out-dated so I devoted two or three years to thoroughly revising it and bringing it up-to-date. My *Rural Sociology* of 1936 is the result of that work.

Edmund deS. Brunner

Most of the pioneer rural sociologists spent their early years in rural environments, but there were exceptions. Brunner was born in the industrial town of Bethlehem, Pennsylvania, in 1889. He took B.A., B.D., M.A., and Ph.D. degrees from Moravian College and Theological Seminary. After ordination he served pastorates in Pennsylvania from 1911 to 1918. In 1919–20 he directed the town and country survey department of the Interchurch World Movement, and from 1921 to 1933 he was director of town and country surveys of the Institute for Social and Religious Research in New York City. During this period he became associate in rural education at Teachers College, Columbia University, and in 1933 professor of sociology in the Graduate Faculty of Political Science at Columbia. The following statement was prepared at my request in 1965.

My drift into rural sociology began in my senior year, 1908–9, at Moravian College, Bethlehem, Pennsylvania. I had had a most disappointing semester in sociology but continued with the subject because a new faculty member, Albert G. Rau, took it over.[5] At the first meeting of the class he directed me to find out what the coming of a new interurban trolley and of electric lights had done to the life of a small hamlet seven miles from the college. Let me emphasize that this was in September 1908. Giddings at Columbia was just beginning to start a few doctoral candidates on field investigations in connection with their dissertations, notably James M. Williams and Warren H. Wilson.

My college was church related and I was seriously considering the Christian ministry as a career. My father, however, insisted on paying the small tuition fee so that I would be under no legal obligation to serve the denomination. Soon after I entered the theological seminary there was a long and serious strike at the Bethlehem Steel Company. It was covered for a Philadelphia newspaper by a favorite cousin of mine. Since we both knew the town well and also some of the strikers it was not long before I had a lot of practical education in the problems of labor. This extracurricular education was continued during two succeeding summers when I worked for a local graphite mill, the second summer as assistant shipping clerk at four dollars a week for an eleven-hour day, nine hours on Saturday. Among other things I made up the payroll and found that married men were earning only eight to ten dollars a week. These experiences convinced me I should enter the ministry and seek to serve labor in what was then called an institutional church.

However, upon graduation from the theological seminary I was sent to a country village of seven hundred population and to a church with less than a hundred adults and children listed on its rolls. There were between four hundred and five hundred persons within the community area but outside the village boundary. There were also five other churches to serve the total population.

I began to try to look at the community as Rau had taught us to analyze a social situation. To get to know it better, and to the horror of many people, I offered myself to the semipro baseball team. (I was a letter man from my college.) The team was sponsored by one of the two local industries, a cigar factory. It met in one of the town's many saloons. I was one of the two pitchers

174

of this team for the three years I stayed in the community. (Benson Y. Landis was bat and water boy the first year and after that, first baseman.) The parsonage had a large garden and it was clear I was expected to use it. I had one scientific farmer in my congregation who helped me and I also took courses in home vegetable gardening by mail from Pennsylvania State. The garden won praise from my farmer members and I acquired a love for the soil, both its feel and the things that it can produce, which has never left me. A close friendship was formed very soon with a doctor in a neighboring community who was the manager of its baseball team and a keen amateur sociologist. (He afterward became the first doctor of rural public health to graduate from Harvard and had a very distinguished career.) From all these contacts I soon saw that there were plenty of problems and opportunities in the country as well as the city.

In the meantime I'd heard of the Federal Council of Churches and learned that it had a rural church commission. A few like-minded individuals among our clergy persuaded the official board of my denomination to set up a country church commission. I was made secretary of the commission and for this reason became the denominational representative on the Federal Council commission mentioned above. There I met Warren Wilson, Paul Vogt, Henry Israel of the rural department of the YMCA, and others. Wilson and Israel became lifelong friends. Wilson loaned me one of his staff to conduct a social survey of the community I served. It was sponsored by a recently organized neighborhood association, which won a good bit of recognition in eastern Pennsylvania and a feature story and later news in the leading Philadelphia daily paper. I was made the executive secretary of this association. My own analysis of the situation, I trust in the Rau tradition, is in my first book, *Cooperation in Coopersburg*, published in 1916 by the Library of Christian Progress of the Missionary Education Movement, now the Friendship Press.

In the fall of 1914 I was transferred to a small county-seat city, Easton, Pennsylvania, in part because successive pastors had had difficulties with a group of retired farmers in the congregation. It was hoped that with my rural experience I could tame them somewhat. I retained the secretaryship of the denominational country church commission and the interdenominational contacts this meant.

The United States entered World War 1 in April 1917. The Federal Council immediately formed a wartime commission of the churches which in view of the "Food will Win the War" slogan set up a rural division. There were few persons in those days with experience, training, or interest in rural social life. Warren Wilson and H. Paul Douglass had gone to France for the YMCA to work among the troops. Herman Nelson Morse was holding Wilson's post as rural secretary for the Presbyterians; Vogt had just gone from Ohio State to the Methodists to organize their rural church work. Hence I was asked to be executive officer of this rural division and accepted.

With the war's end about thirty Protestant bodies organized the Interchurch World Movement with the objective "to win the world for Christ in this generation." The appeal for the funds to do this was to be based on careful surveys of all pertinent facts from which would come an understanding of needs to be met and the cost. A few major divisions were set up — foreign missions, educational institutions, home lands, etc. Under the last, two major departments

175

were city and town and country surveys. Warren Wilson was asked to head the last named. He had just returned to his Presbyterian post and was not anxious to request further leave. He suggested that I be made administrative head with his chief assistant, Herman Morse, in a coordinate position with major responsibility for the methods and techniques. Morse had participated in most of Wilson's score of county-wide church and community studies that had been conducted in every major region of the United States. This proved for me a most happy association throughout. Moreover, under Wilson's leadership, Morse had become completely committed to a sound, objective, technical approach so that intellectually we had been similarly disciplined. We did have a number of troubles with church board secretaries and some of our own state survey supervisors who wanted questions inserted in our instrument that would "prove" what they thought they knew!

This experience was, of course, definitive for me. I abandoned all idea of returning to the service of a specific church. When the Institute of Social and Religious Research was organized to salvage what it could of scientific value from the Interchurch studies (the Interchurch World Movement had failed financially), my career as a rural sociologist, as my profession knows it, began.

Ezra Dwight Sanderson

Sanderson, like Brunner, was the product of an urban environment. He grew up in the city of Detroit and took B.S. degrees from Michigan State College and Cornell. As noted in Chapter 6, Sanderson — after twenty successful years as an entomologist — abruptly decided to abandon this career for a wholly new vocation in sociology. In 1915, at the age of 37, he went to the University of Chicago to begin graduate study. The following brief account was written about 1938.

There was nothing in my work in Michigan or Cornell which gave me ideas about sociology. In fact, there was no rural sociology at that time. I got acquainted with Butterfield and Bailey in later years.

The thing that probably stimulated my interest in rural sociology was the organization of agricultural extension work at the University of West Virginia, which was under way when I went there in 1910 and which was more definitely organized while I was there in 1912 and 1913. I was quite familiar with work in farm management and agricultural economics at that time and was aware that research in that field was well under way. It seemed, however, that no one had given much study to the problems of social organization and the improvement of rural life. The report of the Roosevelt Country Life Commission was undoubtedly a factor in this thinking, as was my contact with the rural surveys of the late Warren H. Wilson.

The way in which I became definitely interested in sociology was about as follows. As I remember, I knew little or nothing about the subject in a formal way. It happened that I had a rather unusual secretary, who had been an instructor in law and who presented me with a subscription to the *American Journal of Sociology* for a Christmas present. I got to reading the journal and got some ideas as to what sociology was all about. I then took my first course in the subject by correspondence with the University of Chicago, before going there for graduate work.

Possibly the situation in West Virginia as regards the organization of extension work may have been peculiarly striking in showing the need for such study, for at that time there was very little, if any, organization of the farmers or rural life and it was one of the most backward states in the union.

Fred R. Yoder

Yoder was born near Hickory, North Carolina, in 1888. He received a bachelor's degree in 1910 from Lenoir Rhyne College at Hickory. The following statement recounts some details of his graduate study at the University of North Carolina, where he took his M.A. in 1915, and at the University of Wisconsin, where he received his Ph.D. in 1923. Further information about his career can be found in Chapter 7.

The first time I heard about anything that had to do with the rural life of the people of the United States was around 1908, when Theodore Roosevelt's Commission on Country Life began to gather some information about rural problems, and sent a questionnaire to the school district where I had gone to elementary school in North Carolina. When the questionnaire arrived, I had left my country school and was in attendance as a freshman at Lenoir Rhyne College. According to reports given me by my father, the people assembled at the little schoolhouse were somewhat baffled and even cynical about any commission making any inquiries about the way people were living in the country communities, and there was a great deal of discussion whether the questionnaire should be thrown into the wastebasket or whether the people assembled should undertake to give answers to the questions. As I recall, the people finally voted to answer the questionnaire.

At this time the agrarian rebel, Tom Watson of Georgia, was rather widely read in the community. In an article in his weekly newspaper or monthly magazine, he had ridiculed the whole idea of the undertaking of Roosevelt's Country Life Commission.

All through my undergraduate college course, 1906–10, I had planned to become a lawyer. Debating was my hobby in college and I must have spent one-third of my time preparing for the Saturday-night debate. I did not really study economics or sociology until my senior year. In the fall of 1909, I took my first course in economics and in the second semester (1910) I took a course in sociology. The college offered only one course in each of these subjects. So far as I had any special taste for knowledge when I left college with my B.A. degree, it was for economics and sociology. For the next four years, I taught in small rural and village high schools in North Carolina, with my strongest interest in teaching history and government.

In the summer of 1911, I attended summer school at the University of Tennessee and at a convocation program heard Warren H. Wilson give a sort of summary of his book on the *Evolution of the Country Community*. He was a very dynamic and inspiring speaker. He was holding a three-week country ministers' institute. There must have been something like fifty ministers from eastern and central Tennessee in daily attendance. After hearing Wilson's convocation address, I attended regularly his one-hour daily sessions, in which he discussed the problems of the rural community with special reference to the country church. At that time, he and his aides in Tennessee were making rural country church surveys in some four or five Tennessee counties. In his daily lectures, Wilson was giving us some of the results of the findings. Later, when these surveys were published, I got copies of all of them.

During this same summer school, I took a course in agricultural economics under John Lee Coulter, who at that time was head of the department of agricultural economics at the University of Minnesota. This course was my first study and experience with agricultural economics.

Also in this summer school there came to the campus for some half dozen daily appearances, O. J. Kern of Winnebago County, Illinois, where he was superintendent of schools and was then or later the author of a book on country schools [*Among Country Schools*, 1906]. He was later called to the University of California as one of the first professors of rural education in the United States. I listened with great interest to his illustrated lectures on the country school and its future possibilities. Interestingly enough, Kern had practically nothing to say about the consolidation of country schools. The great goal that he had in mind was to have well-trained, one-room country school-teachers, who had a love of and enthusiasm for the country and rural people.

Around 1912–13 I first became acquainted with the books on rural life written by Liberty Hyde Bailey of Cornell University. Also, I came into possession of two books on country schools and rural life by a man by the name of McKeever, who was either from the University of Kansas or from Kansas State College. Later I heard him give a series of lectures in the University of North Carolina on problems of rural life as they related to rural education. As soon as Gillette's book, *Constructive Rural Sociology* [1913], came out, I got a copy and read it while I was still teaching in high school.

In the summer of 1913, I went to the University of Wisconsin. I took a course in agricultural economics under H. C. Taylor and a sort of individual seminar course in rural sociology under C. J. Galpin. Galpin had just finished his survey of Walworth County and had its findings on display on a large map in his office. He explained to me and another student how the survey had been made and many of the things that had been found.

After four years of high school [teaching], I was still uncertain whether I wanted to be a college teacher or take up the study of law. I decided I would go to the University of North Carolina and take a master's degree, and make my decision after that. I majored in economics and minored in political science, with a second minor in agricultural economics and rural sociology under E. C. Branson, who had just come to the university from a teachers' college in Georgia. By the end of the year, I had decided I would go into college teaching. Although I had had only twelve hours in sociology, most of which I had had under Ross in summer schools at Wisconsin, I decided that I would prepare to teach in the field of sociology, with special attention to rural sociology. I applied for and received a fellowship in the University of Missouri, and spent two years under Charles A. Ellwood and Luther L. Bernard, serving as Bernard's reading assistant in rural sociology. At the University of Missouri I took all the courses that were offered in agricultural economics and rural sociology, along with courses in general sociology and general economics.

After returning from military service in 1919, I became instructor in sociology at the University of Missouri. During this year I cooperated with Carl Taylor in making a survey of farm tenancy in two counties of southeastern Missouri where farm tenancy ran as high as 90 per cent of the farmers. The report that Carl Taylor, Carle Zimmerman, and I wrote on the tenancy situation in these two counties was so startling and so unbelievable that neither the Missouri College of Agriculture nor the United States Department of Agriculture would publish the bulletin. It lay dormant until Carl Taylor, a decade and a half later, resurrected it and published it in mimeograph form under the title *Rich Land, Poor Man.*[6]

In 1920 I went to Washington State College as assistant professor of agricultural economics and rural sociology. Later I took off one year to go to North Carolina State College as associate professor of agricultural economics and another year to finish my work for the Ph.D. degree at the University of Wisconsin. In my last year of graduate work at Wisconsin, I took all the courses that were offered in agricultural economics and rural sociology as minors along with my major in general sociology under E. A. Ross. I was a fellow under him and assisted him in working up one of his seminar courses on group conflict. I wrote my Ph.D. thesis on the subject "Social Aspects of Farm Tenancy in the United States." Half of the materials that I used for this thesis I had obtained from rural economics and sociological surveys in North Carolina and Missouri.

Carle C. Zimmerman

Zimmerman was born in Raymore, Missouri, in 1897. The following statement describes his education and his early professional years. For a review of his later career, see Chapters 6 and 11.

When I started at Westminster College, Fulton, Missouri, in the fall of 1914, I did not know there was such a thing as sociology or rural sociology. After two years at Westminster, I enrolled in 1916 for summer school at the University of Missouri. There, by accident mostly, I took a class with Luther Lee Bernard, who was teaching in the department with Charles A. Ellwood. I decided to finish my education at the University of Missouri, because, being in a larger community, I could more easily work my way through.

In the fall term of 1916 I registered for all the classes listed under Bernard. To my surprise (and disappointment, at least for a while), the courses were all taught by an unknown person, Carl C. Taylor. However, slowly but surely, I began to recognize the excellent qualities of Taylor. He was a rural sociologist and more a disciple of Thorstein Veblen (then teaching at Missouri) than any sociologist except Charles Horton Cooley.

[After service in World War I] I went [back] to the University of Missouri to finish my B.A. Ellwood hired me as his secretary. Although during World War I, I had changed my mind and decided to be a lawyer, I had beforehand taught myself typing and shorthand. I worked as a secretary only one day when Ellwood promoted me to be his class assistant. At that time Bruce Melvin and Fred Yoder were both doing graduate work in the department.

The spring of 1920, Carl C. Taylor had secured some research funds for

179

field studies of rural tenure and living conditions. His two investigations were to be near the university in Boone County, in the spring months, and in Sikeston, Madrid County, in southeastern Missouri, during the summer of 1920. During the spring of 1920 I had worked with Taylor and had begun to get over my disappointment that Bernard had left. I was intrigued by the method of going out for new information.

That summer Taylor took me and one or two others to Sikeston to do the field work. Fred Yoder was there also, but in the status of supervisor and photographer. We collated the results of our study but the university would not publish them. Later I published some results in a book of mine.[7]

Taylor told me in August 1920 that he had accepted an offer as professor at North Carolina State, and my first request was that he take me along, which he agreed to do. I started working on a master's degree, writing a thesis on standards of living. At the same time I studied sociological theory under Taylor. My first graduate reading was William Graham Sumner's *Folkways*. There were no other courses in the social sciences so I filled out sufficient credit hours in such subjects as English and technical agriculture. I remember taking courses in animal husbandry, including cattle-judging, and in legumes and plant growth.

Taylor had the theory that one first had to become a sociologist, and then, if he so desired, a rural sociologist. I studied the works of Charles Horton Cooley carefully, and I might have read a book by Charles Josiah Galpin; I also studied some agricultural economics. During the first winter Taylor got a small grant from Galpin's division in Washington to help study rural primary groups. I was given the job of doing the field work in rural Wake County, which surrounds Raleigh, the state capital. The result eventually printed was the bulletin on Rural Organization in Wake County. It was an attempt to describe the geographic primary group in Cooley's sense.

In the summer of 1921 Taylor organized a group called the North Carolina Tenancy Commission, which had as its main purpose to find out about the living conditions of sharecroppers and small farmers in the state. Due to my previous experience in Missouri, I was given the main part of the job of making up the schedule and supervising the field work, and later tabulating the material and helping write it up. It served well to give a background for understanding the diverse types of culture in the state. The material was collated in the winter of 1921–22 and published with Taylor and myself as authors.

About that time the prices of cigarette tobacco fell disastrously low. The attempt of the tobacco-growers at organization was grist for my mill. By then I had decided to be a marketing expert. That spring of 1922, without even waiting for graduation, I left immediately for the field for the sign-up campaign. By September the sign-up was completed, and I was offered a job as sort of a traveling field secretary. Although I had agreed to accept an assistantship in sociology with Dwight Sanderson at Cornell University, I resigned it and accepted the position with the tobacco-growers' association. But during that winter I found that the change from academic to business life, no matter how much more remunerative it might be, was not for me. By Christmas of 1922 I had a feeling that I was not going to be happy outside of the academic life, so I took off for Chicago to the meetings of the American Sociological

Society and talked with Bernard. At that time he was a professor at the University of Minnesota.

Bernard gave me to understand that he had sufficient funds at Minnesota to take care of me and that if I would come there in the fall of 1923, I could be an instructor on the sociology staff. I was still awestruck by Bernard. Bernard claimed that Ellwood thought he (Ellwood) was the greatest social thinker since Aristotle, but Bernard was sure that this was not true. Said Bernard, "I am the greatest since Aristotle — not Ellwood." The spring of 1923 finished me with business life. I was made for study and an academic life and that was it. So I decided not to wait until fall but rather to leave North Carolina in June and go to the University of Chicago for preliminary study. Robert E. Park and Ellsworth Faris were the leading professors there. W. I. Thomas was gone. Young Ernest Burgess was around but not teaching that summer. Albion W. Small was retired but working in the library. He was an excellent student of German but he could not read French very well. I had studied French for World War I and felt it a pleasure to help him. I couldn't understand why anyone who could master that difficult sociological German could not also easily read French. However, those few hours in the library enabled me afterward to say that I had studied sociology with the famous Albion W. Small. Chicago was the academic center of sociology at that time.

All at once things began to change. Bernard told me that he had secured a position for me as research assistant in agricultural economics with John D. Black at the University of Minnesota. The fall of 1923 I went to the University of Minnesota. The most I learned that year was in economic theory with F. B. Garver and working for N. S. B. Gras. I had to read economic history, to grade papers in his class. In 1924 I was appointed instructor in sociology. I was also research assistant in agricultural economics. Black asked C. J. Galpin at Washington to allocate money to do fieldwork on a thesis. I made a study of attitudes and practices of cooperative marketing in Minnesota.

I was still both economist and sociologist, veering more toward economics. F. Stuart Chapin, chairman of sociology, asked me to give a seminar in sociology. I agreed to give the seminar but the next day Chapin asked me to give it jointly with a young Russian émigré who had come to the campus — P. A. Sorokin. I agreed because I thought I could learn something as well as get credit for teaching.

I believe it was the challenge of the best of European scholarship, which I met in Sorokin, which finally tipped the scales totally in favor of sociology for me. When I heard Sorokin talk in the seminar, I knew that his training was a standard of scholarship which was challenging. Then or later many persons came to Minnesota to study in that atmosphere.

During this time I had been thinking about rural sociology as a profession and rejecting it. That spring I talked with Garver about making it my profession and he warned me about it, saying it had little prestige and no future. But in the seminar with Sorokin we launched into a study of the city and the country. I found out, to my surprise, that much European literature of the nineteenth century had been about rural-urban differences. In one foray into the library, quite by accident I came upon the book published about 1898 by Adna P. Weber dealing with *The Growth of Cities in the Nineteenth Century*.

This led me into theories of sociology which were based upon the significance of the urbanization process, such as the ideas of George Hanssen, Georges Vacher de Lapouge, Otto Ammon and Livio Livi of Italy, and dozens of others.

At the same time I received an appointment as assistant professor at Minnesota with half my time at the St. Paul [agricultural] campus and half at Minneapolis. Thus began some very fruitful years of writing, research on family budgets, studies of the changing structure of trading communities, using business listings such as those of Dun and Bradstreet, and a thousand other things. But the one overriding consideration was a work which later became four volumes, the *Principles of Rural-Urban Sociology* and the *Systematic Source Book in Rural Sociology*. These works arose out of that seminar in which Sorokin and I had joint responsibility. I had originally conceived these books late in 1924 or early 1925 after finding how rich and how controversial the field had been in Europe. I proposed to Sorokin in this seminar that we together examine this field.

By 1927 we had done not one, not two, but actually three volumes of writing. I had no idea that anyone unsubsidized could publish that amount of material. So I proposed that we ask Galpin if his office would subsidize the work. Galpin asked me to meet him at Michigan State the summer of 1927 at the American Country Life Association meeting where we could talk. I thought that this meant acceptance so I was overjoyed.

We celebrated the Country Life Conference by a picnic in the center of the campus to which everyone brought a basket of food. I arrived there just after talking with Galpin, who had turned down the idea of a subvention for publishing our work. He not only turned it down but deprecated the idea. [My friends the Eduard C.] Lindemans fed me on all the fried chicken I could eat and then Eduard said that he could raise five hundred dollars for us. We could take the money and buy two typewriters, cut down the manuscript to one volume, and publish it as a text. I took the money and returned to Minneapolis, where Sorokin and I purchased our first two portable typewriters through the university. I still have mine.

The textbook *Principles of Rural-Urban Sociology* was published by Henry Holt. After it came out and had been in circulation awhile, I heard that Galpin was coming to Minnesota on an official visit. Galpin had read the *Principles* and was very enthusiastic. He had changed his mind about the *Systematic Source Book*. Now he wanted the whole three volumes published. Finally at the end of the first day his plan came out. The new scheme was for Galpin's office to put up money for the preparation of the manuscript and some translations and the University of Minnesota Agricultural Experiment Station was to subsidize the publication by the University of Minnesota Press. However, the books were now to be published under the joint names of only Sorokin and Galpin. This was Galpin's idea.

This hit me like a bolt of lightning. However, I had counted the chickens too early. Dean Walter C. Coffey, later president of the University of Minnesota, simply said, "no books without Zimmerman." So after a sleepless night I found my way back into the *Source Book*. And when it was published, since the work was all done by Sorokin and myself, I became the second author.[8]

Carl Cleveland Taylor

Taylor, it will be recalled from Chapter 6, was born in 1884 and grew up on an Iowa farm. He received his B.A. degree from Drake University in Des Moines in 1911, his M.A. from the University of Texas in 1914, and his Ph.D. from the University of Missouri in 1917. The following account was prepared in 1950 at the request of Howard W. Odum for inclusion in his *American Sociology*.[9]

As a boy working on the farm until I was almost 20 years of age, never having seen inside a high school, I became tremendously appalled with my lack of intelligence about society and the world. Undoubtedly the things that developed this state of mind were a father who had done some college work away back around 1860, a brother 13 years older than I who had not only completed his undergraduate work but gone into graduate work, and intelligent persons who visited my father in our home — ministers, Chautauqua speakers, editors of farm journals, etc. I therefore decided to leave the farm and study for the ministry. I know no other reason for selecting this profession than that my older brother had pursued it and probably because the majority of the above-normal intelligent persons who visited our home were ministers. In my experience they were the people who saw beyond and reached beyond the local horizons in their conversations with Dad.

When I left the farm, I entered a preparatory department of college and spent three years completing high school work. I had not completed my preparatory work before I became convinced that other fields than the ministry would lead me much further in the understanding of the world and society. I took all the courses in sociology that were available in my undergraduate days but took an even greater number of courses in philosophy, because more courses in that field were available. It was during the first year after my undergraduate work, while I was teaching public speaking at the University of Texas — not too onerous a task — that I read more widely in the fields of philosophy and sociology and decided to do graduate work in sociology. I went into sociology because it was more apprehensible, more graspable. The next summer (1912) I went to the University of Missouri for graduate work and the summer following to Columbia University. Peculiarly enough, I went to the University of Missouri primarily because of men who were teaching in the two fields which I expected to pursue as minors, namely [Herbert J.] Davenport and Veblen in economics and Max Meyer in psychology.

I suppose the reason I selected rural sociology, although there literally was no rural sociology when I made the decision, was my own background on the farm. I remember saying to Clarence Yokum, head of the department of psychology and philosophy at the University of Texas, where I took my Master's degree in psychology in 1914, that I was going to be a rural sociologist. He said "There isn't any such thing as rural sociology, is there? and there may never be." I replied that everything that I had seen from boyhood to that moment convinced me that what I had learned about psychology and sociology needed to be applied to an analysis of rural life. The only rural sociology course I could take at the University of Missouri, or for that matter any place else at that time (1914) was Dr. L. L. Bernard's graduate seminar in which each student followed his separate topic or thesis. I took that course and outlined what I thought were thirty-two lectures in rural sociology. It was the only rural sociology course I ever had, except to audit Kenyon Butterfield's course in rural organization at Massachusetts State College of Agriculture while I was teaching economics and sociology at Mt. Holyoke College in the spring of 1916.

Whether warranted or not, I would like to be featured as a social or cultural psychologist working in the laboratory of rural life. I probably also am thought of by my colleagues as a person who is interested in the practical application of social knowledge. I think I somewhat resent the notion that this interest compromises me as a professional sociologist. My own conviction is that this interest makes me a realist in the correct use of that term. I know that my experience with practical affairs has driven me to a conviction that men of practical affairs have a lot of social knowledge. I should like, therefore, to be featured as a sociologist who is definitely convinced that social knowledge is validated by folk experience and practical effective behavior in everyday human affairs as well as by so-called scientific procedures. Because this conviction is based, I believe, upon social observations, I am convinced that good sociology must be a combination of science and common sense.

Lowry Nelson

At the risk of being charged with immodesty, I decided to include a brief account of my own experiences. My drifting has probably been more circuitous than that of the other men whose statements are included here.

My early ambition was to be a farmer. After my graduation from high school, it was therefore natural for me to go to the Utah State Agricultural College in the fall of 1913. I majored in agronomy and minored in chemistry. I took the one course offered in sociology, taught by the professor of economics. Giddings' text was used.

My advisor and the chairman of the department of agronomy was Franklin S. Harris, who had received his degree from Cornell University in 1911. He was destined to have a marked influence on my career. I have often wondered why, on various occasions, he placed in my hands books by Bailey and Butterfield, along with the bulletins by Galpin which were appearing during this period of my student days (1913–16). I am convinced that Harris himself had been deeply influenced by the so-called Country Life Movement and by the work and spirit of Bailey and others at Cornell University. Harris showed me one time the notes that he had taken in a course at Cornell on the economics of agriculture given by G. N. Lauman. It is almost as if he were a frustrated rural economist or sociologist himself and was projecting his ambition on me.

Nevertheless, I graduated as a major in agronomy in 1916 and like my fellow graduates was looking for a job as an instructor in agriculture in a high school. From that point on until 1923, my vocational meandering was something to behold. I was successively secretary to the newly named president of the college from August 1916 to December 1917; assistant state leader of county agents from December 1917 to March 1919; county agricultural agent from March to December 1919; fieldman for a sugar company during 1920; editor of the *Utah Farmer* during 1921 and 1922. In the latter year I served half time as editor and half time as director (and organizer) of the extension division of Brigham Young University, of which Harris had been appointed president.

In 1923 a crucial thing happened. A close friend invited me to go with him to attend the summer school at the Southern Branch of the University of California, at Los Angeles (later to metamorphose into U.C.L.A.). One of the instructors was to be C. J. Galpin. We enrolled for Galpin's two courses, one based on his *Rural Life*, which had appeared in 1918, and the other on *Rural Social Problems*, which was yet to be published. It was in that course that I first heard of the neighborhood studies of Kolb, Sanderson, and Taylor and Zimmerman.

One morning after class Galpin invited my friend and me to come to his apartment in the afternoon for a visit. I presume he did this with other members of the class as well. In the course of this conversation Galpin asked, "What would you men like to do?" I immediately answered that I would like to make a study of a Utah village. I presume I used the word "community" because nobody called these places villages; they were called towns. I believe I was the first to call them villages. Galpin's response was immediate and, I think, as I reflect now, rather enthusiastic. He said, "That's fine, I think I can help you with a little money. When you get back to your university prepare for me a statement of the project; that is, what you would like to do, make out a questionnaire that you propose to use, and send it to me in Washington. I will then seek the approval of the president of the agricultural college, which is necessary since you are connected with a private institution." Approval was given, and the study of Escalante was begun in October 1923.

In February 1924 I left for the University of Wisconsin with the Escalante schedules in hand and the study partly written up. It was used as thesis for the M.S. degree, which was granted in October 1924. While in Madison, I met T. Lynn Smith, who decided to begin his college work at Brigham Young that fall. Subsequently, the farm village of Ephraim was studied in 1925 and that of American Fork in 1927–28. Lynn Smith assisted with both of them. Nathan L. Whetten, who had majored in languages for the B.A. degree at Brigham Young, decided to switch to sociology and did his thesis on one aspect of the American Fork study, the participation of the population in church organizations.

It is worth pointing out perhaps that one did not major in anything called rural sociology for a higher degree at Wisconsin in 1924. Sociology was a part of economics, and agricultural economics was likewise a part of the department of economics and sociology. The only work I had with Kolb was a seminar. My other courses were in marketing with Theodore Macklin, agricultural economics with B. H. Hibbard, economic institutions with Richard T. Ely, a seminar in economic theory, and a course in economic statistics.

I cannot honestly say that I made any deliberate choices in what I was going to do with my life. It seems in retrospect a matter of pure chance that events during and immediately following World War I happened in such a way that I found myself in contact with Galpin and that he was interested enough in what he later spoke of in his memoirs as a "unique sidelight on American farm life" to encourage me in these studies. That contact was a crucial one and because of it I became irrevocably committed to the field of rural sociology.

NOTES AND INDEX

Notes

THE following abbreviations have been used: AFS, Agricultural Experiment Station; AJS, American Journal of Sociology; ASR, American Sociological Review; RS, Rural Sociology; SF, Social Forces (formerly the Journal of Social Forces).

Historical Studies of Rural Sociology

Two valuable studies of the development of rural sociology are available. T. Lynn Smith's *Rural Sociology: A Trend Report*, occupies the entire issue of *Current Sociology*, Vol. VI, No. 1, published by UNESCO (Paris, 1957). This report includes a valuable 58-page bibliography. A second work of importance is Edmund deS. Brunner's *The Growth of a Science: A Half-Century of Rural Sociological Research in the United States* (New York: Harper, 1957), which contains a selected bibliography. All who undertake historical studies are indebted to the late W. A. Anderson for his comprehensive *Bibliography of Researchers in Rural Sociology*, Cornell AES Rural Sociology Publication No. 52 (1957). This bibliography is marred by many errors and unnecessary repetition, but it nevertheless remains one of the best in existence.

Several articles in *Rural Sociology* have dealt with the history of the field. Particularly noteworthy is Otis Durant Duncan's "Rural Sociology Coming of Age," *RS*, 19:1–12 (March 1954). Charles R. Hoffer discusses the evolution of research in "The Development of Rural Sociology," *RS*, 26:1–14 (March 1961). Other articles of more limited scope include: Paul H. Landis, "Development of Rural Sociology in the United States," in his *Rural Life in Process* (New York: McGraw-Hill, 1940), pp. 573–77; C. E. Lively, "Rural Sociology as an Applied Science," *RS*, 8:331–42 (December 1943); Lowry Nelson, "Constructing Rural Sociology," *RS*, 9:219–25 (September 1944); W. A. Anderson, "Rural Sociology as Science," *RS*, 12:347–56 (December 1947); C. Horace Hamilton, "Some Current Problems in the

Development of Rural Sociology," *RS*, 15:315–21 (December 1950); Paul J. Jehlik, "Rural Sociology and Sociological Reality: An Appraisal," *RS*, 29:355–66 (December 1964).

Helpful as a reference work is Ann Garver Olmsted, "A Critical Review of the Research in Rural Sociology" (dissertation, University of Minnesota, 1954), which reviews representative studies from 1900 to the early 1950s.

Chapter 1. The Social Climate

1. For a discussion of agricultural conditions at the end of the century, see John D. Hicks, *The Populist Revolt* (Minneapolis: University of Minnesota Press, 1931), Chaps. 1–3. For the quotation see p. 84; for farm mortgages, p. 24; and for crop liens, p. 44.

2. Quoted in Carl C. Taylor, *The Farmers' Movement, 1820–1920* (New York: American Book Co., 1950), p. 226.

3. On the Grange and other farm organizations, see Taylor, *Farmers' Movement*, and Solon J. Buck, *The Granger Crusade* (Cambridge: Harvard University Press, 1913).

4. For accounts of this movement see Hicks, *Populist Revolt*, and Taylor, *Farmers' Movement*.

5. Henry C. and Anne Dewees Taylor, *The Story of Agricultural Economics in the United States, 1840–1932* (Ames: Iowa State College Press, 1952), Chap. 3. The quotation from Ward is on p. 44. Before the organization of the American Sociological Association in 1905, sociologists joined the American Economic Association, which had been formed in 1885.

6. *Ibid.*, p. 35.

7. See Richard Hofstadter, *Social Darwinism in American Thought, 1860–1915* (Philadelphia: University of Pennsylvania Press, 1944).

8. On Henderson, see Chapter 3, below. Other sociologists, notably Lester F. Ward, were devastating critics of Spencer.

9. Quoted in Hofstadter, *Social Darwinism*, p. 34.

10. *The New Era or the Coming Kingdom* (New York: Baker and Taylor, 1893).

11. Garland, *Main-Travelled Roads* (New York: Harper, 1930), pp. xiii–xiv.

12. Quoted in Henry Nash Smith, *Virgin Land: The American West as Symbol and Myth* (Cambridge: Harvard University Press, 1950), p. 253.

13. See Pinchot, *The Fight for Conservation* (New York: Doubleday, Page, 1910), and *Breaking New Ground* (New York: Harcourt, Brace, 1947).

14. Philip Dorf, *Liberty Hyde Bailey: An Informal Portrait* (Ithaca, N.Y.: Cornell University Press, 1956), p. 154. For the quotation, see the *New York Times*, July 13, 1910, which gives an account of a meeting between L. H. Bailey and Roosevelt.

15. *Theodore Roosevelt: An Autobiography* (New York: Scribner, 1924), pp. 413–14.

16. Margaret Digby, *Horace Plunkett: An Anglo-American Irishman* (Oxford: Blackwell, 1949), pp. 121–22.

17. *Ibid.*, p. 124.

18. For the quotation, see *ibid.*, p. 124.

19. *Report of the Commission on Country Life* (New York: Sturgis and Walton, 1911), pp. 49–58. Of the 550,000 "circulars of questions" sent out, said the report, "about 115,000 persons have now replied. . . . Nearly 100,000 . . . have been arranged and some of the information tabulated . . . by the Census Bureau." (Pp. 54–55.)

20. Digby, *Plunkett*, p. 126.

21. Dorf, *ibid.*, p. 153. The report was published routinely as *Senate Document*

No. 705, 60th Congress, 2d session. It was not generally available to the public until the Sturgis and Walton edition of 1911, although the Spokane, Washington, Chamber of Commerce had earlier made a reprint "for use in the country life movement in the Northwest," according to a statement by L. H. Bailey in the Sturgis-Walton edition. I have been unable to locate a copy of the Spokane reprint or to verify the date.

22. For the summary, see *Report*, 17–31.

23. For an excellent treatment of this period, see Richard Hofstadter, *The Age of Reform: From Bryan to F.D.R.* (New York: Vintage Books, 1955).

24. Hofstee, "Rural Sociology in Europe," *RS*, 28:329–30 (December 1963).

25. An exception to the rural stability of Europe was Ireland, devastated by the potato famine of 1846–51. This catastrophe led to the development of a nationwide cooperative movement, and, as has been noted, a leader of it, Sir Horace Plunkett, was important in the development of rural sociology in the United States.

Chapter 2. The Herald-Evangelists of Rural Life

1. The idea of applying the word "herald" to these men came from Albion W. Small and George E. Vincent (*An Introduction to the Study of Society* — New York: American Book Co., 1894), who used the term in their evaluations of the importance of August Comte.

2. For biographical information, see Dorf, *Liberty Hyde Bailey*, p. 153.

3. *Ibid.*, p. 244.

4. *The Holy Earth* (New York: Scribner, 1915), p. 61. Other books of interest on this aspect of his thinking are *The State and the Farmer* (New York: Macmillan, 1908); *The Outlook to Nature* (New York: Macmillan, 1908); and *The Country-Life Movement* (New York: Macmillan, 1920).

5. *Outlook to Nature*, p. 87.

6. *Ibid.*, p. 55.

7. *Country-Life Movement*, pp. 19, 20.

8. *Outlook to Nature*, p. 93.

9. *Country-Life Movement*, p. 61.

10. *Ibid.*, p. 63.

11. *The State and the Farmer*, pp. 148–49.

12. *Ibid.*, p. 97.

13. Bailey rarely referred to either rural sociology or agricultural economics as college disciplines. The only specific reference I have found occurs in the *Cyclopedia of American Agriculture* (4:437): "These subjects are practically untouched although the terms 'rural economics' and 'rural sociology' are coming into the curricula of the colleges of agriculture . . . These subjects are in many ways the most important that fall to the field of colleges of agriculture. . . ."

14. There is no formal biography of Butterfield, but see *Who Was Who in America* (Chicago: Marquis, 1943) and *Dictionary of American Biography*, Vol. 21, Supplement One (New York: Scribner, 1944).

15. Butterfield's other books were *The Country Church and the Rural Problem* (Chicago: University of Chicago Press, 1911), *The Farmer and the New Day* (New York: Macmillan, 1919), and *A Christian Program for the Rural Community* (Nashville, Tenn.: Publishing House of the M. E. Church South, 1923).

16. *Chapters in Rural Progress*, pp. 9, 15.

17. *Ibid.*, pp. 5–7.

18. *Ibid.*, pp. 17, 19.

19. *Ibid.*, p. 183.

20. *Ibid.*, pp. 181, 199, 200. Unlike Bailey, Butterfield favored consolidated schools. (See *The Farmer and the New Day*, p. 145.) The truth of his comments on educa-

tion has been discovered anew by students and administrators of foreign-aid programs for economic growth in underdeveloped countries. There is wide agreement that the most important first step in promoting economic development is a massive investment in "human capital." This is also the basic approach of the domestic "war on poverty" program. See C. Arnold Anderson and Mary Jean Bowman, eds., *Education and Economic Development* (Chicago: Aldine, 1965).

21. *Chapters in Rural Progress*, pp. 200–1.

22. *Ibid.*, p. 203.

23. American Academy of Political and Social Sciences, *Annals*, 40:13–18 (March 1912).

Chapter 3. The Academic Milieu

1. Howard W. Odum, ed., *American Masters of Social Science* (New York: Holt, 1927), p. 5.

2. *Ibid.*, p. 131.

3. On Adams and the early days at Johns Hopkins, see John M. Vincent, "Herbert B. Adams," *ibid.*, pp. 99–127. Among the Johns Hopkins studies, the following titles should be mentioned: Adams' *The Germanic Origin of New England Towns* and *Village Communities of Cape Ann and Salem*, both in *Johns Hopkins University Studies*, Vol. 1 (1882); C. M. Andrews, *River Towns of Connecticut*, Vol. 7 (1889); and in Vol. 4 (1886): Irving Elting, *Dutch Village Communities on the Hudson River*; Melville Eggleston, *The Land System of the New England Colonies*; William P. Holcomb, *Pennsylvania Boroughs*.

4. Richard T. Ely, *Ground Under Our Feet* (New York: Macmillan, 1938), p. 179.

5. *Ibid.*, p. 192.

6. *Ibid.*, p. 79.

7. On Small, see Edward C. Hayes, "Albion Woodbury Small," in Odum, *American Masters of Social Science*, pp. 149–87.

8. The four chapters constitute Book II, which, according to the authors, introduced "an anonymous but not fictitious western settlement" (p. 367). Vincent's interest in the sociology of rural life is also indicated by the fact that he chose it for the theme of the 1916 meeting of the American Sociological Society, of which he was then president. For additional evidence of his rural interest, see Lowry Nelson, "On George Edgar Vincent: Rural Social Scientist," *RS*, 31:478–82 (December 1966).

9. On Henderson's 1894 course, see Dwight Sanderson, "The Teaching of Rural Sociology: Particularly in Land-Grant Colleges and Universities," in American Sociological Society, *Proceedings*, 10:181 (1916). Henderson taught a course on "Rural Communities" in 1899–1900, according to a communication received from the late John M. Gillette, who was a student of Henderson.

10. Quoted by Sanderson, in American Sociological Society, *Proceedings*, 10:437 (1916).

11. Biographical material has been taken from a leaflet, "Community Memorial Meeting in Honor of Charles Richmond Henderson, April 11, 1915," in the possession of the author.

12. Quoted by Taylor and Taylor, *Story of Agricultural Economics*, p. 35. See also Lowry Nelson, "The Rise of Rural Sociology," in *RS*, 30:407–27 (December 1965).

13. Sims's comments, here and below, were made in a letter to the author.

14. Quoted in Taylor and Taylor, *Story of Agricultural Economics*, p. 79.

15. *Ibid.*, pp. 89, 90.

16. For example, in his *Agricultural Economics* (New York: Macmillan, 1919),

Taylor defined the field of agricultural economics and said it included the "problems of . . . farm life" (p. vii). Some thirty years later he recalled the time "when
I was objecting to the word 'sociology' and stressing the phrase 'rural life.'" See his
article, "The Development of Rural Life Studies at the University of Wisconsin," in
RS, Vol. 6, No. 3 (September 1941).

17. Carl W. Thompson and Gustav P. Warber, *Social and Economic Survey of a
Rural Township in Southern Minnesota* (1913); Louis D. Harvell Weld, *Social and
Economic Survey of a Community in the Red River Valley* (1915); Warber, *Social
and Economic Survey of a Community in Northeastern Minnesota* (1915).

18. Sanderson, in American Sociological Society, *Proceedings*, 10:181 (1916).

19. American Sociological Society, *Papers and Proceedings*, 1916, p. 163.

Chapter 4. Charles Josiah Galpin

1. Biographical information has been taken from Galpin's modest and sprightly
memoir, *My Drift into Rural Sociology* (Baton Rouge: Louisiana State University
Press, 1938).

2. *Ibid.*, p. 6.

3. *Ibid.*, p. 17.

4. *Ibid.*, pp. 21–22.

5. Published as Wisconsin AES Research Bulletin No. 34 (1915). A preface for
the bulletin, written at Galpin's request by E. A. Ross, professor of sociology, was
deleted by the dean with the comment: "What has Ross got to do with anything in
the College of Agriculture?" The incident typified the isolation of many an agricultural college from the rest of its university during that period. A similar lack of integration existed at the University of Minnesota until George E. Vincent became president in 1911.

6. Galpin, *Rural Life* (New York: Century, 1923), pp. 70, 71. Much of the contents of the bulletin was repeated in this book, which has been cited in the expectation that it would be more accessible.

7. *Ibid.*, pp. 86–87.

8. Warren H. Wilson, *The Evolution of the Country Community* (Boston: Pilgrim
Press, 1912), p. 91. Wilson acknowledges his indebtedness for this definition to Wil-
let M. Hays. L. D. H. Weld used a similar concept; see the frontispiece map of his
Social and Economic Survey of a Community in the Red River Valley (1915).

9. The study was published as Wisconsin AES Bulletin No. 234 (1914). The idea
for this bulletin was conceived in 1912, but Galpin also had the Walworth County
project under way and publication of *Rural Social Centers* was apparently delayed
for this reason.

10. Wisconsin AES Bulletin No. 278 (1917); Bulletin No. 288 (1918); and Research Bulletin No. 44 (1919).

11. Galpin, *My Drift into Rural Sociology*, p. 20.

12. The name of the division underwent several changes, becoming the Division
of Farm Population and Rural Life Studies and later the Division of Farm Population and Rural Welfare. In the reorganization of the Department of Agriculture in
1953, it lost its status as a division within the Bureau of Agricultural Economics
(which was itself abolished) and became a branch of the department's Economic
Research Division. Since that time its work has been almost wholly limited to population studies. As of 1968, the program is referred to as the Human Resources
Branch of the Economic Development Division of the Department of Agriculture.

13. *My Drift into Rural Sociology*, p. 49.

14. *The Standard of Life in a Typical Section of Diversified Farming*, Cornell University AES Bulletin No. 423 (1923). This was apparently the first published study
of the subject. Carl C. Taylor reports that in 1920–21 Carle C. Zimmerman wrote

his master's thesis at North Carolina State College on "The Rural Standard of Living." See Taylor's *Rural Sociology* (New York: Harper, 1933), p. 169.

15. *The Farmer's Standard of Living* (New York: Century, 1929).

16. Galpin, *My Drift into Rural Sociology*, p. 54.

17. *Ibid.*, p. 40.

18. *Rural Life*, pp. 359–60.

19. C. J. Galpin and Veda B. Larson, *Farm Population of Selected Counties* (Washington, D.C.: Government Printing Office, 1924). The eight counties were: Otsego, N.Y., Dane, Wis., New Madrid and Scott, Mo., Cass, N.D., Wake, N.C., Ellis, Texas, and King, Wash.

20. Kolb, *Rural Primary Groups: A Study of Agricultural Neighborhoods*, Wisconsin AES Bulletin No. 51 (1921).

21. *Ibid.*, pp. 5–6.

22. *Rural Social Organization: A Study of Primary Groups in Wake County, N.C.*, North Carolina AES Bulletin No. 245 (1922), p. 31. The field work was done by Zimmerman.

23. *Ibid.*, p. 30.

24. *The Social Areas of Otsego County*, Cornell University AES Bulletin No. 422 (1923), p. 11. This statement is reminiscent of the point made by Zimmerman and Taylor, that "name" communities were not necessarily indicative of groups in the sociological sense.

25. Furthermore, the authors, after concluding that the neighborhood was disappearing as a social unit, noted a distinction "between the rural neighborhood as a social unit, and the neighborliness of farm people. . . . as long as farmers own their places and are not frequently shifting, the nature of their work compels a certain amount of neighborliness." How the neighborhood could disappear as a "social unit," but still remain as an entity because of the "neighborliness of farm people," is an unresolved question. So too is the question of what a neighborhood actually is.

26. *Rural Population Groups*, Missouri AES Research Bulletin No. 74 (1925), p. 10.

27. *Ibid.*, p. 16.

28. It is indicative of the vagueness of sociological concepts, especially in the early development of the science, that the word "community" was used to refer to several different social groups. It was applied variously to neighborhoods, "name" communities, and social areas, as well as to the trade-area rurban concept of Galpin. Indeed, the definition of community is still a problem for sociologists.

Chapter 5. Church and Lay Organizations

1. Information about the publication of these surveys is difficult to find and has not been considered necessary for the purposes of this book. Vogt was instrumental in organizing the Ohio Rural Life Survey, which covered practically the entire state and produced information on several thousand rural churches. It became the basis for C. O. Gill and Gifford Pinchot, *Six Thousand Rural Churches* (New York: Macmillan, 1920). See Vogt's *Introduction to Rural Sociology* (New York: Appleton, 1918), pp. 297ff.

See also Allen Eaton and Shelby M. Harrison, *Bibliography of Social Surveys* (New York: Russell Sage Foundation, 1930), which lists several scores of rural surveys published between 1911 and 1924 and covering nearly half the states.

2. Earl Taylor, head of the Foreign Mission Board of the Methodist Church, and Ralph Diffendorfer, head of its Home Missions Work, were active in promoting a united Protestant campaign, according to Edmund deS. Brunner (letter of September 25, 1965, to the author). See also C. O. Gill, "Interdenominational Cooperation," in American Sociological Society, *Publications*, 1916, pp. 106–12.

3. "The Interchurch World Movement," *The Outlook*, 122:58 (May–August 1919).

4. Earp, "Sociological Evaluation of the Interchurch Movement," in American Sociological Society, *Papers and Proceedings*, 15:74–89. A professor of sociology at Drew Theological Seminary, Earp was the author of a number of books, including *The Rural Church Movement*, *The Rural Church Serving the Community*, and *Rural Social Organizations*. Besides Earp's evaluation of the movement and reports in magazines and newspapers at the time of its demise, there is an extensive manuscript history in the library of Union Theological Seminary, according to information supplied by Benson Y. Landis, but which I have not seen.

5. "Why the Interchurch Movement Failed," *Literary Digest*, 66:42–43 (August 7, 1920); "Discussing the 'Collapse' of the Interchurch Movement," *Current Opinion*, 69:221–22 (August 1920).

6. Federal Council of Churches of Christ in America, *Information Service*, Vol. 8, No. 41 (November 16, 1929).

7. Among the resulting publications were "A Church and Community Survey of Salem County, New Jersey," "A Church and Community Survey of Pend Oreille County, Washington," "Church Life in the Rural South" — all by Brunner; Edmund and Mary V. Brunner, *Irrigation and Religion* (New York: Doran, 1922); Brunner and H. N. Morse, *The Town and Country Church in the United States* (New York: Doran, 1923). The last volume is a summary of the results of the county surveys. Biographical information about Brunner can be found in the Appendix, below.

8. An early publication in the village series was C. Luther Fry, *Diagnosing the Rural Church; A Study in Method* (New York: Doran, 1924). This was a pioneering attempt to apply new methods of analysis, including statistical correlation, to the study of religious institutions. Other books in the series included Fry, *A Census Analysis of American Villages* and *American Villagers* (New York: Doran, 1925 and 1926) — the first analyses of census data on villages; Brunner, Gwendolyn Hughes, and Marjorie Patten, *American Agricultural Villages* (New York: Doubleday, Doran, 1927); Brunner, *Village Communities* (New York: Doran, 1927). The last volume was a summarization of the village series.

9. Brunner, *Village Communities*, p. 27.

10. Brunner and J. H. Kolb, *Rural Social Trends* (New York: McGraw-Hill, 1933); Brunner and Irving Lorge, *Rural Trends in Depression Years* (New York: Columbia University Press, 1937).

11. Brunner, *Immigrant Farmers and Their Children* (New York: Doubleday, Doran, 1929), pp. vii, 277. Part II of the book consisted of special studies of four immigrant communities: Castle Hayne, N.C., Askov, Minn., Petersburg, Va., and Sunderland, Mass. They were written by Robert W. McCollock, David Lloyd, Nels Anderson, and Theodore Abel, respectively.

12. Brunner to the author, September 25, 1965. The work of Douglass is of interest to rural sociologists not only because of his studies of churches — largely but not entirely city and metropolitan institutions — but also because of his pioneer study of suburbanization. His *The Little Town* (1919) is discussed in Chapter 9, below. It is worth noting that the National Council of Churches has established in New York City the Harlan Paul Douglass Collection of Religious Research Studies, which includes some 80 titles by Douglass, along with a substantial number of other studies and publications.

13. Carl C. Taylor, "Country Life Movement," in *Encyclopedia of the Social Sciences*, 4:497–98. See also Bailey, *The Country-Life Movement*. For a discussion of the influence of the country life movement on textbooks in rural sociology, see Chapter 9, below.

14. For the quotation, see American Country Life Association, *Rural Health: Proceedings of the Second National Country Life Conference*, 1919, p. 219. In the

first years of the organization, the annual meeting was called the National Country Life Conference. At some time in the 1930s it became the American Country Life Conference and finally the National Rural Forum. *Rural America* began publication with the March-April issue of 1923 and ended in May 1941. Vols. 1 and 2 have the title of *Country Life Bulletin*. It was issued monthly except during the summer. Benson Y. Landis served as editor and the early sociologists were prominent contributors.

15. *Proceedings*, 1919, p. 209.

16. The full financial history of the organization is impossible to reconstruct. Only certain volumes of the *Proceedings*, such as those for 1926 and 1934, contain reports on finances. The office files of the association disappeared sometime after its dissolution and my efforts to locate them have proved unavailing. My personal files included the mimeographed reports (including financial statements) of the executive secretary for 1940–41, when I was an officer of the organization; these and a few other items once in my possession are now in the archives of rural sociology in the library of the University of Missouri.

17. The members of the committee were Floyd Reeves, professor of education, University of Chicago, and chairman of the Advisory Committee on Education, Washington, D.C.; Mabel Carney, professor of rural education, Teachers College, Columbia University; Leo M. Favrot, General Education Board, Baton Rouge, La.; Agnes Samuelson, Des Moines, Iowa, former president of the National Education Association; Maurice L. Seay, professor of education, University of Kentucky; J. F. Waddell, assistant state superintendent of schools, Wisconsin; Roscoe Pulliam, president of State Teachers College, Carbondale, Ill.; Lowry Nelson, professor of sociology, University of Minnesota; Mrs. Raymond Sayre, Ackworth, Iowa.

Among the tangible outcomes of the committee's work were a book by the executive director, Iman Elsie Schatzman, *The Country School* (Chicago: University of Chicago Press, 1942); and an article by Lowry Nelson, "Education in a Changing Rural Life," in Nelson B. Henry, ed., *Education in Rural Communities* (University of Chicago Press, 1952), pp. 6–47.

18. The association lived on, in name at least, as a council in which membership was held by organizations rather than individuals. Since World War II, it has continued to hold annual meetings.

19. The association, of course, was not a farm organization, nor was it ever meant to be; its goal was to solve farm problems, particularly social ones. It was never able to establish a broad base of membership among farm people.

Chapter 6. Sending Down the Roots

1. Sanderson, *Relation of Community Areas to Town Government in the State of New York*, with Chester R. Wasson, Cornell University AES Bulletin No. 555 (1933); *Social and Economic Areas of Broome County, New York, 1928*, No. 559 (1933); *Rural Social and Economic Areas in Central New York*, No. 614 (1934); *Locating the Rural Community*, No. 413 (1939).

2. Sanderson, *A Survey of Sickness in Rural Areas in Cortland County, New York*, Cornell AES Memoir No. 112 (1929).

3. New York: Harcourt, Brace, 1922.

4. New York: Wiley, 1942. Sanderson's other books include *The Rural Community* (New York: Ginn, 1932); *Rural Community Organization*, with Robert A. Polson (New York: Wiley, 1939); *Leadership for Rural Life* (New York: Association Press, 1940). The March 1946 issue of *RS* was in large part devoted to a discussion and evaluation of Sanderson's work.

5. See his "Group Description" and "A Preliminary Group Classification Based on Structure," *SF*, 16:309–19 (March 1938) and 17:196–201 (October 1938).

6. Sanderson, "Scientific Research in Rural Sociology," *AJS*, 33:181–82 (September 1927).

7. W. A. Anderson, *Bibliography of the Department of Rural Sociology, Cornell University*, Cornell University AES (May 1953). See also an address made by O. F. Larson at Cornell's Fiftieth Anniversary dinner (1965).

8. Anderson coined the word *Hurelures* from the phrase "Human Relationship Structures." In Anderson's system the phrase comprehended small groups, formal organizations, institutions, collectivities, and ecological entities. The following titles are representative of his work: *Mobility of Rural Families*, I and II, Cornell AES Bulletin Nos. 607 (1934) and 623 (1935); *Rural Youth: Activities, Interests and Problems*, I and II, Cornell AES Bulletin Nos. 649 (1936) and 661 (1937); *The Social Participation of Farm Families*, with Hans Plambeck, Cornell AES Department of Rural Sociology Bulletin No. 8 (1943); *A Study of Values in Rural Living*, Part I, Cornell AES Memoir No. 277 (1947) — the first of a seven-part series, some numbers of which were mimeographed bulletins of the Department of Rural Sociology.

9. Kolb, *Service Relations of Town and Country*, Wisconsin AES Research Bulletin No. 58 (1923); *Service Institutions for Town and Country*, No. 66 (1925). Both studies were cooperative with Galpin.

10. Kolb and Charles J. Bornman, *Rural Religious Organization*, Wisconsin AES Research Bulletin No. 60 (1924).

11. Kolb and Arthur F. Wileden, *Special Interest Groups in Rural Society*, Wisconsin AES Research Bulletin No. 84 (1927). The coauthor was a native of Wisconsin who took his B.S. and M.S. degrees from the University of Wisconsin. He was the first extension rural sociologist in the state. His major concern was the translation of rural sociology into usefulness to agricultural extension service personnel and to the communities of the state.

12. Kolb and Wileden, *Rural Community Organization Handbook*, Wisconsin AES Bulletin No. 384 (1926).

13. Kolb and Wileden, *Making Rural Organization Effective*, Wisconsin AES Bulletin No. 403 (1928).

14. Kolb, *Emerging Rural Communities: Group Relations in Rural Society, A Review of Wisconsin Research in Action* (Madison: University of Wisconsin Press, 1959), p. 5.

15. For this quotation and the following one, see *ibid.*, p. 7.

16. *Ibid.*, p. 13.

17. See p. 39, above.

18. Kirkpatrick, John H. Kolb, Creagh Inge, and Arthur F. Wileden, *Rural Organizations and the Family*, Wisconsin AES Research Bulletin No. 96 (1929); Kirkpatrick, Rosalind Tough, and Mary L. Cowles, *How Farm Families Meet the Emergency*, No. 126 (1935); Kirkpatrick, *et al.*, *The Life Cycle of the Farm Family*, No. 121 (1934).

19. Bernard's publications on rural themes include "A Theory of Rural Attitudes," *AJS*, 22:630–49 (March 1917); "Education of the Rural Ministry," *School and Society*, 11:68–73 (January 17, 1920); "Research Problems in the Psychology of Rural Life," *SF*, 4:446–53 (March 1925); "A Classification of Environments," *AJS*, 30: 318–22 (November 1925); "Research in Rural Social Control," American Sociological Society, *Publications*, 19:249–59 (December 1925); "The Fundamental Values in Farm Life," *South Atlantic Quarterly*, 27:142–60 (April 1928); "Standards of Living and Planes of Living," *SF*, 7:190–202 (December 1928).

In addition to the names mentioned in the text, professional rural sociologists who acknowledged Bernard's influence include Otis Durant Duncan, Charles R. Hoffer, Charles E. Lively, and Rupert Vance. See Read Bain, "L. L. Bernard: Sociological

Theorist (1881–1951)," *ASR*, 16:285–97 (June 1951); and Carle C. Zimmerman, "Luther Lee Bernard," *RS*, 16:309–13 (September 1951).

20. New York: Crowell, 1943.

21. Morgan, *Rural Community Organization: What It Is. How It May Be Done. The Benefits to Be Derived*, Massachusetts Agricultural College Extension Service (1918).

22. Morgan and Burt, *Community Relations of Rural Young People*, Missouri AES Research Bulletin No. 110 (1927). Before Burt decided to leave the field of sociology for the ministry, he was the author of another important work, *Contacts in a Rural Community*, Missouri AES Research Bulletin No. 125 (1929). This study, made cooperatively with the Division of Farm Population, was one of the earlier investigations of social participation. It was preceded only by J. L. Hypes, *Social Participation in a Rural New England Town* (Contribution to Education No. 258, Columbia University, Teachers College — 1927), and by H. B. Hawthorn's studies in Iowa as reported in his *Sociology of Rural Life* (New York: Century, 1926).

23. Morgan and Melvin W. Sneed, *The Activities of Rural Youth in Missouri*, Missouri AES Research Bulletin No. 269 (1937); Morgan, J. D. Ensminger, and Sneed, *Rural Women and the Works Progress Administration: A Partial Analysis of Levels of Living*, Missouri AES Research Bulletin No. 253 (1937).

24. Lively and Beck, *The Rural Health Facilities of Ross County, Ohio*, Ohio AES Bulletin No. 412 (1927). This publication preceded Sanderson's study of Cortland County, New York, by six months. See Note 2, above.

25. Lively, *Some Rural Social Agencies in Ohio*, Bulletin of the Ohio State University Extension Service, Vol. 18, No. 4 (1922–23). Ten years later he made a follow-up study, *Some Rural Social Agencies in Ohio: A Study of Trends, 1921–1931*, Ohio AES Bulletin No. 529 (1933). This was followed by *Some Aspects of Rural Social Organization in Fairfield County, Ohio*, Ohio AES Mimeographed Bulletin No. 91 (1936), written with R. C. Smith and Martha Fry.

26. Lively and Taeuber, *Rural Migration in the United States*, Works Progress Administration Research Monograph No. 19 (1939). For further discussion of this study, see Chapter 8 below. The Ohio AES publications included: Lively and P. G. Beck, *Movement of Open Country Population in Ohio*, Bulletin No. 467 (1930); Lively and C. L. Folse, *The Trend of Births, Deaths, Natural Increase and Migration in the Rural Population of Ohio*, Mimeographed Bulletin No. 87 (1936); Lively and Frances Foott, *Population Mobility in Selected Areas of Rural Ohio, 1928–1935*, Bulletin No. 582 (1937).

27. Typical examples are Howard W. Odum, *Southern Regions of the United States* (Chapel Hill: University of North Carolina Press, 1936); P. G. Beck and M. C. Forster, *Six Rural Problem Areas*, Federal Emergency Relief Administration Research Monograph No. 1 (1935); A. R. Mangus, *Rural Regions of the United States*, Works Progress Administration (1940); Margaret J. Hagood, *Rural Level of Living Indexes for Counties of the United States, 1940* (Washington, D.C.: Bureau of Agricultural Economics, 1943).

28. Lively and R. B. Almack, *A Method of Determining Rural Social Sub-Areas with Application to Ohio*, Ohio AES Department of Rural Economics Bulletin No. 106 (1938); Lively and C. L. Gregory, *Rural Social Areas in Missouri*, Missouri AES Research Bulletin No. 414 (1948).

Galpin had another Ohio collaborator in Perry P. Denune, a graduate student and instructor in sociology at Ohio State University, who published *Some Town-Country Relations in Union County, Ohio*, Ohio State University Studies, Sociology Series No. 1 (1924); and *The Social and Economic Relations of the Farmers with the Towns in Pickaway County, Ohio*, Ohio State University Bureau of Business Research Monograph No. 9 (1927).

29. The textbooks referred to are *Rural Sociology* (New York: Harper, 1926; rev. ed. 1933); and Taylor, Douglas Ensminger, T. Wilson Longmore, Louis J. Ducoff, Arthur F. Raper, Margaret J. Hagood, Walter C. McKain, Jr., and Edgar A. Schuler, *Rural Life in the United States* (New York: Knopf, 1949). *The Farmers' Movement, 1620–1920* (New York: American Book Co.) was published in 1950; a second volume is projected. In addition Taylor wrote with B. F. Brown, a colleague at North Carolina State College, *Human Relations: A College Textbook in Citizenship* (New York: Harper, 1926). For a fuller account of his work in Argentina and India, see Chapter 11, below.

30. Dickey and Branson, *How Farm Tenants Live*, University of North Carolina Extension Bulletin, Vol. 2, No. 6 (1922). The quotation is on the flyleaf. Carl Taylor, then at the State College of North Carolina, was also a member of this commission; he and Carle C. Zimmerman prepared the final report.

31. Odum, *American Sociology* (New York: Longmans, Green, 1951), p. 299. Branson also published *Farm Life Abroad*, based on a year's travel in Europe. See Chapter 11, below.

32. Tribute to Odum, in *RS*, 20:89–90 (March 1955).

33. See Chapter 11, below.

34. Zimmerman and Black, *Marketing Attitudes of Minnesota Farmers*, Minnesota AES Technical Bulletin No. 45 (1926); *How Minnesota Farm Families' Incomes Are Spent: An Interpretation of a One Year's Study, 1924–1925*, AES Bulletin No. 234 (1927); *Family Living on Successful Farms*, AES Bulletin No. 240 (1927); and *Factors Affecting Expenditures of Farm Families' Incomes in Minnesota*, AES Bulletin No. 246 (1928).

35. Zimmerman, *Farm Trade Centers in Minnesota: A Study in Rural Social Organization*, Minnesota AES Bulletin No. 269 (1930).

36. New York: Holt, 1929.

37. Minneapolis: University of Minnesota Press, 1930–32. See also Zimmerman's account of the book in the Appendix, below.

Chapter 7. The Growth and the Spread

1. See Chapter 8, below.

2. Von Tungeln, *A Rural Survey of Orange Township, Blackhawk County, Iowa*, Iowa AES Bulletin No. 184 (1918). In 1915 the experiment station had published his Circular No. 24, entitled *The Survey as a Guide to Rural Social Progress*, one of the earliest such guides to be published.

3. Von Tungeln, *A Rural Social Survey of Lone Tree Township, Clay County, Iowa*, with W. A. Brindley, Iowa AES Bulletin No. 193 (1920); Von Tungeln, E. L. Kirkpatrick, C. R. Hoffer, and J. F. Thaden, *The Social Aspects of Rural Life and Farm Tenantry in Cedar County, Iowa*, Iowa AES Bulletin No. 217 (1923) — apparently the only study which Galpin supported financially; Von Tungeln and Harry L. Eells, *Rural Social Survey of Hudson, Orange, and Jesup Consolidated School Districts, Blackhawk and Buchanan Counties, Iowa*, Iowa AES Bulletin No. 224 (1924).

4. Examples of Wakeley's publications are *Rural Organization and Land Utilization on Muscatine Island*, with J. Edwin Losey, Iowa AES Bulletin No. 353 (1936); *Rural Organization in Process: A Study of Hamilton County, Iowa*, with Paul J. Jehlik, Iowa AES Bulletin No. 365 (1949); "Selecting Leaders for Agricultural Programs," *Sociometry*, Vol. 10, No. 4 (November 1947).

5. Mumford, "Relation of Economic Success of Farmers to Their Standard of Living," in *Farm Income and Farm Life: Proceedings of the American Country Life Association* (Chicago: University of Chicago Press, 1927); "The Agricultural Problem from the Point of View of the Sociologist," in *Proceedings of the Land-Grant*

Colleges and Universities, 1927; "The Next Steps in Sociological Research," in American Sociological Society *Proceedings*, 1927; Mumford and John F. Thaden, *The Standard of Living of Farm Families in Selected Michigan Communities* and *High School Communities in Michigan*, Michigan AES Special Bulletin No. 287 (1937) and No. 289 (1938). See also an obituary notice by Thaden in *ASR*, 8:88–89 (February 1943).

6. See, for example, Thaden's articles "Effect of the Increased Birth Rate on School Enrollment and School Building Needs" and "Forecast of Future Public School Enrollment by Grades in Michigan," Michigan AES *Quarterly Bulletin*, 31: 1–11 (August 1948) and 31:378–86 (May 1949). This *Bulletin* published many other articles on the same theme.

7. Mumford and Thaden, *High School Communities in Michigan*, cited in note 5, above. The results of this study were significant in showing that the "high school attendance area was a more satisfactory single factor in determining a community boundary than any other, as it did not come and go erratically as other service areas, and tended to oscillate less."

8. H. Bruce Price and Hoffer, *Services of Rural Trade Centers in Distribution of Farm Supplies*, Minnesota AES Bulletin No. 249 (1928) — supported with funds provided by Galpin.

9. Hoffer, *The Community Situation as It Affects Agricultural Extension Work*, Michigan AES Special Bulletin No. 312 (1941); *Selected Factors Affecting Participation of Farmers in Agricultural Extension Work*, Special Bulletin No. 331 (1944); *Social Organization in Relation to Extension Service in Eaton County, Michigan*, Special Bulletin No. 338 (1946). See also *Acceptance of Approved Practices Among Farmers of Dutch Descent*, Special Bulletin No. 316 (1942); *Farmers' Reactions to New Practices in Corn Growing in Michigan*, Technical Bulletin No. 264 (1958).

10. Among Lindstrom's publications are the following: *Forces Affecting Participation of Farm People in Rural Organizations*, Illinois AES Bulletin No. 423 (1936); *Local Group Organization Among Illinois Farm People*, Bulletin No. 392; *Selectivity of 4-H Club Work: An Analysis of Factors Influencing Membership*, Bulletin No. 426 (1936). His books include *Rural Life and the Church* (Champaign, Ill.: Garrard Press, 1946); *American Farmers and Rural Organizations* (Garrard Press, 1948); *American Rural Life: A Textbook in Sociology* (New York: Ronald Press, 1948). See also Chapter 11, notes 29 and 33.

11. Willson, *Social Organizations and Agencies in North Dakota* and *Rural Community Clubs in North Dakota: Influencing Their Success or Failure*, North Dakota AES Bulletin No. 221 (1928) and No. 251 (1931); Willson, Hoffsommer, and Alva H. Benton, *Rural Changes in Western North Dakota*, No. 214 (1928). Hoffsommer, who did the bulk of the field work for the last-mentioned bulletin, received a Ph.D. from Cornell University in 1929. His major professional positions have been as professor of sociology at Alabama Polytechnic Institute (1929–35), rural sociologist for the Louisiana Agricultural Experiment Station (1936–42), and head of the department of sociology and chairman of the division of social sciences at the University of Maryland (1945–).

12. University of Virginia Record, Extension Series, Vol. 10, No. 9 (May 1926).

13. Gee and John J. Corson, *Rural Depopulation in Certain Tidewater and Piedmont Counties of Virginia*, University of Virginia, Institute for Research in the Social Sciences, Monograph No. 3 (1929); Gee and William Henry Stauffer, *Rural and Urban Living Standards in Virginia*, Institute Monograph No. 6 (1929).

14. Garnett, *Attitudes of Rural People Towards Organizations*, Virginia AES Bulletin No. 250 (1927); Hamilton and Garnett, *The Role of the Church in Rural Community Life in Virginia*, Bulletin No. 267 (1929); Garnett and Hamilton, *Forward Steps for Rural Churches*, Bulletin of the Polytechnic Institute, Vol. 24, No. 8 (1931).

15. Smith's research studies were published by Louisiana State University as, respectively, Bulletin No. 234 (1933) and No. 264 (1935). His textbook is reviewed in Chapter 9, below, and his work in Latin America in Chapter 11.

16. Hayes, *Examples of Community Enterprise in Louisiana*, Tulane University Research Bulletin No. 3 (1928); *Some Factors in Town and Country Relations*, Tulane University Research Bulletin [unnumbered] (September 1922).

17. Examples of Duncan's work are: *Some Social and Economic Aspects of the Problem of Rural Health in Oklahoma*, Oklahoma AES Circular No. 78 (September 1931); "A Sociological Approach to Farm Tenancy Research," *RS*, Vol. 5, No. 3 (September 1940); *Oklahoma's Farm Population*, Oklahoma AES Bulletin No. B-379 (1952).

18. Chicago: University of Chicago Press, 1934.

19. Nelson, *A Social Survey of Escalante, Utah*, Brigham Young University Studies No. 1 (1925); *The Utah Farm Village of Ephraim*, No. 2 (1928); *Some Social and Economic Features of American Fork, Utah*, No. 4 (1930). T. Lynn Smith assisted with the Ephraim study, and Nathan L. Whetten with that on American Fork. For a contemporary review of the Escalante bulletin, see *New York Times*, January 31, 1926 (editorial page).

20. Nelson, *The Mormon Village: A Pattern and Technique of Land Settlement* (Salt Lake City: University of Utah Press, 1952).

21. See, for example, "Speaking of Tongues," *AJS*, 54:202–10 (1948); "The Farm Laborer," in *Proceedings of the Twenty-First American Country Life Conference*, pp. 96–107 (1939); *Education of the Farm Population of Minnesota*, Minnesota AES Bulletin No. 377 (1944); *Population Trends in Minnesota*, Bulletin No. 387 (1945); *Farm Retirement In Minnesota*, Bulletin No. 394 (1947); *Red Wing Churches During the War* (Minneapolis: University of Minnesota Press, 1946); "Distribution, Age, and Mobility of Minnesota Physicians, 1912–1936," *ASR*, 7: 792–801 (1942).

Other publications by Nelson include *Rural Sociology* (New York: American Book Co., 1948; rev. ed. 1956); *Rural Cuba* (Minneapolis: University of Minnesota Press, 1950); *American Farm Life* (Cambridge: Harvard University Press, 1954); *The Minnesota Community* (University of Minnesota Press, 1960); *Community Structure and Change*, with Charles E. Ramsey and Coolie Verner (New York: Macmillan, 1960). See also Chapter 10, below.

22. Geddes, *Farm Versus Village Living in Utah, Plain City, Type "A" Village*, Utah AES Bulletin No. 249, Parts I and II (1934); No. 269, Parts III and IV (1936).

23. E. A. Taylor and Yoder, *Rural Social Organization in Whitman County*; *Rural Social Organization in Whatcom County*; and *Rural Social Organization of Clark County* — Washington AES Bulletin No. 203 (1926), No. 215 (1927), and No. 225 (1928).

24. See Tetreau's *Migration of Agricultural Wealth by Inheritance in Two Ohio Counties*, Ohio AES Bulletin No. 65 (1933). In Arizona he produced the first bulletins based on sociological research, *Arizona's Farm Laborers*, Arizona AES Bulletin No. 163 (1939), and *Arizona's Agricultural Population*, Technical Bulletin No. 88 (1940).

25. Hypes, *Social Participation in a Rural New England Town*, Teachers College, Columbia University, Contribution to Education No. 258 (1927).

26. Groves, *Using the Resources of the Country Church* (New York: Association Press, 1917); *Rural Problems of Today* (Association Press, 1918); *The Rural Mind and Social Welfare* (Chicago: University of Chicago Press, 1922). His bibliography after this period lists no items on rural themes.

27. *Rural Health: Proceedings of the Second National Country Life Conference*, 1919, p. 210. See also pp. 51–52, above.

28. The quotations from Elmer are in a letter to the author, dated November 9,

1965. The account of his contact with Gillette is also told in his book, *Contemporary Social Thought* (Pittsburgh: University of Pittsburgh Press, 1956), p. 97.

29. Elmer, *Stillwater: The Queen of the St. Croix* (Stillwater, Minn., 1920). Charles E. Lively assisted in this study. "Park and Burgess," Elmer observed in the communication cited above, "made an extensive quote from that study and most people assumed it was Stillwater, Oklahoma, where Burgess attended college."

30. These studies were discussed in Elmer's article, "Evaluating Community Activities," *SF*, Vol. 6, No. 1 (September 1927). Robert W. Murchie and George A. Lundberg assisted him. Elmer's *The Technique of the Social Survey* (Lawrence, Kan.: World, 1917) was one of the earliest published guides in this field.

31. McCormick, *Rural Social Organization in South-Central Arkansas*, Arkansas AES Bulletin No. 311 (1934).

32. McCormick, "Major Trends in Rural Life in the United States," *AJS*, 36:721–34 (March 1931).

33. Among Taylor's perceptive field studies, one is especially important in the early literature of rural life: *An American-Mexican Frontier: Nueces County, Texas* (Chapel Hill: University of North Carolina Press, 1934). Typically, Taylor did all his own field interviewing for this study, which is an illuminating treatment of the social stratification and the inter-ethnic attitudes associated with the contact of two cultures. See also his *Adrift on the Land* (New York: Public Affairs Pamphlet No. 42, 1940) and *An American Exodus*, with Dorothea Lange (New York: Reynal and Hitchcock, 1939).

Chapter 8. Federal Subsidies for Rural Research

1. L. H. Bailey, *Cyclopedia of American Agriculture* (New York: Macmillan, 1911), p. 425.

2. *Preliminary Report on Rural Sociological Research in the United States During the Year July 1, 1926–June 30, 1927* (mimeographed; n.p., n.d.). The report was prepared under the direction of the Advisory Committee in Social and Economic Research in Agriculture of the Social Science Research Council by C. J. Galpin, with the assistance of J. H. Kolb, Dwight Sanderson, and C. C. Taylor.

3. *Ibid.*, p. 40. Curiously, Galpin's office was also supporting projects in 17 states, sometimes jointly with Purnell funds, but more often not. Some of his cooperators were in private institutions, such as the Institute for Social and Religious Research.

4. *Handbook of Workers in Subjects Pertaining to Agriculture in Land-Grant Colleges and Experiment Stations, 1964–65* (Agricultural Handbook No. 116, published by the Division of Farm Population and Rural Life).

5. "Status and Prospects for Research in Rural Life Under the New Deal," *AJS*, 41:180–93 (September 1935). Sanderson did not give a specific figure for the expenditures; however, on the basis of other remarks in his article, the amount appears to have been about $2,500,000.

6. The field work was carried out by the following area directors: E. L. Kirkpatrick, the lake states cut-over area; Paul H. Landis (South Dakota State College), the wheat area; T. G. Standing (University of Iowa), Appalachian-Ozark area; B. F. Coen (Colorado State College), winter wheat area; Harold C. Hoffsommer (Alabama Polytechnic Institute), the eastern cotton belt; and Z. B. Wallin (Oklahoma State College), the western cotton area. The quotation below is from p. 5.

7. Mangus, *Rural Regions of the United States* (Washington, D.C.: Government Printing Office, 1940). Mangus is a native of Virginia, born in 1900. His degrees: B.A., Illinois Wesleyan, 1927; M.A., Chicago, 1929; Ph.D., Wisconsin, 1934. He taught at the University of North Dakota from 1929 to 1934, then became senior research supervisor (with Berta Asch) of FERA-WPA, 1934–39. Mangus was also the author of *Changing Aspects of Rural Relief*, WPA Monograph No. 14 (Wash-

ington, D.C.: Government Printing Office, 1938); and *Farmers on Relief and Rehabilitation*, WPA Monograph No. 8 (Government Printing Office, 1937). He has made pioneer studies of mental health in the rural population. He has been professor of rural sociology at Ohio State University since 1939.

8. See Odum, *Southern Regions of the United States* (Chapel Hill: University of North Carolina Press, 1936); Odum and H. E. Moore, *American Regionalism* (New York: Holt, 1938). Lively wrote "Social Planning and the Sociology of Sub-Regions," *RS*, 2:288–98 (September 1937); and, with R. B. Almack, *A Method of Determining Rural Social Sub-Areas with Application to Ohio*, Ohio AES Department of Rural Economics Bulletin No. 106 (1938).

9. Elliott, *Types of Farming in the United States* (Washington, D.C.: Bureau of the Census, 1938).

10. Carle C. Zimmerman and Nathan L. Whetten, *Rural Families on Relief*, WPA Monograph No. 17 (Washington, D.C.: Government Printing Office, 1938). The data were collected under the supervision of A. R. Mangus and T. C. McCormick, and the analysis was made under the supervision of T. J. Woofter, Jr., coordinator of rural research.

Whetten was born in Colonia Juarez, Mexico, in 1900. His B.A. and M.A. degrees were granted by Brigham Young University in 1926 and 1928. His Ph.D. is from Harvard, 1932. He has been professor of rural sociology and dean of the Graduate School at Storrs Agricultural College (now University of Connecticut). He has written various studies of suburbanization in Connecticut. For his books on Latin America, see Chapter 11, below.

11. Woofter, *et al.*, *Landlord and Tenant on the Cotton Plantation*, WPA Research Monograph No. 5 (Washington, D.C.: Government Printing Office, 1936). The collaborators were Gordon Blackwell, Harold Hoffsommer, James G. Maddox, B. O. Williams, Waller Wynne, Jr., and Jean M. Masselli. Woofter was born in Georgia. His Ph.D. came from Columbia University in 1920. From 1921 to 1928 he was engaged in research on race relations; in 1928 he joined the staff of the department of sociology at the University of North Carolina, remaining there until he was appointed in 1935 as coordinator of rural research for FERA-WPA, a position he held until 1940. During World War II he served with the Federal Security Agency.

12. *Ibid.*, p. xvii.

13. Such a program was enacted in 1937 when Congress created the Farm Security Administration, the most important aspect of which was the tenant-purchase program.

14. C. E. Lively and Conrad Taeuber, *Rural Migration in the United States*, WPA Monograph No. 19 (Washington, D.C.: Government Printing Office, 1939). The census and survey data analysis was made under the supervision of T. J. Woofter, then chief of the Rural Surveys Section, and Carl C. Taylor, head of the Division of Farm Population. Both the WPA and the Farm Security Administration participated in this study.

Taeuber was born in South Dakota in 1906. His degrees are all from the University of Minnesota: B.A., 1927; M.A., 1929; Ph.D., 1931. He also studied at the University of Heidelberg in 1929–30 and the University of Wisconsin in 1930–31. Since 1933 he has been employed by the federal government, except for the years 1946–51, when he worked with the United Nations Food and Agriculture Organization. His early years of service were in the Bureau of Agricultural Economics and its Division of Farm Population. In 1951 he became assistant director of the Bureau of the Census.

15. See, for example, Francis D. Cronin and Howard W. Beers, *Social Problems of the Drought Area*, WPA Research Bulletin Series 5 (Washington, D.C.: Government Printing Office, 1937). This volume contains three bulletins.

16. Loomis, *Social Relationships and Institutions in Seven New Rural Communities*, Social Research Report No. 18 (U.S. Department of Agriculture, 1940). Loomis was born in Colorado in 1905. He took his B.S. degree from New Mexico State College in 1928, his M.S. from North Carolina State College in 1929, and his Ph.D. from Harvard in 1933. He served in the Division of Farm Population, 1934–42, and then as assistant chief of the Division of Extension and Training in the Office of Foreign Agricultural Relations until 1944, when he became head of the department of sociology and anthropology at Michigan State University.

17. John B. Holt, *An Analysis of Methods and Criteria Used in Selecting Families for Colonization Projects*, and Marie Jasny, *Family Selection on a Federal Reclamation Project — Tule Lake Division of the Klamath Irrigation Project, Oregon-California*, Social Research Reports Nos. 1 and 5 (U.S. Department of Agriculture, 1937 and 1938).

18. E. A. Schuler, *Social Status and Farm Tenure — Attitudes and Social Conditions of Corn Belt and Cotton Belt Farmers*; Carl C. Taylor, Helen W. Wheeler, and E. L. Kirkpatrick, *Disadvantaged Classes in American Agriculture*, Social Research Reports Nos. 4 and 8 (U.S. Department of Agriculture, 1938). Edgar A. Schuler was born in Iowa in 1905. He earned his B.A. degree at Morningside College in 1928, his M.A. degree at Minnesota in 1929, and his Ph.D. at Harvard in 1933. He was at Louisiana State University from 1933 until 1943, when he joined the Division of Farm Population. In 1946 he went to Michigan State University; in 1949 he became chairman of the department of sociology and anthropology at Wayne State University, a position he held until he returned to Michigan State as professor of sociology and anthropology.

19. Olen E. Leonard and C. P. Loomis, *El Cerrito, New Mexico*; Earl H. Bell, *Sublette, Kansas*; Kenneth MacLeish and Kimball Young, *Landaff, New Hampshire*; Walter M. Kollmorgen, *The Old Order Amish of Lancaster, Pennsylvania*; Edward O. Moe and Carl C. Taylor, *Irwin, Iowa*; Waller Wynne, *Harmony, Georgia* — Rural Life Studies Nos. 1–6 (U.S. Department of Agriculture, 1941–43).

20. See, for example, Frank D. Alexander and Lowry Nelson, *Rural Social Organization, Goodhue County*, Minnesota AES Bulletin No. 401 (1949).

21. See Charles M. Hardin, "The Bureau of Agricultural Economics Under Fire: A Study in Valuation Conflicts," *Journal of Farm Economics*, 28:635–68 (August 1946), an excellent analysis of the developments which brought congressional action to limit activities, including those of the Division of Farm Population.

22. Quoted in *ibid.*, p. 653.

23. The author has read the document and found it to be an honest report of a competent observer, who admittedly was not expected to make a detailed study of Coahoma County.

24. Quoted by Hardin, in *Journal of Farm Economics*, 28:655. This was one of the few quotations from the document inserted in the record by the Mississippi congressmen.

25. During the middle 1940s, the Division of Farm Population was an anthill of activity. Never before had so many individuals been employed in Washington and in the field; nor did the division enjoy any comparable period afterward. As of January 1945, Carl Taylor reported a professional staff of 45 persons. Twenty of them were in the Washington office and the remainder in seven regional offices. See *RS*, 10:125 (March 1945). A bibliography for the years 1944–46 includes 363 entries, all of them listing one or more of the employees of the division as author or joint author. The list includes all sorts of publications, including mimeographed reports, journal articles, and bulletins published in cooperation with the states or with other federal agencies. See *Publications and Releases of the Division of Farm Population and Rural Welfare and its Staff Members Between July 1944 and June 1946* (Washington, D.C., 1946).

Chapter 9. Scope and Content

1. Kern, *Among Country Schools* (New York: Ginn, 1906).

2. Carney, *Country Life and the Country School* (Chicago: Row, Peterson, 1912). Miss Carney was a native of Illinois. She had served as country training teacher at Western Illinois State Normal School at McComb, and at the time of publication of the book was director of the country school department of Illinois State Normal University. She later went to Teachers College, Columbia University, as professor of rural education.

3. Hart, *Educational Resources of Village and Rural Communities* (New York: Macmillan, 1913). A native of Indiana, Hart obtained his Ph.D. degree at Columbia University in 1909. His major interest was in relating education to the whole community. He taught at a number of universities, including Washington and Wisconsin, with a longer period at Teachers College from 1934 to 1940. His *Community Organization* (1920) was widely used as a textbook in sociology.

4. Cubberly, *Rural Life and Education: A Study of the Rural School Problem as a Phase of the Rural Life Problem* (Boston: Houghton Mifflin, 1914). He also published *The Improvement of Rural Schools* (Houghton Mifflin, 1912).

5. Anderson, *The Country Town: A Study in Rural Evolution* (New York: Baker and Taylor, 1906). There is an introduction by Josiah Strong, an early commentator on the condition of the rural church.

6. Wilson, *The Evolution of the Country Community: A Study in Religious Sociology* (Boston: Pilgrim Press, 1912). Franklin Giddings wrote the preface.

7. *Ibid.*, pp. 91–92.

8. *Ibid.*, p. 93.

9. Earp, *Rural Social Organization* (New York: Abingdon Press, 1921).

10. Douglass, *The Little Town, Especially in its Rural Relationships* (New York: Macmillan, 1919). At the time he wrote this book, he was secretary of the American Missionary Association. His work in connection with the Institute for Social and Religious Research has been mentioned in Chapter 5, above.

11. New York: Sturgis and Walton, 1913. There is an introduction by George E. Vincent, then president of the University of Minnesota.

12. As Kenyon L. Butterfield put it: "We cannot very well consider the rural problem in its social aspects without becoming convinced that the teacher of rural sociology should also be to some degree a propagandist. The rural problem itself is so significant and vital, the need for cooperative planning is so apparent, that it becomes necessary to develop a program for rural betterment, to indicate the means by which we may secure a larger development of the rural community. Therefore this work constitutes a distinct phase of rural sociology." "Rural Sociology as a College Discipline," in American Academy of Political and Social Science, *Annals*, 40: 14 (March 1912).

13. Gillette, *Rural Sociology* (New York: Macmillan, 1923). A revised edition appeared in 1928.

14. *Ibid.*, p. 6.

15. *Ibid.*, p. 11.

16. *Rural Sociology*, 3rd ed. (New York: Macmillan, 1936).

17. *Ibid.*, p. 32.

18. Vogt, *Introduction to Rural Sociology* (New York: D. Appleton, 1917). A second edition, appearing in 1921, was apparently a new printing rather than a revision.

19. *Ibid.*, p. 15.

20. For an interesting piece of information regarding Vogt and the efforts to define rural sociology, see Manuel Elmer, *Contemporary Social Thought*, p. 97.

21. For Smith's remark, see "Rural Sociology: A Trend Report and Bibliography,"

Current Sociology, 6:29 (1957). The 15 textbooks are: Newell L. Sims, *The Rural Community: Ancient and Modern* (New York: Scribner, 1920); Walter Burr, *Rural Organization* (New York: Macmillan, 1921); Augustus W. Hayes, *Rural Community Organization* (Chicago: University of Chicago Press, 1921); Eduard C. Lindeman, *The Community: An Introduction to the Study of Community Leadership and Organization* (New York: Association Press, 1921); Ernest R. Groves, *The Rural Mind and Social Welfare* (University of Chicago Press, 1922); Dwight Sanderson, *The Farmer and His Community* (New York: Harcourt, Brace, 1922); John M. Gillette, *Rural Sociology* (New York: Macmillan, 1923 — a new book, not a revision of the 1913 work); Charles J. Galpin, *Rural Social Problems* (New York: Century, 1924); John Phelan, *Readings in Rural Sociology* (New York: Macmillan, 1924); Horace B. Hawthorn, *The Sociology of Rural Life* (New York: Century, 1926); Carl C. Taylor, *Rural Sociology* (New York: Harper, 1926); Gustav A. Lundquist and Thomas N. Carver, *Principles of Rural Sociology* (Boston and New York: Ginn, 1927); Newell L. Sims, *Elements of Rural Sociology* (New York: Crowell, 1928); Augustus W. Hayes, *Rural Sociology* (New York: Longmans, Green, 1929); P. A. Sorokin and Carle C. Zimmerman, *Principles of Rural-Urban Sociology* (New York: Holt, 1929).

22. Burr, *Rural Organization*, p. 3.

23. Hayes, *Rural Community Organization*, pp. 1–2.

24. Lindeman, *The Community*, p. 55.

25. Phelan, *Readings*, p. 612.

26. Hawthorn, *Sociology of Rural Life*, p. 66. Hawthorn was born in Iowa in 1889. He obtained B.S. and M.S. degrees from Iowa State University in 1914 and 1915 and his Ph.D. from the University of Wisconsin in 1922. He was assistant professor of rural sociology at Iowa State (1921–26) and associate professor of sociology at the University of Akron (1926–30). He became professor of sociology at Morningside College at Sioux City, Iowa, in 1931 and spent the remainder of his academic career there.

27. *Ibid.*, p. 114.

28. Notably that of F. Stuart Chapin, "Social Participation and Social Intelligence," *ASR*, 4:157–66 (April 1939), and *The Social Participation Scale* (Minneapolis: University of Minnesota Press, 1938).

29. Taylor, *Rural Sociology*, p. 3. The quotation in the following paragraph is on p. 4.

30. The first two quotations in the paragraph are from the first edition of *Elements of Rural Sociology* (1928), pp. 14, 18. The quotations from the third edition (1940) can be found on pp. 19, 20.

31. Sims, *The Problem of Social Change* (New York: Crowell, 1939).

32. For Zimmerman's account of how the book came to be written, see the Appendix, below.

33. *Principles of Rural-Urban Sociology*, p. 10.

34. See Sorokin, "Sociology of Yesterday, Today, and Tomorrow," *ASR*, 30:833–43 (December 1965).

35. Charles R. Hoffer, *Introduction to Rural Sociology* (New York: Richard R. Smith, 1930); Roy H. Holmes, *Rural Sociology: The Family-Farm Institution* (New York: McGraw-Hill, 1932); J. H. Kolb and Edmund deS. Brunner, *A Study of Rural Society: Its Organization and Changes* (Boston: Houghton Mifflin, 1935). Gillette, Taylor, and Sims, as noted previously, brought out revisions during the thirties. Another work of this period was Dwight Sanderson and Robert A. Polson, *Rural Community Organization* (New York: Wiley, 1939).

36. Hoffer, *Introduction to Rural Sociology*, p. 12.

37. In the preface to *Rural Sociology*, Holmes paid the following tribute to Cooley: "although he concerned himself relatively little in any specific way with

rural-urban relationships, he aided his students to see the relatedness of all people, wherever they may chance to live and whatever they may chance to do." Incidentally, Holmes was the only author of a text in the field who spent his career in a major state university (Michigan).

38. Brunner and Kolb produced one of the monographs in the Recent Social Trends project directed by William F. Ogburn. Their book, *Rural Social Trends* (New York: McGraw-Hill, 1923), was a restudy of the 140 villages first surveyed by Brunner in the 1920s under auspices of the Institute for Social and Religious Research. These studies, along with Kolb's restudies of Galpin's Walworth County study and his work with Dane County neighborhoods, provided an excellent basis for discussion of changes in the morphology of rural society.

39. T. Lynn Smith, *The Sociology of Rural Life* (New York: Harper, 1940); Paul H. Landis, *Rural Life in Process* (New York: McGraw-Hill, 1940); Dwight Sanderson, *Rural Sociology and Rural Social Organization* (New York: Wiley, 1942); David E. Lindstrom, *American Rural Life* (New York: Ronald Press, 1948); Lowry Nelson, *Rural Sociology* (New York: American Book Co., 1948); Carl C. Taylor, Douglas Ensminger, Margaret Jarman Hagood, T. Wilson Longmore, Louis J. Ducoff, Arthur F. Raper, Walter C. McKain, Jr., and Edgar A. Schuler, *Rural Life in the United States* (New York: Knopf, 1949); Charles P. Loomis and J. Allan Beegle, *Rural Social Systems* (New York: Prentice-Hall, 1950).

40. Born in Sanford, Colo., in 1903, Smith received his bachelor's degree at Brigham Young University in 1928, his M.A. degree at Minnesota in 1929, and his Ph.D. in 1932. He was a research fellow at Harvard in 1930–31. He joined the faculty of Louisiana State University as professor of sociology and rural sociology in 1931, serving as chairman from 1937 to 1947. In 1947–49 he was director of the Institute of Brazilian Studies at Vanderbilt University. He joined the staff of the University of Florida in 1949. His major research interests have been rural and urban population analysis and social organization, gerontology, and the community, but see also Chapter 11, below.

41. Landis was born in Illinois in 1901. He took his B.A. at Greenville College in 1926, his M.A. at Michigan in 1927, and his Ph.D. at Minnesota in 1933. He has held the following positions: instructor in sociology, University of Minnesota, 1928–31; rural sociologist, South Dakota State College, 1931–34; associate professor of sociology and rural sociology, Washington State College, 1935–39, and professor of sociology, head of rural sociology, and dean of the graduate school, 1939–47. Since 1947 he has held the position of State Professor of Rural Sociology and Rural Sociologist of Washington State University. He has written on the family, social control, and general sociology.

42. Sanderson, *Rural Sociology and Rural Social Organization*, pp. ix–x.

43. Lindstrom, *American Rural Life*, p. v.

44. Nelson, *Rural Sociology*, p. 3. For a more ample discussion of this topic, see Nelson, "Rural Sociology: Dimensions and Horizons," *RS*, 10:131–35 (June 1945).

45. Taylor, *et al., Rural Life in the United States*, p. 4.

46. Joseph Allan Beegle was born in Pennsylvania in 1918. He obtained the B.S. degree at Pennsylvania State University in 1939; the M.A. from Iowa State University in 1941, and the Ph.D. from Louisiana State University in 1946. In 1946 he joined the staff of the department of sociology and anthropology at Michigan State University. For biographical information on Loomis, see p. 204, above.

47. For the quotations here and below, see Loomis and Beegle, *Rural Social Systems*, pp. 4–5.

48. Translated by Loomis and published as *Fundamental Concepts of Sociology* (*Gemeinschaft und Gesellschaft*) (New York: American Book Co., 1940).

49. In a review of the book, Otis Durant Duncan said: "the fiction called regions is used as guilelessly as when the term was invented." *RS*, 15:383 (December 1950).

Nevertheless, one would have difficulty in denying the existence of agricultural regions. They are, indeed, basically derived from climatic and soil conditions, but the agriculture responding to these conditions under the ministering hand of man is part of "culture." The very nature of farming and the farming systems associated with various types of crop production give rise to different social environments in addition to those environments inherent in nature. Our main objection to the use of regions in this book is their treatment as social systems. On the definition of "system," see, for example, the entry in *Webster's New International Dictionary of the English Language* (2nd ed., unabridged, 1934).

50. Duncan, in *RS*, 15:387.

51. Alvin L. Bertrand, *et al.*, *Rural Sociology: An Analysis of Contemporary Rural Life* (New York: McGraw-Hill, 1958); Irwin T. Sanders, *The Community* (New York: Ronald Press, 1958); Everett M. Rogers, *Social Change in Rural Society* (New York: Appleton-Century-Crofts, 1960); Walter L. Slocum, *Agricultural Society* (New York: Harper and Row, 1960); Lee Taylor and Arthur R. Jones, *Rural Life and Urbanized Society* (New York: Oxford University Press, 1964); James H. Copp, ed., *Our Changing Rural Society: Perspectives and Trends* (Ames: Iowa State University Press, 1964).

Chapter 10. The Profession

1. This has also been the experience of other professions. The first organization of social scientists was the American Historical Association in 1884. Economists, political scientists, and sociologists all participated. In 1885 economists and sociologists withdrew to form the American Economic Society. The sociologists formed their own American Sociological Society in 1906. Another offshoot was the American Farm Economic Association, formed in 1919.

2. Brunner, *Growth of a Science*, p. 3.

3. Elmer, *Contemporary Social Thought*, p. 97.

4. *AJS*, 24:303–10 (November 1918). It is worth noting that the definitions of "rural" and "community," in particular, unmistakably reflect the experience of Galpin, who was the committee's chairman. No doubt he prepared the entire report.

5. On financial arrangements for the yearbook, see American Sociological Society, *Publications*, 26:168–69 (1932).

6. For the minutes of this meeting, see *RS*, 1:113–14 (March 1936).

7. For a brief history of the journal and a list of editors through 1957, see *RS*, 22:313–18 (December 1957).

8. *RS*, 1:5–7 (March 1936).

9. See, for example, a letter of January 6, 1937, from Sanderson to Ellsworth Faris and H. A. Phelps, respectively president and secretary of the society. In particular, the opposition of Sanderson and other members to a separate organization is reflected in the chairman's interpretation of the purpose of the committee. Frey's motion had called for a study of the possibility of forming an "autonomous organization," whereas Sanderson in the letter speaks of a "separate organization" that would be affiliated with, and a section of, the parent society.

10. *RS*, 3:124 (March 1938).

11. *Directory of Teachers Giving Courses in Rural Sociology and Rural Life* (Bureau of Agricultural Economics, U.S. Department of Agriculture, 1936).

12. Figures were gleaned from the annual reports as published in *Rural Sociology*. The method of reporting was not consistent from year to year. Nevertheless, the figures are indicative of trends.

13. *RS*, 30:538 (December 1965).

14. It is appropriate to note that rural sociologists have also been active in the various regional sociological societies including the Eastern (established in 1929),

the Ohio Valley (1924), the Southern (1935), the Pacific (1935), the District of Columbia (1934), and the Midwest (1936). In addition several states now have societies, including Michigan, Missouri, and Wisconsin.

15. For the full report, see Wilson Gee, ed., *Proceedings of the Southern Conference-Seminar on Teaching and Research in Rural Sociology, Blue Ridge, North Carolina, August 26–30, 1940* (mimeographed; Charlottesville, Va.).

16. The report was published in *RS*, 10:76–85 (March 1945).

17. It was not yet clear just how the so-called GI Bill would affect demobilized servicemen.

18. It is important to note here that from its beginning the society has had standing committees on teaching, research, and extension which have made annual reports over the years. How much real attention is given to their work has always been questionable.

19. *Human Relations in Agriculture and Farm Life: the Status of Rural Sociology in the Land-Grant Colleges* (Chicago, 1950). The committee making the study was composed of F. D. Farrell, chairman, Clyde H. Bailey, Howard W. Beers, John Kolb, and H. C. Ramsower. Acting as consultants were Douglas Ensminger, Frank W. Peck, and Joseph Ackerman.

20. *Ibid.*, p. 29.

21. *Ibid.*, p. 51.

Chapter 11. Rural Sociologists Abroad

1. Chapel Hill: University of North Carolina Press, 1924. Branson's letters had been published earlier in the University of North Carolina newsletter and in newspapers of the state.

2. Kulp, *Country Life in South China* (New York: Bureau of Publications, Teachers College, Columbia University, 1925).

3. Buck, *Land Utilization in China* (Nanking: University of Nanking, 1937).

4. Brunner, *Rural Australia and New Zealand* (New York: Institute of Pacific Relations, 1938). J. H. Kolb later made a study of the standard of living of dairy farmers in New Zealand.

5. But see Yoder, "The Japanese Rural Community," *RS*, 1:420–29 (December, 1936).

6. Zimmerman, *Siam: Rural Economic Survey, 1930–31* (Bangkok: Bangkok Times Press, 1931).

7. Terpenning, *Village and Open-Country Neighborhoods* (New York: Century, 1931).

8. Smith, *Brazil: People and Institutions* (Baton Rouge: Louisiana State University Press, 1946).

9. Revisions appeared in 1954 and 1963. See also Smith and Alexander Marchant, *Brazil: Portrait of Half a Continent* (New York: Dryden Press, 1951). Smith's textbook, *The Sociology of Rural Life*, was translated into Portuguese as *Sociologia da Vida Rural* (Rio de Janeiro: Casa do Estudante do Brazil, 1946).

10. Smith, *Agrarian Reform in Latin America* (New York: Knopf, 1965).

11. Smith, Justo Diaz Rodriguez, and Luis Roberto Garcia, *Tabio: A Study in Rural Social Organization* (Washington, D.C.: Department of Agriculture, Office of Foreign Relations, 1945; Spanish ed., Bogotá: Ministerio de la Economia Nacional, 1944).

12. Smith, *Social Structure and the Process of Development* (Gainesville: University of Florida Press, 1967); *Latin American Population Studies* (University of Florida Press, 1961).

13. See, for example, Thomas R. Ford, *Man and Land in Peru* (Gainesville: University of Florida Press, 1955); John V. D. Saunders, *Differential Fertility in Bra-*

zil (University of Florida Press, 1959). While he is not a North American, Orlando Fals Borda did both his undergraduate and graduate work in the U.S. His *Peasant Society in the Colombian Andes* (University of Florida Press, 1955), was based largely on his M.A. thesis at the University of Minnesota. His Ph.D. thesis at Florida was published as *El Hombre y la Tierra en Boyaca* (Bogotá: Editore Antares, 1957).

14. Taylor, *Rural Life in Argentina* (Baton Rouge: Louisiana State University Press, 1948).

15. Leonard, *Canton Chullpas: A Socioeconomic Study in the Cochabamba Valley of Bolivia* (Washington, D.C.: Department of Agriculture, 1948; Spanish ed., La Paz: Ministerio de Agricultura, 1947); *Santa Cruz: A Socioeconomic Study of an Area in Bolivia* (Washington, D.C.: Department of Agriculture, Office of Foreign Agricultural Relations, 1948; Spanish ed., La Paz: Ministerio de Agricultura, Ganaderia y Colonizacion, 1948); *Bolivia: Land, People and Institutions* (Washington, D.C.: Scarecrow Press, 1952).

16. Leonard, *Pichilingue: A Study of Rural Life in Coastal Ecuador* (Washington, D.C.: U.S. Department of Agriculture, 1947). A more recent study is John V. D. Saunders, "Man-Land Relations in Ecuador," *RS*, 26:57–69 (March 1961).

17. Loomis, "Extension for Tingo Maria, Peru," *Applied Anthropology*, Vol. 3, No. 1 (December 1943). See also his *Studies in Rural Social Organization* (1945); *Studies in Applied and Theoretical Social Science* (1950); and, with Olen Leonard, *Readings in Latin American Social Organization and Institutions* (1953) — all published at East Lansing by Michigan State College Press.

18. Loomis, Julio O. Morales, Roy A. Clifford, and Olen E. Leonard, eds., *Turrialba: Social Systems and the Introduction of Change* (Glencoe, Ill.: Free Press, 1953).

19. Loomis and Reed M. Powell, "Class Status in Rural Costa Rica," in Theo R. Crevenna, ed., *Materiales para el estudio de la clase media en la America latina*, Vol. 5 (Washington, D.C.: Pan American Union, 1951).

20. Whetten, *Rural Mexico* (Chicago: University of Chicago Press, 1948), and *Guatemala: The Land and the People* (New Haven: Yale University Press, 1961). An important journal article is Whetten and Robert G. Burnight, "Internal Migration in Mexico," *RS*, 21:63–68 (March 1956).

21. Whetten, *Guatemala*, p. 355.

22. Nelson, *Rural Cuba* (Minneapolis: University of Minnesota Press, 1950).

23. Ferragút became one of the chief administrators in the Cuban agricultural bank, and after Castro came to power he was made its director. He broke with Castro in 1961 and joined the Inter-American Development Bank in Washington, D.C.

24. As it turned out, this was something of an understatement. I am told that in the early days of his regime Castro carried a well-marked copy of the book with him. It is a fact that when he came to Washington, D.C., in April 1959 to address the American Association of Newspaper Editors, he had the book with him and at one point declared: "We are getting many of our ideas from this book by Professor Nelson of the University of Minnesota."

25. Hill, *El Campesino Venezolano* and *El Estado Sucre: sus Recursos Humanos* (Caracas: Universidad Central de Venezuela, 1959 and 1961).

26. Zimmerman, "Family Organization and Standards of Living," in *Problems of the New Cuba* (New York: Foreign Policy Association, 1935).

27. Biesanz and Biesanz, *Costa Rican Life* and *The People of Panama* (New York: Columbia University Press, 1944 and 1955).

28. Theo Crevenna, ed., *Materiales para el estudio de la clase media en la America latina*, 6 vols. (Washington, D.C.: Pan American Union, 1950–51).

29. Joseph Lopreato, "Social Classes in an Italian Farm Village," *RS*, 26:266–80 (September 1961). Lowry Nelson, *Land Reform in Italy* (Washington, D.C.: Na-

tional Planning Association, Planning Pamphlet No. 97, 1956); "An Italian Farm and Family — 1934 and 1955," *Land Economics*, 35:362–65 (November 1959); "Life at Peruzzi — A Century Ago and Now," *RS*, 25:232–35 (June 1960). David Lindstrom, "The Changing Rural Community in Sweden," *RS*, 16:49–55 (March 1951).

30. Sanders, *Balkan Village* (Lexington: University of Kentucky Press, 1949); *Rainbow in the Rock: The People of Rural Greece* (Cambridge: Harvard University Press, 1962). See also his "Village Social Organization in Greece," *RS*, 18:366–75 (December 1953), and "The Nomadic Peoples of Northern Greece: Ethnic Puzzle and Cultural Survival," *SF*, 33:122–29 (December 1954). Sanders has sought to derive principles for the technical assistance programs. See his "Research with Peasants in Underdeveloped Areas," *SF*, 35:1–10 (October 1956).

31. Tannous, "Trends of Social and Cultural Change in Bishmizzeen: An Arab Village in North Lebanon" (Ph.D. thesis, Cornell University, 1940); "Social Change in an Arab Village," *ASR*, 6:650–62 (October 1941). See also his "Rural Problems and Village Welfare in the Middle East," *RS*, 8:269–80 (March 1943); "Agricultural Production and Food Consumption in Iran," *Foreign Agriculture*, 8:27–42 (February 1944); "Technical Exchange and Cultural Values: Case of the Middle East," *RS*, 21:76–79 (March 1956).

Born in Lebanon, Tannous did his undergraduate work at the University of Beirut. He completed his work for the Ph.D at Cornell in 1940 and joined the staff of the University of Minnesota. In 1942 he was appointed to the Near East branch of the Office of Foreign Agricultural Relations (now the Foreign Agricultural Service) and has remained in that work. In this capacity, he has visited all the countries of the Near and Middle East as well as those of Africa.

32. Raper, Tamie Tsuchiyama, Herbert Passim, and David L. Sills, *The Japanese Village in Transition* (Tokyo: General Headquarters, Supreme Commander for the Allied Powers, Natural Resources Section, Report No. 136, 1950). See also Raper, "Some Recent Changes in Japanese Village Life," *RS*, 16:1–16 (March 1951).

33. Lindstrom, "Outlook for the Land Reform in Japan," *RS*, 21:164–70 (June 1956), and "Diffusion of Agricultural and Home Economics Practices in a Japanese Rural Community," *RS*, 23:171–83 (June 1958).

34. Raper, *Rural Taiwan — Problem and Promise* (Taipei: Taiwan China Good Earth Press, 1953). See also Bernard Gallin, "Rural Development in Taiwan: The Role of Government," *RS*, 29:313–23 (September 1964).

35. For a description of the program see Schuler, "The Origin and Nature of the Pakistan Academies for Village Development," *RS*, 29:304–12 (September 1964).

36. Generoso F. Rivera and McMillan, *The Rural Philippines* (Manila: Mutual Security Agency, 1952). See also McMillan, "Land Tenure in the Philippines," *RS*, 20:25–33 (March 1955).

37. Taylor, Ensminger, Helen W. Johnson, and Jean Joyce, *India's Roots of Democracy: A Sociological Analysis of Rural India's Experience in Planned Development Since Independence* (Bombay: Orient Longmans, 1965).

38. Ryan, *Caste in Modern Ceylon: The Sinhalese System in Transition* (New Brunswick, N.J.: Rutgers University Press, 1953); "Socio-cultural Regions of Ceylon," *RS*, 15:3–19 (March 1950); "The Ceylonese Village and the New Value System," *RS*, 17:9–28 (March 1952); "Primary and Secondary Contacts in a Ceylonese Peasant Community," *RS*, 17:311–21 (December 1952); "The Agricultural Systems of Ceylon," *RS*, 20:8–15 (March 1955). See also Murray A. Straus, "Cultural Factors in the Functioning of Agricultural Extension in Ceylon," *RS*, 18:249–56 (September 1953).

39. Edmund deS. Brunner, Irwin T. Sanders, and Douglas Ensminger, eds., *Farmers of the World: The Development of Agricultural Extension* (New York: Columbia University Press, 1945).

40. The European Society for Rural Sociology held its first congress in 1960. Since 1962 *Sociologia Ruralis* has been published biannually by Royal VanGorcum, Ltd., Assen, The Netherlands. For more information see Carl C. Taylor, "The Development of Rural Sociology Abroad," *RS*, 30:462–73 (December 1965).

Chapter 12. Progress, Problems, Perspectives

1. Galpin appropriately called this the humanitarian stage: "the stage of pity, sympathy, and active desire to better rural life by means already known and fairly near at hand." See "The Development of the Science and Philosophy of American Rural Society," *Agricultural History*, 12:195–208 (July 1938).

2. Chapin, *Contemporary American Institutions* (New York: Harper, 1935), pp. 373–97; Sewell, "The Construction and Standardization of a Scale for the Measurement of the Socio-economic Status of Oklahoma Farm Families," Oklahoma AES Technical Bulletin No. 9 (1940).

3. Madge, *The Origins of Scientific Sociology* (New York: Free Press of Glencoe, 1962), p. 1.

4. Sewell, "Rural Sociological Research 1936–1965," *RS*, 30:428–51 (December 1965). The table is on p. 433; it will be noted that the righthand column does not total 100.

5. Worth mention too is the earlier "continuum" of Hoe Farmer–Machine Farmer suggested by C. J. Galpin. It anticipated current emphasis on change theory in the typology of Toennies, Durkheim, Redfield, Becker, and others.

6. Sewell, in *RS*, 30:444ff.

7. *Human Relations in Agriculture and Farm Life*, p. 12.

8. On this dilemma, see Lowry Nelson, "Rural Sociology — Dimensions and Horizons," *RS*, 10:131–35 (March 1945). See also *Human Relations in Agriculture and Farm Life*, pp. 37–38.

9. Olson, "Rural American Community Studies: The Survival of Public Ideology," *Human Organization*, 23:342–50 (Winter 1964).

10. Witness the congressional uproar over "rural social surveys" and "land-use planning" as a result of the Coahoma County, Mississippi, survey (pp. 97–99, above) and the consequent strictures imposed on the use of funds.

11. See Herbert F. Lionberger, *Adoption of New Ideas and Practices* (Ames: Iowa State University Press, 1960).

12. Copp, ed., *Our Changing Rural Society: Perspectives and Trends.*

13. "This is a task not of deductive theory but rather a measurement of contingencies; the determination of prevalent configurations in structural attributes of developing societies." See Ryan, "The Resuscitation of Social Change," *SF*, 44:1–7 (September 1965).

14. Hoffsommer, "Rural Sociological Intradisciplinary Relations with the Field of Sociology," *RS*, 25:175–96 (June 1960).

Memoirs

1. This remark appears in *An American Town: A Sociological Study* (New York: James Dempster Printing Co., 1906). In *The Expansion of Rural Life* (New York: Knopf, 1926), Williams also gives credit for inspiration and stimulus to Franklin Giddings and Charles A. Beard (p. xiii). His other works are *The Foundations of Social Science* (Knopf, 1920), *Our Rural Heritage* (Knopf, 1925), and *Principles of Social Psychology* (Knopf, 1922). *Our Rural Heritage* and *Expansion of Rural Life* were based largely on *An American Town.*

2. P. 38n. During a conversation in 1927, I asked Williams to talk about his meth-

ods. He replied approximately as follows: "I think of my students as my parish. They invite me to their homes and I talk with their parents. There are repeated visits. After they become better acquainted with me, they talk frankly and I try to remember what they say. I do not take notes. Sometimes when I get outside and fear I might forget, I stop and write down something." For a fuller statement on methodology, including a stricture against "putting interpretation before observation," see *Our Rural Heritage*, pp. 9, 13.

3. In his letter to me, Sims criticized Robert S. and Helen M. Lynd for failing to acknowledge these three community studies in their *Middletown — A Study in Contemporary American Culture* (1929). More particularly he took issue with Clark Wissler for the "specious claim" in the foreword to *Middletown* that "No one has ever subjected an American community to such a scrutiny. . . . It is a pioneer attempt to deal with a sample American community after the manner of social anthropology. . . . It is in this that the contribution lies, an experiment not only in method, but in a new field, the social anthropology of contemporary life."

4. In the preface to *Constructive Rural Sociology* Gillette wrote: "A course of lectures entitled 'North Dakota Sociology' was offered to students of the University of North Dakota in 1908. But in order to interpret many local conditions a larger comparative study was necessary. This larger undertaking furnished the foundation for the present volume."

5. Brunner also commented: "Rau was a great teacher and save for a double tragedy would doubtless be counted among the great sociologists. His book on sociology was delivered to him one day in October 1912, all typed copies and the manuscript. That night the main building of the college was gutted by fire. The typescript, manuscript, notes, and library were completely destroyed. Shortly before, both of Rau's sons had been stricken with infantile paralysis. All his spare time from then on went into earning extra money to care for the medical bills. He never began to rewrite. But his point of view, his social interpretation of history, his insistence on the factual basis for opinions and on objectivity, and his equal insistence that sociology could and should be applied, have never left me."

6. See Zimmerman's reference to this report in the following account, as well as Galpin's comment in *My Drift Into Rural Sociology*, pp. 51ff.

7. See Chapter 6 in *The Changing Community* (New York: Harper, 1938).

8. For Galpin's own and slightly different account, see *My Drift Into Rural Sociology*, pp. 59–63.

9. New York: Longmans, Green, 1951, pp. 223–24, 226.

Index